ALSO BY TIM DLUGOS

High There
    (Some of Us Press, 1973)

For Years
    (Jawbone, 1977)

Je Suis Ein Americano
    (Little Caesar Press, 1979)

A Fast Life
    (Sherwood Press, 1982)

Entre Nous
    (Little Caesar Press, 1982)

Strong Place
    (Amethyst Press, 1992)

Powerless: Selected Poems 1973-1990
    (High Risk Books/Serpent's Tail, 1996)

TIM DLUGOS

Tim
Dlugos
reads his poems
Monday,
January 26, 8 pm
The Poetry Project
St. Mark's Church
Second Ave. & 10th St.
New York, N.Y.

A
FAST
LIFE THE COLLECTED POEMS OF

TIM DLUGOS

EDITED BY DAVID TRINIDAD

NIGHTBOAT BOOKS
CALLICOON, NEW YORK

Poems copyright © 2011 by the Estate of Tim Dlugos
Editing, Introduction, Chronology, and Notes
    copyright © 2011 by David Trinidad
Second Printing, 2013
All rights reserved
Printed in the United States

ISBN: 978-0-98445-983-4

Design and typesetting by HR Hegnauer
Text set in Palatino

Cataloging-in-publication data is available
    from the Library of Congress

Distributed by University Press of New England
One Court Street
Lebanon, NH 03766
www.upne.com

Nightboat Books
Callicoon, New York
www.nightboat.org

Photo Credits:
Cover: Photo by Jack Shear, 1982
Frontispiece: Postcard for reading at The Poetry Project, 1981
Page 2: Student Identification, La Salle College, 1971
Page 64: Cover of *High There* (Some of Us Press, 1973),
    Photo by Tom Farley
Page 188: Cover of *Entre Nous* (Little Caesar Press, 1982),
    Photo by Rudy Burckhardt, 1982
Page 424: New Year's Day Marathon, The Poetry Project;
    January 1, 1988; Photo by Vivian Selbo

CONTENTS

WASHINGTON, D.C.: 1973-1976

MANHATTAN AND BROOKLYN: 1976-1988

INTRODUCTION

As he says in the title poem of this book, Tim Dlugos led a fast life. He started writing poetry at the age of twenty, in 1970, and almost immediately developed a mature voice. A year later he came out (the Gay Liberation movement was at its height) and thereafter had a prolific number of boyfriends and lovers. He was at the center of two of the most exciting alternative poetry scenes of the seventies: the Mass Transit group in Washington, D.C., and the community of writers, largely affiliated with the New York School, that revolved around the Poetry Project at St. Mark's Church in downtown Manhattan. Between 1973 and 1982, he published four chapbooks and one full-length collection, *Entre Nous*. Charismatic and gregarious, Tim lived, in many ways, by his wits. During the day he supported himself by writing copy for non-profit organizations (often composing poems when he should have been "working"); his nights were a glamorous whirl of art openings and poetry readings, gay bars and bathhouses.

This fast-track lifestyle eventually caught up with him. He got sober in 1984 and reevaluated his priorities. Somewhat disillusioned with the poetry world, he began to pursue, in earnest, the religious life that he had set aside in the early seventies. In 1986, he met and entered into a relationship with Christopher Wiss. The following year, two months after his mother died, he tested positive for HIV. Then, in 1988, he enrolled in Yale Divinity School and moved to New Haven. The last two years of his life he devoted to his studies, to Christopher, to his many friends, to travel abroad, and to his writing. Although he'd given up, in some respects, on poetry (he wrote comparatively little his first few years of sobriety), poetry never gave up on him. Once he settled in New Haven, Tim started writing regularly again, and produced some of his most remarkable poems as he was dying of AIDS. He left behind an amazing body of work: nearly 600

poems, written during a twenty-year period. He also left be-
hind two unpublished manuscripts: "Strong Place," which con-
tained work from the early eighties, and "Powerless," which
contained his last poems.

The week before he died, I visited Tim in his room at
Roosevelt Hospital. It was late afternoon, and we sat, mostly
in silence, as the light faded; I remember everything as gray.
It was during this final visit that he asked me to look after his
work. It's something I would have done even if he hadn't
asked. Christopher, Tim's executor, entrusted me with Tim's
papers; for several years they sat, in four or five boxes, in my
living room. I sorted through and cataloged the poems as best
I could; it was a slow, emotional process. In the meantime,
I oversaw the production of *Strong Place*, which Amethyst
Press published in 1992. I also placed some of Tim's unpub-
lished poems in journals. The "Powerless" manuscript was
shown to—and rejected by—a long list of publishers. It would
remain unpublished.

Ira Silverberg, my partner at the time, who was the publish-
er of High Risk Books, offered to put out a selected volume of
Tim's poems. I edited this volume, which bore the same title as
the unpublished manuscript, *Powerless*. Because I had to adhere
to a limit of 125 pages, I thought of *Powerless* as Tim's "greatest
hits." I began the book with "Poem After Dinner," which Tim
wrote in 1973, and which he was obviously fond of (it's the ear-
liest poem that he included in *Entre Nous*), and ended it with
"D.O.A.," Tim's last poem, written in August of 1990, three
months before his death. In between were such popular and
important poems as "Gilligan's Island," "At the Point," "Heal-
ing the World from Battery Park," "Powerless," and "G-9." Still,
I was aware of the wealth of writing that would remain, for the
time being, unavailable; I hoped that one day someone would
come along and edit a more substantial collection. *Powerless*
was published in 1996. That same year, Tim's papers were de-

posited in the Downtown Collection at the Fales Library at New York University.

Poems usually circulate in the world in a quiet, if not imperceptible way; even when a poet is alive, and successful, it's not easy to gauge their effect. I never doubted that Tim's poems would continue to find readers who would appreciate his particular brand of pop prophecy ("America is turning into a culture / with reruns instead of a memory") and be moved by his chameleon-like (sometimes artfully cloaked, sometimes nakedly exposed) mode of self-disclosure. Tim had put himself on the map: he'd given electric readings, published well (mostly in small press venues, though every now and then he'd make it into a more mainstream journal like *The Paris Review*), and socialized (or should I say "dazzled") his way into a far-reaching reputation. Now it was *solely* up to the poems to do the work, and the poems, some of us believed, would stand up over time. Occasionally I'd hear from a reader who had discovered and fallen in love with Tim's work. The feeling among such readers was that they were always left wanting more.

In 2000, Patrick Merla edited a tribute to Tim that appeared in *The James White Review*. He included uncollected poems (reprinting, in its entirety, the long-out-of-print "A Fast Life"), photographs (Tim talking with William Burroughs in 1977; Tim and Christopher smiling from Tim's bed in G-9, the AIDS ward at Roosevelt Hospital, in 1989, on Tim's thirty-ninth birthday; etc.), and ephemera (such as a flier for an East Coast reading tour Tim did with Dennis Cooper in 1981). The magazine's distribution was limited primarily to a gay audience, but Merla's effort helped keep Tim in the spotlight. Several years later, Christian Smith, a student at New York University, wrote, as a project for a journalism class, a biographical sketch of Tim. He interviewed a number of Tim's friends, chronicled the major events in Tim's life. Smith's sketch was not published; it was comforting, however, to know that someone was gathering this information, and making use of Tim's papers at the Fales Library.

Things then got very quiet. There were no requests to reprint Tim's poems, and only infrequent emails from fans who had found one of Tim's books (at this point collectible) in a used bookstore. In January of 2006, I wrote an elegy, "To Tim Dlugos," which I modeled after "Pastorale," Tim's elegy to his friend Virgil Moore. (My friendship with Tim had begun, in 1981, with him sending me a signed typescript of "Pastorale," which I'd admired, so the poem held a special significance for me.) It had taken me a long time (fifteen years) to talk to Tim in a poem, and now that I had, it appeared he intended to stick around. *Powerless* had gone out of print; it pained me to think of Tim's work slipping into obscurity. And since the devoted graduate student I had always imagined (who would transcribe and compile every poem Tim had ever written) had failed to materialize, I decided to undertake the project myself. It was a decision that seemed to descend, slowly, upon me. A year would pass before I'd proceed. The following March, while on a trip to New York City, I met with Christopher, who gave me his blessing to edit a comprehensive volume of Tim's poetry. I also met with Marvin Taylor, Director of the Fales Library and Special Collections at NYU, who agreed, in a generous display of cart blanche assistance, to provide me with copies of all of Tim's poems. After an interval of several months, a box containing Xeroxes of the very papers that had, all those years earlier, sat in my living room, arrived.

As I began to sift through and reacquaint myself with these papers, I realized I'd already laid the groundwork, when I initially cataloged Tim's poems in the years after his death, for assembling this collection. Each poem was accounted for and arranged in files by year of composition. It was fairly easy, as I now typed the poems and decided—where there were variants—on definitive versions, to place them in chronological order. Tim rarely held on to worksheets (the yellow lined legal pages he liked to write on), but he did date the typescripts of completed poems—almost meticulously so, often noting the location ("Brooklyn Hts.," for example) where individual poems were written. Sometimes there were lapses. I had the sense that dated copies of some poems might have been lost in one of his many moves (from Philadelphia to Washington, D.C., to Manhattan to Brooklyn, back to Manhattan, then back and forth between New Haven and Manhattan), or that in the turmoil of certain moments (such as a dramatic love affair), poems were simply left undated. Where there were gaps, I tried to put poems where they seemed to belong, within a given time frame, or relied on the order of Tim's books and manuscripts for placement (for instance, I inserted the undated "Song of Bernadette" in front of the dated "Entre Nous" because that's where it falls in the book *Entre Nous*).

In the year it took me to type the poems—579 in total—an intimate portrait of Tim gradually emerged. By running, as it were, his entire artistic output through my head, I got to know Tim far better than I knew him in life. Those who were as taken as I was with Tim's ingratiatingly clever public persona may be surprised by the strong autobiographical impulse that propels the poems, and by the quasi-diaristic story they collectively tell. Tim chose not to publish his most confessional poems (at least not until the end; it's hard to imagine a more revealing poem than "G-9"), but he saved them nonetheless. Particularly in his New York years, he got great satisfaction from straddling the line between literary camouflage and explicitness, as in "Desire Under the Pines" (a poem of which he was proud), where he could construct impeccable rhymed stanzas and infuse them with striking imagery, and be naughty at the same time. Even at his most oblique (experimenting with found poems or cut-ups, or lost in labyrinthian, Roussel-inspired wordplay), something private invariably shines through. As Bernard Welt has said,

Tim's "forward-driving means of writing poetry . . . grew out of his personality rather than his poetics. He picked it up and ran with it." A poem like "East Longmeadow" is a perfect fusion of the two strains that Tim so dextrously juggled: it's an ingenious New York School list poem, a wonderfully exhaustive tour de force, but it's also the story of his youth.

In terms of selection, I gave myself only one mandate: to include, without question, any poem that Tim had included in his own books and manuscripts. Other than that, my goal was merely to bring together his best and most interesting poems. I had at first thought that I would put in all 579 poems, but quickly came to see that a "collected"—rather than a "complete"—poems would better showcase Tim's talent. It would have done him a disservice to publish his lesser efforts, no matter how useful they might be biographically, or in charting the evolution of his craft. Excluded were poems that, for one reason or another, fell short of their mark (for example, a handful of "mash notes" that he wrote to Jim Carroll in the early seventies, none of which are particularly successful) or lacked Tim's usual verve. This collection represents half of his extant poems, and has the feeling of abundance I'd hoped it would. I included four of the poems that Tim titled "From Journal" (he wrote twenty-three of them between 1974 and 1982). They give the impression that they were extracted from a longer journal, but were in fact written as individual pieces. They would make a terrific book in their own right. I included the collaboration "Columbus Day" not only because it has merit (and happens to have been written with me), but also because it's the only work of this kind among Tim's papers.

The idea of sectioning the book by cities in which Tim lived came early on, and proved a suitable one. The four sections highlight distinct phases in Tim's development: youthful romantic, burgeoning artist, urbane New Yorker, vigorous supplicant. A unifying sensibility runs through the whole of Tim's work, as he moves from city to city, as the "young poet gets a little older, and his poetry matures" (as he says in "The Young Poet"), while the flavor of poems produced in each locale remains discrete. Tim used a John Cheever quote about setting as an epigraph for part four of *Entre Nous*, and since a sense of place is always prevalent in Tim's poems (especially Manhattan, with its persistent siren song—"the clear-eyed smiles of [the] pale and lovely young"—present from the very beginning), it seemed an ideal epigraph for this book as well.

The notes are primarily meant to provide dates of composition and—in a scattershot fashion—background and factual information, and to give interested readers a sense of the publishing history of the poems—both before and after Tim's death. Less than half of these poems—and only five of the forty-seven he wrote during the last two years—were actually published in his lifetime. For Tim, publishing was largely a "family affair." He tended to publish his poems in magazines edited by his friends: *Mass Transit* (Ed Cox, Tina Darragh, Peter Inman, Beth Joselow, Michael Lally, Terence Winch), *Z Magazine* (Kenward Elmslie), *Little Caesar* (Dennis Cooper), and so on. Similarly, his books were published by friends' presses: Some of Us Press, run by Michael Lally, Terence Winch, and others; Dennis Cooper's Little Caesar Press; my own Sherwood Press. Tim was too busy living and writing to manage what we now think of as a "poetry career." This helps to explain the number of marvelous poems that were left unpublished. But this is not to say that he lacked ambition. Ultimately, he was drawn more to the warmth and excitement of "the scene" than to the politics of power and prestige. When the poetry world became overrun with "canny grant recipients of many hues," whom he derides in "It Used To Be More Fun," Tim just wasn't as interested. He preferred "the poise and energy and grace / of black poets and gay poets and Dadaists / and unschooled natural artists / who fell into the workshops through the open doors."

Personally, it was gratifying to witness the resurgence that Tim underwent when he was writing his last poems. I remember when he called from Roosevelt Hospital, in November of 1989, to tell me that he had put me in a poem he had just finished. He said it was too long to read over the phone (as was his custom), he would send it in the mail, but I could tell from the ebullience in his voice that he knew he'd written something important—a masterpiece, the poem of his life. Tim submitted "G-9" to *The Paris Review*; Patricia Storace, then the poetry editor, accepted it, and it was published the following summer, only months before Tim's death. In a letter to his friend Joe Brainard, dated July 9, 1990, Tim wrote, "When I was in the hospital last Nov., I wrote a poem about a day in the hospital, and about having AIDS. Well, the Paris Review accepted it, and it's going to be in the issue that comes out in August. I'm really happy about it, both to have the work 'out there' and to be able to incorporate AIDS into my poetry. It feels good when my writing is in the same place I am, & when that gets affirmed." Two months after he died, I read "G-9" at Tim's memorial service at St. Mark's Church. Someone said to me afterwards, "I can't believe you didn't cry." I can't say the same was true when I typed it for this book.

—David Trinidad
Chicago, 2010

ACKNOWLEDGMENTS

My gratitude to the following individuals, whose assistance and support helped make this book possible:

Christopher Wiss, executor of the Tim Dlugos Estate, has always entrusted me with Tim's work. I thank him for his faith in my decisions. He was there each step of the way to encourage and facilitate the progress of this collection.

Marvin Taylor, Director of the Fales Library and Special Collections at New York University, offered, from the outset, his unbridled assistance. He and his staff were continually helpful and generous with my requests.

Stephen Motika, publisher of Nightboat Books, expressed interest in this project when it was still in the editing phase. He was, therefore, the first publisher to whom I submitted the completed manuscript; his immediate acceptance of it was a great boon. His enthusiasm and care are much appreciated.

Joe Eldridge and Cora Jacobs read and discussed all of the poems with me. Their input was instrumental in the shaping of this book.

Michael Lally and Terence Winch freely offered their support from the very beginning. Their dedication to Tim and his legacy is heartening. Every poet should have such loyal and devoted friends.

John Dlugos, Tim's younger brother, provided valuable information about Tim's childhood and family history. Regrettably, he died before this book went to press. In October 2008, he wrote to me, "It makes me happy to know that Tim and his poetry are still alive and loved."

Kenneth Daley, Chair of the English Department at Columbia College Chicago, actively supported this project from its inception. I am also grateful to Columbia College for a Faculty Development Award that enabled me to conduct research at Fales Library.

Stacy Szymaszek, Artistic Director of the Poetry Project at St. Mark's Church, kindly made materials available to me.

Holly Amos and Jessica Dyer proofread the galleys. I am grateful for their time and expertise.

Rebecca Burrier, Jeffery Conway, Aaron Smith, and Tony Trigilio provided moral support and assistance throughout.

A number of Tim's friends took the time to share their memories and knowledge. I thank: Michael Card, Tom Carey, Tina Darragh, Jane DeLynn, Kenward Elmslie, Richard Elovich, Cheri Fein, Michael Friedman, Amy Gerstler, Brad Gooch, Duncan Hannah, Beth Joselow, Scott McKinley, Patrick Merla, Philip Monaghan, Eileen Myles, Mary Ellen O'Donnell, Ron Padgett, Ken Schwartz, Marty Watt, Father Edgar Wells, and Bernard Welt. I'm sure all would agree with Marty Watt: "Tim gave me wonderful moments."

CHRONOLOGY

1950

- Born on August 5 in Springfield, Massachusetts. Named Francis Timothy Dlugos by adoptive parents Frank Joseph Dlugos and Mary Collins Dlugos. His father, a native of Connecticut, is an industrial safety engineer in a defense plant. His mother, who had grown up in Springfield, is a registered nurse turned full-time homemaker.

1952

- Adoptive brother John Anthony Dlugos born on September 30.
- Family moves to East Longmeadow, Massachusetts, where they reside at 49 Merriam Street.

From Tim's own description of his youth: "Externally, it was a 'Leave It To Beaver' childhood, a model of TV-sitcom Fifties normality. . . . My brother and I attended local public schools, played baseball, hiked through the woods and climbed the hills, participated in Scouts and altar boys. . . . I was a 'nervous' child, well-behaved, good around adults, an over-achiever at school, adept at controlling social situations with peers, most happy when I was reading a book on my own, rather than engaging in group activities."

1962

- While a student at Birchland Park Junior High School, joins "Catholic Vocation Club" for students with possible religious vocations and attends weekend meetings at nearby monastery of the Passionist Fathers.

1964

- His father accepts job as highway safety engineer for the federal government and family moves to Arlington, Virginia.

1965

- Attends Bishop Denis J. O'Connell High School, a Catholic college-preparatory school, where he is taught by the Christian Brothers. Tim will later write, "I was certainly attracted to a structure of community in which men shared their lives and possessions, with a ministry of education to the poor and primary emotional commitments to one's brothers in the community."

1968

- One week after graduation from high school, enters the Christian Brothers as a postulant.
- During his novitiate, he becomes involved in the Catholic draft resistance movement, discovers marijuana, and has "an abortive and guilt-ridden romance with a classmate."
- Begins therapy after having a "major anxiety attack."

1969

- Attends La Salle College in Philadelphia. Receives full-tuition scholarship and majors in English. Lives "in a commune with a confrere, a former confrere, and three others."

1970

- Involved in anti-Vietnam War movement.
- Starts writing poetry. Early influences include John Ashbery, Robert Bly, Jim Carroll, Kenward Elmslie, Allen Ginsberg, Robert Lowell, Thomas Merton, and Frank O'Hara.

1971

- April 16: Acknowledges for the first time that he is gay after he meets a student (Rob) in New York and spends the night with him at the Plaza Hotel. He later refers to this as "the most grace-filled moment / of my life." An affair ensues.
- Leaves the Christian Brothers.

1972

- Becomes president of La Salle's first gay student group, as well as national gay male representative to the Board of Supervisors of the National Student Association.
- April 21: Placed on disciplinary probation for failing to vacate the office of the Vice-President for Student Affairs during a student protest the day before.
- August: Hears poets Ed Cox and Michael Lally give a reading at Catholic University of America in Washington, D.C. Tim is impressed by their "inexhaustible enthusiasm for the Frank O'Hara-style writing" he admires, and by the "sharp political focus" of their work.

1973

- April: Less and less motivated to complete term papers and academic assignments, drops out of college in his senior year. Moves back to his parents' home in Arlington, where he spends "a year or so at loose ends."
- Immerses himself in the Mass Transit poetry scene in Washington, D.C., regularly attending open readings at the Community Book Shop in Dupont Circle. His friends during this period include Ed Cox, Tina Darragh, Michael Lally, Bernard Welt, and Terence Winch.
- First chapbook, *High There*, published by Some of Us Press.

1974

- Moves to apartment at 1437 Rhode Island Avenue, N.W. in Washington, D.C.
- Works for Ralph Nader's "Public Citizen," a non-profit public interest advocacy group, as fundraising assistant and first editor of *Public Citizen* newspaper. This leads to a successful career as a fundraising consultant and copywriter for liberal and charitable organizations.
- September 4: Reads with John Ashbery and Kenward Elmslie at the Pyramid Gallery in Washington, D.C.

1975
- August: Trip to San Francisco.

1976
- June 1: Moves to Manhattan, renting the top floor of Kenward Elmslie's townhouse at 104 Greenwich Avenue in Greenwich Village.
- June 8: Attends party for John Ashbery at the Fischbach Gallery; meets Brad Gooch, who will become a longtime friend. Other friends, from this point on, include Joe Brainard, Jane DeLynn, Cheri Fein, Morris Golde, Steve Hamilton, and Eileen Myles.
- August: Hired as copywriter for the U.S. Committee for UNICEF.
- December: Begins writing monthly column for *Christopher Street* magazine, "Rough Trade," featuring "behind-the-scenes news of the publishing world that involves gay books and books of interest to gay people."

1977
- Chapbook *For Years* published by Jawbone Press.
- Begins correspondence and friendship with Dennis Cooper; publishes poems in Cooper's *Little Caesar* magazine.
- September 26: Interviews Joe Brainard. Published as "The Joe Brainard Interview" in *Little Caesar* in 1980.
- Through 1984, supports himself as freelance copywriter and journalist.

1978
- Winters in Key West. Meets and begins dating Bobby Thompson.
- Moves in with Thompson at 45 West 68th Street, off Central Park West.

1979

- *Je Suis Ein Americano* published by Little Caesar Press.
- Writes cover story, "A Cruel God: The Gay Challenge to the Catholic Church," for September issue of *Christopher Street*.
- October: As Director of Programming, Dennis Cooper invites Tim to read at Beyond Baroque Literary / Arts Center in Venice, California.

1980

- Assists Dennis Cooper in editing *Coming Attractions: An Anthology of American Poets in Their Twenties*.
- February 12: Moves with Bobby Thompson to 111 Hicks Street (formerly the St. George Hotel) in Brooklyn Heights.
- Coordinates reading series (through 1982) at The Ear Inn, 326 Spring Street in Manhattan.
- March 7: First of four readings (through 1984) at Beyond Baroque.
- June 8: Hosts party for Dennis Cooper in apartment at Hicks Street.
- Fall: Begins working as copywriter for Sanky Perlowin Associates, a direct-mail consulting firm for non-profit organizations. Solicits money for such causes as the Fresh Air Fund, the American Friends Service Committee, Food for Survival, and Recording for the Blind.
- Starts writing "Naked Brunch" gossip column for *New York Native*.

1981

- February 20: Reading with Bob Flanagan at Beyond Baroque. While in California, meets Amy Gerstler, David Trinidad, and others in Cooper's circle.
- May: East Coast reading tour (Philadelphia, Washington, D.C., and Boston) with Dennis Cooper.
- June 11: Father dies of heart attack.

- Fall: Takes his own apartment at 31 Strong Place in Cobble Hill section of Brooklyn, remarking that as he'd just turned thirty-one years old, he was in a "strong place" in his life.
- Begins attending services at St. Paul's Episcopal Church on Carroll Street in Brooklyn. "It was a small parish with an Anglo-Catholic tradition, which enabled me to realize that I could express my Catholicism in an Anglican mode without rejecting any substantial part of it, and without being a collaborator with the oppressive authoritarianism which had clearly infected the current generation of Roman Catholic leadership."
- Starts dating Steven Abbott, a twenty-two-year-old architecture student.

1982

- *Entre Nous* published by Little Caesar Press and *A Fast Life* by Sherwood Press. February 26: Publication reading for both books at Beyond Baroque.
- September: Though they have an "open" relationship, tensions arise when Steven Abbott "distort[s] the romantic implications" of an outside affair.
- December: Tim's drinking escalates when Abbott leaves for eight-month trip to Europe and Africa.
- Circulates private edition of "Strong Place" manuscript (different from eventual book manuscript) to friends as New Year's present.

1983

- April 2: Co-hosts (with Donald Britton, Brad Gooch, and Doug Milford) party at Piezo Electric gallery to celebrate Dennis Cooper's move to New York City. About Tim's lifestyle at this time, Cooper has written, "One was always trailing after Tim as he flew between cocktail parties, poetry readings, art openings, the baths, services at his local church, and elsewhere, often over the course of a single evening."

- April 13: Reads at Museum of Modern Art.
- Still in Europe, Steven Abbott informs Tim that he has a new lover—a boy in Paris, younger than himself—with whom he's deeply in love and with whom he plans to move back to New York. His relationship with Tim is, therefore, "inoperative."
- June: Received into the Episcopal Church. Seriously considers entering the priesthood.
- Summer: Poses with Donald Britton and Dennis Cooper for Larry Stanton's painting *Three Poets*. Dates David Craig, who later becomes involved with Donald Britton.
- September: Upset that Steven Abbott has returned from Europe and "insinuated" himself into his circle of friends ("all of whom he met through me") and that Britton is dating David Craig ("despite my crush on him"), Tim writes that he is "in the process of dropping old friends and making new ones. . . . The perfidy level rivals the pollen level in this September of the terrible queers."
- Attends "Ladies Party" (drag party) at Howard Brookner and Brad Gooch's apartment in the Chelsea Hotel. Steven Abbott also present. Tim gets "*blind* drunk, in the sense of not remembering anything," and causes scene. "So several of my friends have been *rather* cool since then."

1984

- May: Goes to his first Alcoholics Anonymous meeting while on visit to Los Angeles; gets sober after returning to New York, on June 23. Tim will later write that his "spiritual growth . . . has been largely facilitated by my participation in a twelve-step recovery program. I do my best to make its principles the hallmark of my life."
- July 14-16: Writes "Healing the World from Battery Park."
- Becomes Creative Director of Sanky Perlowin Associates.
- Edits *The Poetry Project Newsletter*, overseeing publication of seven issues, October 1984 to May 1985.

1985

- Travels to London with his mother.
- Creates his own imprint, Mary House, to publish Michael Friedman's first book of poems, *Distinctive Belt*. This will be the only book the press publishes.
- May: Trip to the South of France. Sees Menton, Monaco, Nice, Saint-Tropez, Aix, Arles, and Avignon.
- Interval during which Tim's interest in poetry wanes. "From about 1985 until late 1987, I wasn't excited by poetry. I wrote only sporadically during that period."
- Feels "quietly but increasingly drawn toward" religious vocation. Starts taking night classes at Hunter College in order to complete requirements for his B.A. and enter a Master's program in divinity.
- Becomes member of the Board of Directors of the Poetry Project at St. Mark's Church.

1986

- July 4: Meets Christopher Wiss on Fire Island. They continue to see each other in Manhattan and a relationship develops.
- Fall: At invitation of Father Edgar Wells, moves into rectory at the Church of St. Mary the Virgin, 144 West 47th Street in Manhattan. "My contribution for the [room] is far less than my high rent in Brooklyn, and will enable me to save a great deal of money toward my theological education."
- Unable to find publisher for *Strong Place* manuscript.

1987

- Spring: Trip to San Francisco.
- September 11: Mother dies of leukemia.
- November: Tests positive for HIV.
- Christmastime: Travels alone to Amsterdam and Bruges (Belgium).

1988

- Completes degree requirements at Hunter College; credits transferred to La Salle and B.A. awarded.
- Enrolls in Yale Divinity School.
- June: Travels to Geneva and Paris with Steve Hamilton.
- August 4: Ex-lover Bobby Thompson dies of AIDS.
- August: Moves to 29 Rowe Street in New Haven, Connecticut, where he pursues graduate studies at Yale Divinity School. His intention is to become a priest in the Episcopal Church. On subsequent visits to Manhattan, Tim stays with Christopher Wiss at 165 West 83rd Street.
- September 22: Accepted as a postulant for Holy Orders in the Episcopal Church by the Bishop of New York.
- Begins writing poems regularly again.

1989

- May: Travels to the South of France and Catalonia with Christopher Wiss.
- July: Admitted to G-9 (AIDS ward) at Roosevelt Hospital with pneumocystis pneumonia. Spends his thirty-ninth birthday in hospital. Diagnosed with Kaposi's sarcoma and AIDS.
- October 23: Again admitted to Roosevelt Hospital with pneumocystis pneumonia. Writes "Powerless," "G-9," and other poems during monthlong hospitalization.
- Withdraws from fall semester at Yale due to illness.
- Collaborates with gay activist and businessman Sean Strub on fundraising projects for ACT UP, Gay Men's Health Crisis, and the AIDS Action Council.

1990

- March: Participates in first OutWrite (gay writers' conference) in San Francisco.
- May: Travels with Christopher Wiss to Amsterdam, Bruges, and Paris.

- Summer: As requirement for graduate degree, works as chaplain-in-training counseling seriously ill patients and their families at Jersey City Medical Center. According to Jane DeLynn, Tim "derived huge satisfaction from his work and thought that he had found the form of his vocation; some of these people, he told me, had never had anybody listen to them in their entire lives."
- August: Moves to one-bedroom apartment at 352 Canner Street; building located on campus at Yale Divinity School.
- "G-9" published in *The Paris Review*.
- After writing last poem, "D.O.A.," on August 29, completes "Powerless" manuscript.
- October 31: Appears on *Good Morning America*, reading an excerpt from "G-9."
- Mid-November: Admitted to Roosevelt Hospital. Friends and relatives visit him during next two weeks. Jane DeLynn, John Dlugos, Edgar Wells, and Christopher Wiss are among the last to see him.
- December 3: Dies of complications due to AIDS.
- December 6: Funeral at the Church of St. Mary the Virgin, 145 West 46th Street, New York, New York.
- Ashes interred in columbarium at the Cathedral Church of St. John the Divine in Manhattan.
- December 23: Memorial Service, Beyond Baroque Literary/ Arts Center, Venice, California. Participants include Dennis Cooper, Bob Flanagan, Amy Gerstler, James Krusoe, Michael Lally, Sheree Levin, Jack Skelley, Ed Smith, David Trinidad, and Benjamin Weissman.

1991

- February 3: Memorial Service, the Poetry Project at St. Mark's Church, New York, New York. Participants include Tom Carey, Cheri Fein, Michael Friedman, Morris Golde, Brad Gooch, Duncan Hannah, James McCourt, Jaime Manrique, Honor

Moore, Eileen Myles, Mary Ellen O'Donnell, David Trinidad, and Christopher Wiss.

1992
- *Strong Place* published by Amethyst Press.

1993
- "Healing the World from Battery Park" included in *The Best American Poetry 1993*.

1996
- *Powerless: Selected Poems 1973-1990*, edited by David Trinidad, published by High Risk Books/Serpent's Tail.
- The Tim Dlugos Papers acquired by Fales Library, New York University.

ABOUT MY WORK

1. I try to write out of the time and space I find myself in.

2. My best work takes the "timeless"—spontaneous goofs, flights, body motions—and drags it onto timeline, the "real world" where we live. I am "successful" when the language (clean combination of words) takes me or someone else back to the original combination of feelings and perceptions "out there," or somewhere equally nice.

3. My work is part of the nostalgia craze; all of it reminds me of where I used to be. That spurs me on to greater achievements, so I can look back at those, too, from a point even further in the future.

4. Grace, in a very orthodox sense, is my major preoccupation.

—Tim Dlugos
10 April 1975

A
FAST
LIFE THE COLLECTED POEMS OF
TIM DLUGOS

The setting seems in some way to be at the heart of the matter.
—John Cheever, *Bullet Park*

LA SALLE COLLEGE

Phila., Pa. 19141

STUDENT IDENTIFICATION

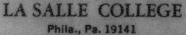

Valid 1971-1972

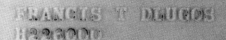

FRANCIS T. DLUGOS

H236000

PHILADELPHIA

1970-1973

COSMOGONY

Down country
across the steel bridge right out of *Easy Rider*
and up a hill's long yellow dusty road

Walked in the sunlight
Walked among the briars
Walked past bare-faced silent rocks
Walked to the river
Walked beneath branches
A slowly-forming form:

spoken out of evanescence
captured, like a banshee, from the mist
(twilight shadows growing realer,
passions planting roots, like holy mountains.)

Turn your face from orchards
and roadside stands that stay closed in the spring.
Watch where you stand,
eyes clear as the river
whose imitative branches know
that corpses cannot speak,
not even lies.

Sit on the mountain, young gentlemen.
Prophesy! I sit before a fire of logs,
see across the valley many points of light,
across the black sky fewer.

Music,
order from the edge,
fills my ears.
The primal rhythm:
our hearts pumped together
when together we lay
in the city, in the season of death.
Our tongues did not speak then.
Breath within us,
we gave and took in rhythm with the world,
in rhythm, in heart, melded.

In ritual, one great heart
laid down, stops again ever.
Fire after water in ritual,
the rage of saints, and appetite quenched.

Music drifts upward from the cliff.
The blinking lights, the lovers' rhythm,
rise under the eyes of
prophets on a dry mountain,
who hear the long space between deep breaths
and call it spirit.

BEYOND THE LIGHT AND THE ROCKS

Let's take a walk along the walnut-colored wharf,
Stroll by the fishing-boats and touch the bristly pilings.

We can say Hi to the Portuguese
Who squat on their trawlers' decks
And fiddle with flashlights.

We can dodge puddles, and, toes dangling,
Hang our sneaks down
Over the spotted water.

We can see the ocean-smell
As it oozes up from the wharf's green bottom
And sticks in layers to the walls of a rotting shed.

We can smell the ocean-smell
That sticks in our noses in a stiff breeze
With a little whiff of mustard from the hot-dog stand nearby.

We can look out at the light
And see, beyond the light and the rocks,
The bumpy blue playground where both of us could roll.

We'd be surrounded by splashes.
We'd touch both the air and the water.
We'd see where the sun comes up from, and where it goes down.

Let's take a walk along the oil-covered docks,
Sit along a fishing-wharf and watch beyond the light and the rocks.

GUILLAUME DE LORRIS

May is the month when the land relaxes,
and I'm at the river.

Thin grass cracks and clods the soil.
Pent-up flowers burst from their pods, and breathe.
Out of the city, I walk downstream
stretching, bend and pick the blossoms,
breathe in the fresh smells near the water
in which reflected I see rippled
my face, new leaves

and a wall. Not ever, not within my memory,
that in this place. Strung along its turrets
one by one in the languid air,
frenzied women are facing the world
to guard their garden wall.

May is the month when things turn inside out.
From a barred window, tinkling laughter,
and a green-sleeved lady at the gate.
From her the promise of a dance;
a glance through the bars at water, which glances back—
I glimpsed myself, and entered.

SURF MUSIC, TEA WITH HONEY

in the pickle-light of a January morning.
And talking: questions bring out that
ours is Canadian, rather than Chinese tea.
We remember Tony the Augurer,
casting chicken bones, reading Tarot.
One night, stoned, in his fourth-floor walkup,
we asked his Ouija, Spirit, Are You Mad?
Ouija answered You Eat Garbage.
We laugh—Tony crossed our conversation
on his way to Chicago, a thousand miles away—
and drink sweet heavy tea from ivory mugs.
Hot gold burns the white film
off the city, off the wet green tealeaves.

NIGHT KITCHEN

luminous
eyes peeping over
the rim of a Skippy jar

crumbs, such chunks
under green fluorescent
and the black gap in a shiny wall

oh make yourself a sandwich after the Late Show
greenly spread peanut butter over flaky bread
flaunt it, cosmic dimensions,
layers and lights in the window
don't forget to tuck in your napkin and
mash that old stickum with all your teeth

a crunch in the night kitchen

LINDFORS AS MOTHER COURAGE

I shall pull my longings and belongings over the fields.
(Her chin is out, and eyes of earth and fire
rivet mine to the screen behind the newsman.
A spotted hand, earth and time,
slaps me hard on the shoulder.
Past Brecht's imagination . . .)
Shit on Brecht's imagination!
I do not know what socialism means!
The horse is dead, long rotted;
my two morons rotting also.
The mute, shot from her tower,
never called out Mother in the middle of the night,
but ached so. I knew what she meant.

I am still crafty (arch your eyebrows,
old wicked woman.) I am not burned
when I make fair trade with the soldiers.
You shall not know whether I'm burned or not.
And I am still strong (plant your
legs in the earth.) I strap myself to the wagon
and pull my wares through fields of mud,
silently follow the ragged, aching column.

No reason for my choice: what I pull
from the cold earth, the odds and ends
of departed armies, fills my cart.
From them (the gypsy life, always cold November)
the choice is merely the mud or the wagon,
but still they choose, you see?
(Again her chin is out; she quivers.)
One holds onto what she can.

LOON DANCE

My grandfather speaks:
In the morning, at the first false light,
the loons danced upon the lake for us.
Your Uncle Tom, who died when you were small,
and I had hiked from Skow the afternoon
before. We set off through the hills, and reached
the lake in time to see the sun go down.
It hung above the pines and stretched our shadows
longer and longer behind us; it dropped
behind the trees and tarnished the whole forest;
and when it went away and the birds flew
home for the night, we built a fire and watched
the smoky flames cast shadows on the lake.
We slept after lying awhile listening
to the water: no dark corners to watch,
but darkness all around, and just the dying
gold of our dark pinefire to know directions
by. In the blue half-light, we woke hours
later. The dew had started to grow. Grayly
down on the lake, the loons were dancing.
They threw out their wings, turning and turning,
half obscured by the mist. They whirled in rows
like Shakers, and were dressed like Mennonites
in their drab feathers. By the time the sun
came back to see their dance, they'd flown away.
Tom and I had bobbed our heads like loons
to keep from being seen. We watched from
behind a blackberry bush, both afraid
we'd sneeze, and both embarrassed to be present
at a loon dance, that early in the morning.
I wonder, Tom said later, as we walked
along an orange-needled path toward home,

if after doing whatever loons do
during the day, they come to dance in darkness
on the lake before they sleep. I said I
didn't know, and thought about it in silence
as your uncle and I descended the hill
and walked beneath the pinetrees toward Skowhegan.

LAST POEM, FIRST MORNING

fragments from a life in progress

The road led nowhere
and could have led any place,
but the sun was up, so we chose
the street beneath our window to rejoice in.
••••••
We danced on the sidewalk,
joining night-spliced energies
to the human current, the New York stream,
the clear-eyed smiles of pale and lovely young,
to the broken sea, to Saturday morning crowds,
and sunfall into the gorge, Fifth Avenue.

I really like your poems,
I said to Ron Padgett
after he and Indian Dick Gallup
had read for a while.
I really liked only one of
Dick Gallup's poems,
so I couldn't say
I really like your poems
to him.
Thank you said Ron Padgett,
it's nice of you to say so.
I like Ron Padgett's poem
about flowers and a girl
the best of all, because it is November.
I like Dick Gallup's poem
"Charged Particles"
because we learned what they are
in physics class.

Who will have whom in the next life?
Will we all be stars with satellites?

I can only speak for Friday,
when snow dropped on our rhinestones
and Liza Minnelli,
and we were together
for evening's sake.

I could not find a pen
on the second floor of my
parents' house

to write that the end of the world
will hum like a swarm
of electrical bees

or sirens on the radio.
The jukebox in the closety bar
will sign off

with Jesus Christ Superstar
preceded by the end of
American Pie.

I shall remember a young man
once whose body and mine
never melded.

He was seventeen or twenty,
and I, with my glasses,
seemed to be complete.

MICHAEL

My fantasy is walking hand in hand
with you; then we stop to
face each other, and to join
our empty hands as well.
I am too cautious and you too fragile
for your warmth or mine to perfectly warm;
but in your eyes and in my back and chest
there is the same ocean—I can hear it
pound, like sex or the night tide breaking.

Nicotiana-Sensation
will bloom every night
in the sour front yard
that has not yielded
a single strand of grass,
according to Burpee,
the seed-magnate.
Forget the past, he tells us;
trust moonflowers.

DAVID CASSIDY

Someone said your teeth are capped,
and makeup hides the blemishes
you haven't gotten rid of at 22.
One pays, I suppose, for looking so young:
but even if the clearness of your features
is the product of massive and daily cosmetic efforts
by a team of specialists,
and even though your lines are blurred
by the blue horizontals of my TV,
I still watch you Friday after Friday,
and save your pictures, as though you came
with baseball bubblegum.

I speculate the Real David
comes straining through your perfect skin
like blackberries through fine mesh—
evenly, with maybe a seed
or two. I can tell that inside
you are damp, warm, and purple like the rest
by the way you laugh easily,
put down pettiness, and carry your TV sister,
Suzanne Crough, upon your shoulders.
When your voice quavers I want you in my livingroom
to watch yourself on television with me,
and wonder whether our repaired
surfaces will ever interlock.

LAST LETTER

This will be the last time I set down
in writing a request for your watery
gaze. I want it to be there, mostly;
not to set it on my dresser next to
the cactus and telephone, nor to save it
for the year you will spend in the mountains.
I am afraid it will fade with your tan
which will take a long time to go away.
There is no well I can think of
as colorful in its darkness as your eyes:
whatever I look down I want to see them
endless and reflecting, but am unwilling
to take them outside of your face, in which
you make me travel the whole route between us,
the distance of my poems and desires. So
this is goodbye, the last time I plead
that you keep the sparkle always there by leaving,
and that you wake beside me every morning forever
to show me what good today can possibly bring.

All the poems I ever write won't tell me
whom I really love, probably

but still there is that tiny chance
so I keep bouncing

between Virginia and Germantown
with East Longmeadow as patron saint

and New York as religion
meanwhile I'm still as afraid of the woods

as ever, and of the Northeast Corridor
Freud would tie it to birthpangs, maybe

and I to a Woody Allen film
(not really, I'm only saying that for effect)

maybe I would love it
in the west

POEM FOR PASCAL, I'M GOING AWAY

I am going away now

The sun will shine for another six weeks
or so before the maple leaves are burning in the street
on long afternoons it will slowly hit the trees by my window

then there would be time to watch the lights
and shadows in your face and your mahogany eyes
but I am going away now

and want the times we shared all back again—
no, not really, I was only summoning
our hazy memories and suntan futures

we have walked for all time down Wisconsin Avenue
I have for all time directed you from Georgetown to my home
and our love stands in the late-summer sunshine

for all time to stop and to say, What's this,
that is burning and arisen
like your Eastertime name

in the warmth of morning and the fire behind your smile
I am going away now
we shall always be where we have been

AFTER PARTING

Two sets of footsteps
on rainy sidewalks late in the afternoon
are certainly worth it
for the river and their own eccentric tapping

but times like now
when all I see is sunny hair and smiles
the eyes that know we're walking
and a shirt that says I Love You

when my hand is in the rainstorm
and cannot quite touch its parts
like my chin straining toward
the freckles on your back

when everything is washed down the stream on the mountain—
such times are worthless.
I'm only writing this because of the moments
you streak through like a river and a laughing power line

a golden train stretching toward New York.

Here is the blond world of Sunday morning:
white pine furniture, your lemon robe
(I am wearing yesterday's shirt)
and we are drinking morning tea
it's all very hazy and golden
and nobody's speaking anywhere I can hear
(we have entered the silent dimension)
sun keeps rising while I am a denim boy
and oh, you are blond

AN UNDELIVERED CLASS
PRESENTATION ON THE SUBJECT
OF GAY CONSCIOUSNESS

We splashed around in such great manly joy
that the night should have melted when we did, together,
so what do you all want, charts? I will kiss you
and breathe the real gay consciousness
into your open mouths, and that will be
my project for the semester. Take notes all over
your not-afraid-to-be-beautiful bodies
with hands that tremble and eyes that are fuller
of wonder than the world.

David Cassidy, I want to fuck you!
Arrrgh! Ummmmm!

What a body, like a teenaged boy's,
and love eyes in the fan magazines!

You're a pussy,
but I crave you—oh!

I want to fuck you, David Cassidy!

A NOTE

I should apologize
I knew we would end up in bed two days before you came to
    see me
I cleaned the house and took down the pictures that you might
    find offensive
I washed my hair in herbs and dried it with an electric dryer
    (but did not shave)
I brewed the tea five minutes before you walked in the door
And was not surprised when our young bodies (yours
    younger) finally meshed
Accept, please, the apologies of your seducer
And come again

HEADING INTO THE CITY

Even the conductors on the Reading
are blinking their eyes, for a new
day is with us seven minutes
now, and I (as Young Fool) head
for Lombard Street, where I shall
blink at the Late Show, a Fu
Manchu film I could see with
equal ease at home (but by myself)
or in Mark Smith's room,
accepting his ambiguous
schoolboy invitation,
                              and spend
the night with Joe. Youth, what won't
I do for you, I question and pose, as
persons dead and living whom I haven't seen
for years climb on the train in twos
and threes at every half-lit station.

NIAGARA

He is going over the edge
and knows it. The pleasurecraft
he is trapped in will crumple
like a bright leaf under tons
of pressure. Only Jean Peters
will be saved, by a copter
out of the sky: the end
of the beer, the end of the ammunition

and of him. Once
he looks upstream, after
she has jumped for her life,
toward the tower where he locked
the body of his wife, the beautiful
and faithless Marilyn Monroe.

WATCHING *PSYCHO* FOR THE FIRST TIME

I know that Martin Balsam will fall
down the stairs of the old house backwards,
and that somebody gets stabbed in a shower,
but so far there's only been Janet Leigh
driving on the Western highways of *Play It As It Lays*
and *Zabriskie Point,* only ten years earlier,
and Tony Perkins playing a disturbed
young man   stuffing things, indeed!   and
hinting at how his mother's lover died.

Now it's getting better   People always call a madhouse
"someplace," don't they?   I'm sorry.
Have you ever seen the inside of one   and
we are slipping into *The Snake Pit* with
Olivia de Havilland, but no now the Perkins
temper is flaring   he gets it under control
and they say goodnight   milk and cookies
indeed!   Stuffed birds surround him,
and Tony Perkins is hawk, is Theodore Roosevelt.

She is in the shower   this is it I guess
she's stepping into the shower   no, she's
checking how much money she has left
here she goes at last, like a Zest commercial
he's here   he has the knife
she screams and her blood is washed
down the drain as soon as it leaves her body
that is the awful part   at the station break
both my hands go up in front of my face

FOR MICHAEL LALLY

When I am surrounded
by the steamy, hard
and twitching cloud Too
Weary upon lying down

to write, I think about
the boy in rhinestones
who sees his angel napping
when he drinks;

and when I plant inside
me the geography I pass
through, so I can feel
its tendrils in my heart,

there crop up wise hands
from a black-haired field,
that gather in amazement
what they never knew had grown.

FOR MY COUSIN, CHRISTINE SPRING
(1948-1971)

You are the only woman I shall wed
because you are dead
because you died going home

The last kiss stayed inside me
when on my knees I watched
the shell of you, knowing

it would be the last time,
knowing how you tried to get away.
You are a place of pilgrimage

now that you have gone.
Holy Acceptance: it was not
of her choosing. They

raise their voices to an empty sky.
Sometimes when you flew,
you glided earthward

like a human, in spurts,
with faltering start. "Familiar"
means beneath the line of flight,

and there were always airports:
your boyfriend was your mother
in disguise. The last lost weekend

when the lost driver hit you
from behind, and crushed your skull,
you soared through the windshield

saying I won't go back
there, I love you all,
Goodbye, and flew away.

Chrissie fly beside me
glide me over the beach
and into the ocean

where it is burning
and cold like your
body this winter

crack my skull and
we will both dream into
the empty sea

WERE WOLF

I wash
my face
with Breck
shampoo, once
a month,
faithfully.

SMALL POEM

The eagle
is on its
side, flapping
one wing awk-
wardly. There
are two black
stars. The back-
ground is red.

How long can one be blackly humorous?
Oh, for a long time

MORNING OFFERING

I send skyward this morning's offering
upon the smoke of patchouli incense
to the paradise of memory and the things to come
which might happen anywhere, even in the sky.

I drain myself of love and possibility,
and am full of every possibility
when I give myself the moment I awake
to my lovers and all whom I desire.

I peak at the press
of a body I have not known
or have known, many times:
I shudder, reach down

and know what is real as I emerge from the dreamworld,
and know it in the shower and the steam
as I carefully scrub and chant
in a voice full of longing my litany of names.

JOHN TONGUE

Tongue in the city   John Tongue
running the edge of his tongue against
the side of his mouth, you watching

always have loved the tongueman, honey
always have watched for slips of the tongue
on the street, and always have washed your own tongue
first thing clean in the morning, baby
your tongue ready to face the day

and John Tongue under the streetlight smiling
John at noon with his tongue in the sky
raining tongues in the twilight, honey
won't you take off your raincoat?

Tongue in his head, tongues in his shoes,
one tongue into your deep throat, baby
tongues you have cared for, tongues to be used,
one up into your wet insides you

never have known the gift of tongues
never have tongued your way to stardom
never have licked that bad boy, honey
never have done it, have you?

but John has. BUT JOHN HAS!

Nobody's baby is John Tongue
nobody's daddy
or mother, nobody's
lover is John Tongue
but warm sometimes

that John is. THAT JOHN IS!

You've done it John Tongue
you've done it all, honey
what you wanted to do those
nights on the corner all has been
done, those things you were wet
and wonderful at

in the cradle, John Tongue
in school, in the army
John Tongue a commander,
in the San Francisco Tongue War
John Tongue grievously wounded

but whole of tongue
and running its edge
against the side of
your mouth tonight

tongue on the sidewalk, tongue in church,
tongue in my head to sing your tongue-song,
tongue in the gastank, tongue in your pants,
tongue at your feet when you do the tongue-dance

with John Tongue. WITH! JOHN TONGUE!

AFTER SEPARATION

We hug so tightly! as if
a constant pain at apartness has been
in the back of our minds. It hasn't.

Still, there is warmth in a body
reclaimed by a body, and genuine sparks of joy
when I know where to touch you however you move:

hardly passionate, though, not quite romantic.
We are not really electric; when something silent
springs out of us both, we don't even know its name.

The look in your eyes at the moment they close
and both your arms jump out to surround
my back is the only reason

that we stay together all night in a single bed
when both of us know the closeness
will only annoy by dawn

and that we make love anyway in the morning,
regardless of how our hair looks, the two of us straining
through night-clogged noses so our breath won't offend.

SHELLEY WINTERS

Shelley Winters you're such a pig I love you
Not "even though" you're ugly and never shut up
    and dress like the wife of a cabbie who won
    the Lottery, but because of it!
I think you're a miserable actress, and didn't
    even care when you drowned in *The Poseidon*
    Adventure, it was a terrible movie and you
    were just wretched all the way through.
I agree with Neal Freeman that, objectively, you
    are ALWAYS unsatisfactory
And incredibly tacky: I know someone who
    saw you stinking drunk and stumbling down a
    corridor in the Traymore, now you always
    remind me of Atlantic City, and that's *dreary*.
Every time you're on Dick Cavett I get embarrassed
    for him just watching you talk.
You never answer the questions. You never *remotely*
    answer the questions.
Shelley, sometimes I don't think I can take it you
    depress me so, but you fascinate the hell out of
    me just the same
And I say with a sigh, "It's okay, it's just the
    way Shelley *is*."
I'm so young, you're so dumb, it never could work
    still I watch you every chance I get and love
    you, you're such a mess

LETTER POEM

to Rob

       I really ought to carry a notebook:
had three Poetical Moments today and
no pen, no paper. I lost three poems
that way. The first (and most inspired)
would have been about Sally's party
on Saturday, her 21st birthday, when
I arrived two hours early carrying
Transformations by Anne Sexton, and
wearing pink jeans, my big rhinestone star,
a scoopneck top, the Vera scarf of life,
and drank LOTS of beer for my nerves:
it was the first time I'd gone in for
Androgyny.

       Well, the results were
Terrific. I got called Mick Jagger three times
in the first half-hour by hunky kids from
the Cardinal Dougherty H.S. Football Team
who'd shown up because they needed a place
to smoke. I thought What a wonderful
compliment. Danced with Tim, which made us
both feel giddy with glamour—open mouths,
etc., but everyone basically cool—and most
amazing of all, a girl I've known for years
kept trying to pick me up, which must say
something for Radical Drag: I'm so unrefined
anymore, my dear,

                  without your eye for Appearance.
Next I was going to write a terrible poem on
sunset at Chestnut Hill. I had remembered
Merton seeing whatever it was between the trees.
That was the least inspired. "The sun descends/
among the shrines . . ." How dreary, how 1946.
Finally on the fluorescent night train, reading
The Crystal Lithium and wondering, Skyler or Shyler?
instead of composing a poem about the red-haired
girl who walked to the back of the car supremely
confident of finding a station, even though
the windows only showed her own reflection.
Rob, she must know something

                        we don't.

ALLENTOWN

waking to
rain and
still being
drunk and
trying again
to fuck before
the bus came

ON TV

cop pulls up
in car in
voice of a cop

block all
exits stop
anyone leaving

No Way To Treat
A Lady is
on tv

tonight they've
almost caught
Rod Steiger

his mother is
watching his mother
is on the wall in

every shot he
may have escaped
detection

by dressing in
mother drag
one time he

tried Interior
Decoration he
tried everything

slipped up once
though now the
tv swarming

with cops
he beats
them off

they love
it of course his
mother is watching

his mother is treating
the ladies her son is
beating the cop by dressing

in cop drag
on tv he even
did that

put on the
leather as soon
as they came

ducked through Stage
Door no way to
treat the son of

a lady who
knows that his
mother is

watching it all
last year on tv
when he was being

On Stage when
no one was ever
allowed to get out

fell asleep stoned second
night in a row not
wanting to, and dreamed

we were together in
bed in a green bedroom
and slept apart

DAN PROPPER

"Precocious w/ missile-age glitter,"
anthologized by Seymour Krim in
paperback *The Beats*, DAN PROPPER
you are 34 or 5 years old now and
I wonder whether you're still
writing Allen Ginsberg imitations

and lying through your teeth when you
say that you know the Apocalypse will
bring us to sweetness and light

or if you're writing at all:
you may be dead or have blown
your mind apart in the Sixties
and be in some bin. I don't
recall your assassination. Maybe
you're running a coffeehouse somewhere,

although I hope not. Maybe
you're married and teaching in college;
I hope too you're not doing that.

I would like to have met you,
a 22-year-old Beatnik poet, in
1960 when the book appeared but
I was just 9 years old then, posing
for snapshots with my arm around
Freddy Geoffrion's shoulder

in June, when school let out. You were
probably in San Francisco then, or NYC
(I'm so familiar now with NYC).

Nine-year-olds were skating down
Camac Street on Saturday after I'd read
your "Fable of the Final Hour." I
wondered what I'll be when they're 22
and possibly poets in thirteen years:
beautiful or dead, I hope.

POEM AFTER DINNER

for Tim

some things never run out:
my poverty, for instance,
is never exhausted
sandwiches for dinner again

your blond hair, for instance,
even if we're both exhausted
soothes me when we go outside
you and the forsythias

I get so excited
I think I'll read the Susan Sontag article
in *Partisan Review*
I want to walk beside you in the drizzle

and say you can move in with me
tonight, right away, even though
this time they'll probably evict me
and although I'm moving out in three weeks anyway

NOTE TO BOB CHAMBERLAIN

Frank O'Hara is THE great American
poet and seer of this our century,
he should have been on tv, the most

beautiful is Michael Lally when he thumbs
across D.C. to buy a scarf in Feb. and wearing
corduroy slippers, he's so fucked up

and Marty Watt the half-discovered genius
of the Seventies I love most when he
lets me know we're both still slender

as the body of our works

ASH WEDNESDAY – 5 POEMS

at the children's mass

1.
I'm not at all sure I'm dust;
meat, perhaps, and dying, the way
Swift could see in timelapse, but
what drifts out of the sunbeam down
to the crowd on knees, I guess not.

2.
An eight-year-old with a butch haircut;
only one in his class with a head that way,
and soft and brutal look, like Cuddly
and Deadly the Butch Sisters now
that everyone knows there's no such thing

3.
The choir of children! my desire
unready for perfection
I stayed though, daubed
with ashes wet as mud
crawled across small bodies to communicate

4.
When I was a small boy I was never
as small as these, never sang Hymns
for Organ, never saw Sister watch
my back at recess when I watched
the long-haired leather jacket boys.

5.
Priest smudges forehead with Inquiring Look
I say Take my picture, please
Black Cross Features, Black Star Photo
Stars Convene In Emergency Session to ask
who doused the fire to make these ashes

CHRIS STREET

Sky of iron, I clang my head against
your edge when I wake up. I forgot.
No scars, though. This is the morning.
I go back to sleep until one o'clock.

All my days are getting to be that way:
half-finished. Even when I wake alone
the room is full of smoke. It hangs there
from nights ago and does not move.
My window has been open all week.

If I could see a corner of the river.
Even if the street outside were wet.
Paper sky, sky of fire-escapes,
I sit like Dick Van Dyke among the chimneys
smoking with my lovers, my poison cigarettes.

CHRIS STREET II

in David's Potbelly, which I persist
in calling Danny's Potbelly, because
there's a bar named Danny's,
we eat Vienna chocolate cake

and talk
it's dark
but sunny
outside

there are a dozen ways to write this poem
this is my Most Poetic Day, I bristle
with ways, like New York,
like the hair of Joey

that shouldn't bristle
at all, but does
or the windowful
of stained glass birds

that knocks me down when we walk
outside: How did that glass
get stained, we ask a cop
who thinks we're crazy

FRIDAY NIGHT

Michael Lally refuses to talk about poetry
while cruising! which is okay, I guess,
although he was rather rude when I tried
to start a conversation. He dances with
sensuous vigor, a saving grace. His eyes

are a saving grace. And Eliot must be
indefensible: Franny never showed up
tonight to swap his virtues for O'Hara's tit for tat
although we'd made a date. The disappointing poets

at the Pier. Chuck likes a muscular boy
in a red plaid shirt, he tells me when we
dance. David, who swims, likes Chuck. And
Michael (not Lally, another one) has taken
five Quaaludes, and wants to go home with

anyone, but David especially. I like them
all. I'd go to bed with any one of them,
although I'm Gregarious Barfly rather than
Slut tonight, passing messages, making

introductions. Finally split with Chuck,
2:45 a.m., to Blimpie's Georgetown for ice cream
and high school memory talk. Gerry was gay;
was Terry gay? We hope so, and wonder
where he is: back then, if only we'd known!

JOE

It's cold, you note
(correctly) as we walk
to the train

it's midnight, it
will be colder
when you leave
6 a.m. or so

What I Have To Do:
think about Robert Lowell
so I can be coherent
tomorrow a.m.

I don't think
I have to think about
you, but I do
anyway

about you next to me anyway
(such an ego!) under
the dim lights

in a blue seat
on an old train
that has not started to move

CRABS? NO CRABS

crabs? no
crabs, though I
thought Not Again
after you stayed
overnight

last time got them
from Tom, they stayed
in bed, in pubic
hair all spring

no good blue
ointment no good
poison shampoo

what I finally
had to do:

shave bald as the
moon for hernia
cut before the
good news Crabs
Evacuate Craters

finally hit the papers

SECOND ANNIVERSARY

for Rob

1.
Two years ago tonight made love with you
for the first time, first time with any boy

on 12th floor Plaza Hotel New York: like Cary Grant,
like Barefoot in the Park, in the dark—

your slimness pressed
against my corduroy chest

your gaze a spike
in the tenderest spot

—with you was the final time it happened that way.

2.
All my lovers here tonight:
it's some star's birthday fallen
on our anniversary.

Tom, for whom I left you
has taken Quaaludes

Tim is with another boy
his woman-lover fixes him a drink

and Joey came from Jersey to reassure himself
that he can be always happy tomorrow
by having me in every tonight.

It is so different, trivial now. The worst part
is not even Having the Answers. I want to

phone you again like this afternoon,
our pointless conversation, hidden eyes:

no sky was heard along the line,
just oceans inside
that we used to walk on.

3.
I leave party early to walk home
holding you two years ago in my mind

wearing wet shoes under
fullest moon of the year.

High

There

poems

by Tim Dlugos

WASHINGTON, D.C.

1973-1976

CRAZY

Everybody tells me I'm crazy because I walked around
    muttering and screwed my courses
I'm crazy for losing Financial Aid and living in a crazy old
    house full of rifles and books
where I'm crazy in the attic like a Gothic novel and crazy in
    bed when I yell in my sleep and of course because of the
    other things I do in bed
I'm crazy, but I've known that all along and don't mind a bit
I'm jobless and crazy, crazy with power, crazy for glamour and
    rhinestones and stars,
you'll laugh at me and point your fingers and I'll still be crazy
    when they lock me up but I'll be
crazy about the surgical orderly who shaves my head, that's
    the kind of beautiful crazy I'll be

I'd be crazy to take off my clothes as I read this, and crazy to
    take yours off too,
we'd all be crazy about the policemen with big black boots
    who'd take us away when we were finally naked
they'd think we were crazy when they read all our personal
    records
and saw how I used to be crazy for Jesus, and crazy for real
    when I cared that they said I was crazy,
but now I'm 22 and growing my hair, I'm crazy with joy
when I think how I'll look in a year in the city, out on the street
being crazy about the New York boys, red hair! brown eyes!
    blue jeans! who'll say
You're Crazy when I fall into their eyes

DEATH BY DROWNING

for Yukio Mishima

1.
Death by drowning—
the swimmer paralyzed
by finally learning
the truth about swans:

why they fly at night,
what they do to their necks
to put the curve there,
why they make that noise.

2.
I shall drown in all
probability, he said to
his friends, because of
the things I want you

to know. The words had failed;
their bodies never learned.
He wished they were crewcut.
He wished they wore hats with shiny brims.

3.
He had been swimming
a long time when the swans
arrived. He watched them
settle on the waves.

His friends had gone.
The temple had burned down.
He knew it was his body's turn
to not know.

4.
The sea will wash me
onto the beach, like in
movies, he thought, and fixed
the scene in his mind

for a last thing to look at.
It was no consolation.
He died in the sea, and his body
was not washed up.

NINETY-ONE DEGREES

in college drag not
like you I perspire

like you in my cool jeans
your beige suit not-so-cool

today is wet
and in three pieces

young men take off
your shirts young women

remove what keeps you hot
first take the afternoon

off then take the young men
we both want to take off

with no shirt the corner
of your mouth goes white

the color of the room
you go to like my shirt went

when I took it off
a corner boy

my black shoes coming
untied

THINGS I MIGHT DO

for Terry Winch

Might write a letter to Jim Carroll
this p.m., I finally found his address.
Might get an answer; probably not.
Might start crying when Joey calls
tonight. Might wonder if he slept
with Michael; probably won't ask.
Some time might remember the name of
the star that the statue on the fountain
at the Circle resembles: not Leslie Howard,
but that's pretty close. Might quit
work today, might dream about my job
again tonight, the 4th night in a row.
Might lose something if I keep on
working. Might forget to cash my check
again. Might go out dancing
with Billy whom I might call this afternoon,
and might go to bed with when parents split
for West Coast in just two weeks. Might
look for an apartment. Might make
a tremendous break and move to New York City.
Might do the streets. Might get crabs.
Might be missing the world's most beautiful
boy by writing now. Might get a sunburn.
Might go bald. Might fall asleep on the bench
like some old bum. Might leave the Circle.
Might check the poems out at Discount Books,
find Joe Brainard, find Geraud. Might wave
to Terry as I just walk past, his waving back
a p.m. highlight and distinct possibility.

ON SEEING GARY COOPER WAKE UP
IN BED WITH WALTER BRENNAN IN
THE WESTERNER

After a drunk
like the rest of us
started

boots still on the young
one wonders where
he left his jacket

when they tumble
out of bed
after playing drugged

and macho like dust
and Sunday after a long night
nothing can change

the hearse still driving
around like a clown-
mobile this morning too

COMPENSATION

mad doll
dances
across the bar

I say when
I mean
walks funny

that is how I
always write
in parents' apt.

HIGH THERE

your small hands, your
nipples

flying to Boston

NEXT CHAPTER

I make my first
fortune, then drive
in a white convertible
to the edge of ruin.

THE WAY WE ARE NOW

for Mary Ellen

1.
We both got tired
of people walking away,
and walked away.

Nobody's waiting now
for our next move.
Even the FBI stopped
following you. We stopped
resisting. Now we can
write it down. We both
are faggots, we both
left home. Now we can
say it. Now we are
sounds to each other
on office phones.

2.
When I say I want
to see you, I mean
I want to be you, I mean
I want to know it
the way we used to want
to know each other, as well as
we thought we knew ourselves
and the way we were sure
we'd know the way we are now,
but couldn't have guessed after all.

3.
I write you poems.
I call you up and talk about dykes.
I cut off all your hair and put it in a green envelope.
I fall in love with the space behind your eyes.
I tuck you in and sing to your remaining ovary.
I won't take off your bra.
I think you're so nifty.
I think you're so blue.
Your laughing. Your car.
I think about you, much of the time.
I think I don't know what to think.
I think of the inevitable fireworks
if I were more a man, or you were.

I want to be a woman when I think
I could be like you.

TWO THINGS A STAR WOULDN'T DO

Masturbate.

Write this.

HAIKU

for Ken

August, midnight: after sex,
my face in bathroom mirror, a surprise.

MESCALINE

for Blaine

Looking at each other:
we turned into people
we never had seen before.
Then we were in the same
room somewhere else: in Mexico,
living in the same hacienda.
We were in the living room

looking like Pancho
and Cisco the Good Guys:
right then, anyway, we were
the good guys. This was on
organic mescaline. There were
mugs of tea and an incredible rainbow,
all white. We took off our hats.

Looking away we were everywhere
together. We broke through
again. The arc of light was
between our foreheads. That was
when I knew I could go with him
down the line, and not need anything else.
It was perfect, and I was so sure.

FAMOUS WRITERS

With famous writers you rarely know
what to expect. But sometimes
there are clues. The Maya in
Mayakovsky, for example, as in
"All is . . .". The secret Hem of
Hemingway. Closet writers give us
many clues. Those two blew
their skulls apart with gunshots.
Most famous writers have died, one way

or another. Frank O'Hara: the magnificent
OH in his name is what you say
when you're on the street pretending to be
Frank O'Hara. He may have said it himself
on the beach that night. And the Man
at the end of Berryman, which appears too
in Whitman, but means something different.

SEPTEMBER 12

On June 8, 1968, when I drove
with friends across Key Bridge
to Georgetown for beer at the same time
that Robert Kennedy's coffin was
crossing Memorial Bridge in the other
direction to be buried by candle-
light at Arlington, I felt the way

I felt last night, drinking and
trying to dance while aware that
gentle Allende was probably dead
by now, and Neruda would get hit
next. I couldn't believe it was
happening either time, which didn't stop me
from feeling that way.

TEN MOVIES

None But the Brave

An American airplane crew crashes on a South Pacific island
held by a Japanese army platoon.
A temporary truce is arranged.

Waterloo Bridge

A ballet dancer falls in love with a soldier.
She's told he has been killed and enters prostitution.

The Hustler

A traveling pool hustler takes on the champ.
His girl commits suicide.
Robert Rossen's direction is superb.

Man in the Dark

A convict submits to a brain operation that eliminates
criminal tendencies.
He loses his memory.

Run for the Sun

A woman reporter flies to a remote Mexican fishing village.
She's looking for an American author but finds a hideout for Nazis.

Gentlemen Prefer Blondes

Two show girls go to Paris, hoping to land rich husbands or
plenty of diamonds.

Girls! Girls! Girls!

Elvis is chased by a mass of girls and can't decide which one
he prefers.

I Married a Witch

A witch is released from "the beyond."
She develops a strong yen for a man who is running for governor.

Jungle Woman

A physician returns an ape to life.
It becomes a beautiful woman.

The Killer That Stalked New York

A husband steals diamonds.
His wife smuggles them into the U.S.
But, unknown to both, the wife carries the plague.

FLAMING ANGEL

The animal strings of Prokofiev
can be inside you, too.
That is the hardest thing:
to watch what you have never known
through animal eyes.

Another flaming angel is
in front of you, he wants
you effortless and shining
the way he insists you
can be. But your heart

is full of animals,
the way the earth is
full of them, and empty
as the earth can be
holding them all.

OUT OF LOVE

We forget if there is anything to say.
I call you and remember your shoulders.
Your voice is the same.
What are you remembering.

Saw you last in a dark corridor.
We didn't kiss at all.
Our hug was harder than I had expected.
It was out of love,
out of everything for 2 whole years.

I discover I've written a poem for you.
It's called "High There."
Also, it's three years since we first met, to the week.
I remember these things when you hang up the phone.

NIGHT LIFE

for Ed Cox

The lives we lead at night:
you are on the streets of my
city, and I am asleep. In
my dream you are talking
to an old man, white beard.
You call him Fritz. You
call him Walt. It does not
matter what you call him;
he is just an old man.

You and he have made the same
choices. Now you think there's
something you should know. You
want him to tell you, but he
will not speak. You are both walking
down Spruce Street, and you are alone.

You are in denim. You are
in therapy too. You learn
what you mean when you talk
out loud. Sometimes you learn
in your sleep. In strange cities,
we discover the way we can be.
We learn that we have always
been talking to ourselves. People
lead their lives all the time.

INCREDIBLE RISKS

I take incredible
risks with my poems,
which is why they
always turn out
so fine.

THE HIGH AIR

The high air is
thin.

In the high air you are
never surrounded.

You can breathe in
the high air.

The high air is still
a boy.

In the mountains you can almost
touch the high air.

The high air in the city is
where you sleep.

People sleep together in
bags in the high air.

People fly out of it.
People don't try.

Once the high air used to be
closer.

Now the high air wants to be
higher, and dark

with stars.

AFTER ANNE HERSHON'S PARTY

Ned Rorem lived in Paris
when he was my age

he lived in Philadelphia when young
and had a serious drinking problem

POEM FOR JEANNE

I am afraid of the country,
too. It is not the distances
that frighten me—it is
the way we can be part of
the scene so easily. Rooted

like a tree in a particular
yard. Standing in the darkness
after the film runs out. Our
hands can be nameless. Our branches
can bud anytime. Suddenly

we can be breathing, as
slowly as the trees. Then
someone will cry out in
the silence, and we will be
startled, and faced with it.

THE THIRD SEX

for Tim

While everyone is driving in
the snow, I will remind you
of Sylvia Plath in her novel.
You will remind yourself
of her as well. We will
lie down where it is warm.
I will grow a moustache.
You will shave as quickly
as you can. We will call
what we are holding our
"hands," and try to proceed
from there. We will discover
more sticky details than we
had prepared ourselves for.
After a night of calling
each other "Sylvia," we
will both be very confused.

AFTER A LINE BY TED BERRIGAN

I want Pepsi for breakfast
every day. Every time I look
out the window I want to see
Sheridan Square. The lights
have to be just right.

I want to look as good as
Carroll (Jim), and write as good as
Berrigan (Ted). I want to seem
gentle and wear leather clothes.
The things you might suppose

I want, I probably don't:
for instance, dope. I can be
totally carried away by a face
in the city, a line in a poem:
the moment at my parents' home,

for instance, when I saw that
phrase again and sat up, straight.
"I have been in bed," I said, "in
my lover's underwear long enough!
I want to be feminine, marvelous, and tough!"

NYC DIARY

Drove up w/ 4 people in front seat.

Stopped several times on 95.

Could only buy $2 worth of gas on NJ Tpk.

Big D Discount Store—looked like a cartoon.

Found Prince Street easily.

Moved furniture upstairs—Randall De Leeuw lives there.

Dinner at the Luna, in Little Italy. Decorations:
    Letter from Gov. of Maine, dated Oct 1950.
    Recommendation by Walter Winchell.
    Murals w/ cracks painted on.
    Picture of a bishop (St. Rocco?)

Christmas lights up on streets of Little Italy.

St. Mark's Poetry Project:
    Rob, looking beautiful.
    Anne Waldman, looking sharp (copper hair!)
    Patti Smith (sexy!)
    Paul Violi's great poems
    Allen Ginsberg, gray of beard
    Heckler in back row, Charlie Mingus' son.
    Bad poetry—Oren Eisenberg, Bill Zavatsky.
    Taylor Mead, w/ a huge forehead like Allen Tate's.
    Anthony Dowell's group, incl. his wife who I thought
        was Jim Carroll when I only could see her face, and
        Val Curzon who is having tea w/ John Ashbery the next day.
    The Hasidic Jesus-person who wouldn't give up the mike.

Back at Prince St. (brush teeth).

Ninth Circle—conversation w/ someone who looks like Michael—
at first glance. Freaked out actor.

The Street—beautiful blond boy in green coat.

Road House—conversation w/ chubby speech therapist from
Brooklyn College. He says he'll write me a letter.

David's Potbelly—Ramon's immense piece of chocolate cake—
my tomato juice—nice waitress, 4 or 6 drunken fat disgusting
men at the next table.

Back to Prince St.

Five in a bed (2 mattresses), a la Three Stooges.

Wake up late Sat. Rain. English muffins, then take taxi
from Houston Street to George Faust's house. Michael says
he's an Allen Austin-type person, and his home looks
something like Allen Austin's.

The cute Faust child. (1½? 2?)

Subway uptown to Fifth Ave. Meet Barbara Baracks for lunch
at deli. Heavy talk w/ Michael while Terry & Barbara have
heavy talk. She's 22, bright-eyed, and knows considerably
less abt. poetry than I do. She writes well though. Has
printed a broadside which she gives each of us, w/ autograph.

Then to bookstore at Museum of Modern Art. Joe Brainard's
I Remember Christmas. Joe Brainard's Christmas card.
Much Duchamp material, in connection w/ current exhibit
at MOMA. Book called *The Machine* w/ metal cover.

By now it's sleeting. I'm only wearing a t-shirt under
my coat (the one from New Ingenue).

We run around like maniacs trying to find Terry's brother's
office. Finally manage to, but the brother's not in.
We go to lobby & make phone calls for awhile.

Michael says we can't visit Brainard because he's having a fight
w/ his landlady this afternoon. Bus downtown.

Get off next to a Woolworth's. I need socks and underwear,
so we walk in where we see (fanfare!) Anne Waldman. I
buy underwear; we're going up the street w/ her for coffee.

A long time talking w/ Anne. She likes the way my book looks.
She wants me to send her the review in the *Star* where
Sean Mitchell panned her. She says living in India for
4 months is cheaper than living on St. Mark's Place.
Everyone she knows is poorer than they were last year
at this time. Don't be shy, she says, and I won't. I
am very high. She asks me to autograph my book, and
I write something dumb like "Hope you like these." which
is true, though.

We leave Anne's and get pictures of ourselves in photo booth
at Woolworth's. We get to keep 2, and give the other 2
to each other.

Go to the Eighth Street Bookshop. I'm a little upset that SOUP
books are on racks w/ the little magazines, but they do
show off better that way. I want to buy *Witt* by Patti
Smith, *In Baltic Circles* by Paul Violi, and Alice Notley's
book from Angel Hair. Also *Magellanic Clouds* by

Wakoski, even though Waldman said she's not writing well
anymore. (Other things A.W. said—APR is horrible
(she didn't care, I think, for Parker); Ted Berrigan is
responsible for the St. Mark's group having a bad reputation
because he made them look so cool in lectures around the
country (1968 or so); people get upset not because the
St. Mark's people are *rich* or *successful* in terms of major
publishers, but because they're having fun.) Anyway,
I don't buy any of the books for lack of $. We take
a cab to Prince Street.

Drive w/ Ramon to his cousin's for drinks. 43 Fifth Ave.
(bldg. designed by Stanford White, w/ gargoyles and
cherubs on lobby walls.) His cousin turns out to be
Agustin Fernandez, painter from Cuba who just moved here
from Paris. Wife Lia, from Rumania. 3 beautiful children.
Beautiful apt. Beautiful French houseguest. I get high
on whiskey and soda in beautiful brandy snifter. The
Fernandezs carry on a tri-lingual conversation, mentioning
friends like Anais Nin, Lawrence Durrell, Bowles and Oc-
tavio Paz. Lia thought Burroughs was a disgusting man.
Terry & I talk to Agustin about Irish wakes and anonymous
violence. Ramon leaves in the middle of the conversation.
We split after half an hour, feeling really fine. My
adjectives for Agustin are "magnanimous," "generous," and
"rich." He might do a collaboration w/ Ashbery, whom I
ought to call, who's haunting, in a sense, this trip.

Next, to a restaurant called One Potato for dinner. I spend
a long time on the phone to Jim (who sounds distant, making
me paranoid—I'm sure I sound drunk which makes me even
more paranoid), to Spin & to parents.

Then to Prince St. Michael, Ramon & Randy are going to the
　　Club Baths; they drop Terry and me off at the Ninth Circle.
　　I meet a *very* beautiful boy named Robert Rooney, who
　　lives (damn!) w/ his family in Jersey City, who went
　　to the Christian Brothers school at Hudson, and who works
　　in the Alumni Shop at Lord and Taylor's. Talk abt.
　　coincidences! His birthday is May 9. We can't get together
　　tonight, but we talk all night and exchange addresses.
　　He gives much Rob Dewey cool glamour, which I know
　　exactly how to handle. That makes me feel good. Randy
　　Michael & Ramon arrive at 2, and we go back to Prince St.,
　　again sleeping a la Stooges.

I don't sleep as well as the night before.

Randy seems like he'll be glad to see us go: understandable.

Ramon, Michael & Terry split for breakfast, but I'm out of $
　　so don't. Listen to Michael's tapes of the St. Mark's read-
　　ings, then write these notes so I won't forget what I
　　did in NY. Randy goes out to Canal Street, leaving me
　　in the apt. with his cat, hairy, black and amorous.

NOTE AND SONNET

the way I used "you" in my poems
after June 1973, meaning
nothing I know

1974—it's January 5
It's Washington it was
New York 2 days ago   Prince St.
Outside Randy's window   nothing
I know I thought I was being Shy:
I know Anne Waldman
I know Michael & Terry
I know the church at Prince &
Elizabeth that rings the highspeed
Angelus   6 a.m.   dear Ted I
Know so many people who love you
Read the Sonnets all afternoon in
DC   in my poems   the terrible
Windows   the way I was using "you"

TIM DLUGOS . 99

SO FAR

Saturday, Jan. 12: sky full

of clouds and the sun behind them
"intermittent" "hard-edged"
                                        that's not unusual

got to sleep 5:30 after Heavy Talk w/ Joe
but that was Last Night, even though
the date is the same
                                I don't like remembering
Last Night when I wake w/ achy legs from
too much beer   so put Joni Mitchell on
(Morning Morgantown)   then switch to Bacall
in Applause as perhaps more appropriate

books for the afternoon: Dreaming As One
by Lewis Warsh and Stupid Rabbits by Michael Lally
also the new Art News, but that's a magazine

it's all about New Mexico!   I wanted to ush
all summer at the Santa Fe Opera, but never
got west of Leesburg, Va.
                                unlike Belinda
                                unlike Chuck

some of the people I know live in California
others are talking outside my room   but
everyone, no matter how far the physical distance
is only a phone call away

I am happy when I remember that

GANGSTER OF LOVE

1.

The woman is seated next to the surgeon's desk. Her fingers
press a lump on her hand. She tells him she is afraid it is
a malignant tumor. No, he replies, it is just a cyst. She
sobs. The surgeon strokes her arm. She bends over, kisses
his hand. He strokes her hair. Suddenly she shivers and
places his hand on her leg. The surgeon leaves it there for
a full minute, then removes it and tells her she has abso-
lutely nothing to worry about. Reassured at last, she leaves.

2.

A minister in a small Southern city calls on a bedridden
woman who has less than a year to live. It is his third
visit and they are alone in the house. Her marriage has
always been unhappy, she tells him. The minister slides
into bed next to her. The affair continues for several
weeks. One afternoon her husband discovers them. He
begins divorce proceedings against his dying wife. The
clergyman is dismissed from the ministry, and his wife
divorces him.

3.

He is an experienced West Coast divorce lawyer. He knows
his female clients are often vulnerable to the advances of
any sympathetic man. The woman sitting in his office de-
clares that there is no such thing as a sexually considerate
man. She crosses her legs and her skirt hikes up. But
the lawyer gives her no encouragement, because he remembers
a colleague who had an affair with a client who subsequently
spread the news around town. The colleague decided to move
his practice to another community.

4.

The male college teacher is handsome, scholarly, and enormously
attractive to the numerous female students he makes love to.
He is also attractive to a male homosexual in one of his classes.
After a session of pot-smoking one night, the teacher has
sexual relations with the homosexual. Next day, remorseful,
he tells the student the incident will not be repeated.
The homosexual retaliates by reporting the incident to college
authorities. The teacher is promptly fired and is unable
to get another job.

DAY LIGHT

for Bob Mulderick

There are people, and there is
a man. His face cuts through our eyelids
like a smoky light. Whenever we speak
we are secretly talking to him.

I shall be able to write great books
when I see him, you will be
able to pay your bills. He will make us
woozy with his smoky love. When we are watching
each other we remember these things. We go home
alone or together, with wandering eyes.

There are kisses, and there is
a kiss. It lives among our rumors
like the family dog. We open our eyes
and it's day light, just as we expected.

MALLARMÉ

Stéphane Mallarmé is living in the woods in a
hut, his hair is brown again, the trees are totally
brown against a deep sky (Feb.) and the river
is brown today too. Mallarmé is cooking at a wood fire.
His eyes are teary from the smoke as he welcomes
his visitors. He is dressed as a farmer with dark brown
shoes, but that is just the mud, he confides.
Everywhere you go you run into it; it's commoner
than shit, than infatuation. Mallarmé smokes
Lucky Strikes. He drives a fine car, and lives
in the capital of one of the sophisticated countries.
He is very rich, which is why he can live this way.
Give me bread and goats for milk, and I'm perfectly
happy, he says. None of the visitors understands,
so Mallarmé repeats himself, this time with broad winks
and a sly expression. The visitors burst into applause.

If he had played his cards right, Mallarmé confesses,
he could have been Heidi's grandfather. Now he has to
settle for Heidegger, or Oskar Kokoschka, neither of which
seems to please him. A woman walks in with a pail of
milk, and Mallarmé puts on an Irish accent, showing off how
literate he is. The visitors think that is arch. A brown
rain starts to fall. Everybody senses that somehow it
provides the connection. Mallarmé is going to New York,
so this is the process described as "seeing him off."

DREAM SERIES

after Annabelle Hebert

1.

I'm back in Philadelphia, living on Pulaski Avenue. We
are about to be evicted again, and Ken hasn't packed a
thing. His clothes, his furniture, his personal effects
are strewn all over. Paul Smith is living there too, which
is illegal. I go downstairs, where the landlord and his wife
have begun to clean the kitchen. I overhear the landlord
say, "I'm not gonna rent this house to no more boys."
"Don't say that, darling, most boys are better than these
four," his wife replies.

2.

I pick Spinner up in my car, and we drive around the block
without talking. He is getting angrier and angrier. Finally
he starts to scream at me, telling me very clearly and very
loudly how fucked up I am, and the exact personality defects
that destroyed our relationship. I understand completely, and
am very sad. He gets out of the car. When I wake up, I cannot
remember any of his words.

3.

I am going to Grand Central for dinner with my mother and
somebody else. Outside the restaurant I run into Bill Anderson,
and ask him how his date went the other night. It went okay.
Inside, the bar looks like a coffeehouse, Amanda's, that used to
be in Georgetown when I was in high school. I discover I am not
wearing a shirt, so we sit at a table in the corner.

4.

I am in Provincetown again, at the Back Room Bar. The Columbia
dropout on whom I had a crush one summer is a waiter there.
I can't remember his name. I order Italian food. When the waiter
comes back I realize he's Danny Friedel. We make up with many
happy tears. After dinner he quits his job, and we go to a movie.

DEATH SERIES

1.

Frank Koerner, Tom Bewick and some other people are drinking
beer and driving around McLean at night. It's June, a month
after graduation. Another car pulls up beside them, and
someone inside throws a beer can. A fight ensues, during which
Frank is stabbed with a bayonet. On the way to the hospital
he keeps asking Tom whether he's going to die.

2.

Patsy McGraw is driving back from Ocean City. At the Chesapeake
Bay Bridge there is a traffic jam, as usual. A thunderstorm is
gathering. Patsy gets out of her car and is struck by a bolt
of lightning.

3.

My cousin Chris. She is tired of driving, and pulls her car to
the side of the highway so her boyfriend can take over. He gets
out of the right front door. She begins to slide across the seat.
A speeding car hits hers from behind. She is killed instantly.

4.

Frank McCarthy sits on the roof of The Philadelphian for several
hours, then jumps off. It's the day after Kent State. He leaves
a note with his schoolbooks, saying They Shoot Horses Don't They.
The impact of the fall drives his pelvis up into his chest cavity.

5.

The Christian Brothers dying. David Ryan clutching at his pillow
in an epileptic fit. Tom Swisdak falling down, unable to breathe.
Franny Hickey dying in a van on the Schuylkill Expressway.
Scores of Brothers passing away from old age.

6.

There are the people who almost die. Tom falls asleep at the
wheel after several Quaaludes and runs his car off the Boulevard.
Tim is dragged thirty feet by the Broad St. subway after his foot
gets caught in a door of the train. Judy's hair catches fire
from a candle at the Robert Kennedy memorial mass. Joe
tells me I will die as the result of a terrible accident.

7.

Greg Severin spends the day teaching. He has dinner with Pam
Kinney, and goes home alone. He drinks heavily for several hours,
then shoots himself in the head with a pistol he has borrowed
from his father. He had been planning to enter religious life.

HOMAGE TO P. INMAN

I see you in an airplane, in a
Western hat. In the cockpit you
are chewing baseball bubblegum &
letting the authorities know what
you do in bed. The microphone
keeps laughing back. Behind your
expensive goggles you plot the
major riots of the 60s. Helen Hayes
is drooling at your feet on a
previous flight. You discover theme
music. You fly this fucker right
into the White House. The brilliant
lights go on. The control tower
vanishes. Its absence is as stupid
a preoccupation as anything else.

TOO FAR

for Bernard Welt

In this story the horizon drops. All winter the sky gets higher, which we perceive as the gesture of beckoning. Our heads are in the clouds, we would say. Our feet are in the sky, our hands are lost in the woods with the other animals. Building a nest in another body, pushing a small boat into the filthy river— these can be perceived as gestures of beginning, but gestures nonetheless. There are many small fires ahead in this story. We shoot at birds, at dead wood, into the sky. We open fire at foreigners who love our easy grace. We know it's not easy. We know it requires much suffering. We have to go far enough without going too far. Stiff terms. Your dancing, the odor of the flowers in your yard all point to something. We mean to find it. We take off our hats. We strip the bark off trees. We keep our eyes peeled. There is a quiet glory in what we perceive as our work.

This story is set in a partially empty space with no borders. The only edge we ever find is where water and land meet air, and even that keeps shifting when we breathe, or when our bodies make their terrible gestures.

AMERICAN BASEBALL

It's for real, not for practice, and it's televised,
not secret, the way you'd expect a civilized country
to handle delicate things, it's in color, it's happening
now in Florida, "This Is American Baseball" the announcer
announces as the batter enters the box, we are watching,
and it could be either of us

                     standing there waiting
for the pitch, avoiding the eye of the pitcher as we take
a few practice cuts, turning to him and his tiny friends in
the outfield, facing the situation, knowing that someone
behind our backs is making terrible gestures, standing
there to swing and miss

                     the way I miss you, wanting to be out
of uniform, out of breath, in your car, in love again, learning
all the signals for the first time, the way we learned the rules
of night baseball as high-school freshmen: first base, you kiss
her, second base, her breasts, third, you're in her pants, and
home is where the heart

                     wants to be all the time, but seldom
can reach past the obstacle course of space, the home in our
perfect future we wanted so badly, and want more than ever since
we learned we won't live there, which happens to lovers in civilized
countries all the time, and happens too in American baseball when
you strike out and remember what the game really meant.

GILLIGAN'S ISLAND

The Professor and Ginger are standing in the space in front
of the Skipper's cabin. The Professor is wearing deck shoes,
brushed denim jeans, and a white shirt open at the throat.
Ginger is wearing spike heels, false eyelashes, and a white
satin kimono. The Professor looks at her with veiled lust
in his eyes. He raises an articulate eyebrow and addresses
her as Cio-Cio-San. Ginger blanches and falls on her knife.

*   *   *

Meanwhile it is raining in northern California. In a tiny
village on the coast, Rod Taylor and Tippi Hedren are totally
concerned. They realize that something terrible is happening.
Each has been savagely attacked by a wild songbird within
the last twenty-four hours. Outside their window thousands
of birds have gathered in anticipation of the famous school-
yard scene. Tippi Hedren is wearing a colorful lipstick.

*   *   *

Ginger stares back at the Professor. His sullen good looks
are the perfect foil for her radiant smile. The Skipper and
Gilligan come into sight. The Skipper has been chasing
Gilligan around the lagoon for a long time now. Gilligan
holds onto his hat in the stupid way he has of doing things
like that. The Professor's lips part in a sneer of perfect
contempt. Ginger bares her teeth, as if in appreciation.

*   *   *

Jackie Kennedy bares her teeth. Behind and above her, the muzzle of a high-powered rifle protrudes from a window. A little man is aiming at Jackie Kennedy's husband. The man is wearing bluejeans and a white T-shirt. There isn't a bird to be seen. As he squeezes the trigger, the little man mutters between clenched teeth, "Certs is a candy mint." The hands of Jackie Kennedy's husband jerk automatically toward his head.

* * *

The Professor is noticing Ginger's breasts. He thinks of the wife he left at home, who probably thinks he's dead. He thinks of his mother, and all of the women he has ever known. Mr. and Mrs. Howell are asleep in their hut, secure in their little lives as character actors. Ginger shifts her weight to the other foot. The intensity of the moment reminds the Professor of a Japanese city before the end of the war.

* * *

In his mind he goes down each aisle in his government class, focusing on each face, each body. He is lying on his bed with his white shirt off and his trousers open. Dorothy Kirsten's voice fills the room. He settles on a boy who sits two desks behind him. He begins to masturbate, his body moving in time with the sad music. At moments like these he feels farthest away. As he shoots, his lips part and he bares his teeth.

* * *

The Professor and Ginger are watching each other across the narrow space. The Skipper and Gilligan have disappeared down the beach. The Howells are quietly snoring. The Professor and Ginger are alone. From the woods comes the sound of strange birds. From the water comes a thick and eerie tropical silence. The famous conversation scene is about to start. Clouds appear in the sky, and it begins to snow.

THE BLACK FOREST

we were told   about the famous couples
of history who walk into the Black Forest
when the light is very dim and it's hard
to tell if it's growing or fading away   they
shed their reputations like their history

and leave their Bavarian hats at the forest's
edge   they are certain that the light is
fading when they walk into the Black Forest
and the chunks of sky between the leaves
lose all their light   it suddenly gets dark

in there and we are as afraid as anyone
entering the Black Forest   lugging our pathetic
basket of food   this is where the history
we had forgotten closes in on all the famous
couples, spoiling their picnic   bit by bit

we leave the food behind as a signal
to others in the Black Forest   but
it is too late   the bread has been
broken into chunks of our history and
eaten by birds   the birds fly away

I am here like Gretel when I hold your
hand and we travel through the Black Forest
late at night   we are ready to meet
anybody here, little brother   we know
their reputations from our history

UNDER THE SKY

We were supposed to
have gone to the mountains
but I stayed asleep
and it was too late

to leave by the time
I woke up and called you.
It started to rain.
All of our plans went

out the window, into
the trees with their tiny leaves
and the parking lot.
I watched a movie

and fell asleep with
a headache which hung on
when I reawoke.
It was too late

to call and explain
so I walked to my car
and drove through the rain
to your building. The moon

was perfectly
full. The sky
was perfectly
clear.

PRESIDENT TRUMAN

President Truman is sitting behind his desk at the Missouri
White House. He presses all the buttons next to the phone,
and hears soft chimes in every other room. Generals, steno-
graphers, gardeners, bodyguards, ministers of other countries,
and the chef all rush into the office simultaneously. They
pair up and begin to dance to an imaginary waltz. "By cracky!"
President Truman exclaims. He barks a short laugh, and
immediately becomes bored again. Bess slinks into the room.

Lauren Bacall was already in love with Bogart when they acted
together in *To Have and Have Not*. President Truman had been
the only other man in her life. In the musical *Applause* it was
President Truman who secretly pulled the strings. He made sure
that Lauren Bacall got first crack at the role of Margo Channing.
President Truman never forgot a face. Many people alive today
are secretly grateful for that. Lauren Bacall is one of them.

Bess and Mama did almost everything together. On Monday they
did the laundry; on Monday night they went to the poetry
reading; on Tuesday they washed the floors, and so on. Together
with his daughter Margaret, President Truman referred to them as
"my bosses." The real bosses were very angry at that. At
Margaret's recital they conspired to ruin her career. The rest,
as they say, is history. Years later, Margaret sang on *Omnibus*.

His past was shrouded in total mystery. Some said he had run
guns to the Cuban rebels in a small boat out of the Keys. Others
said he had only been to Florida once: the Orange Bowl, 1933.
Whatever the truth was, people liked him. You could tell by
the look in their eyes as the train was pulling away. They knew
it was he, not MacArthur, who really had balls when it came to
Japan. He was jaunty. Independent. Right on all the big things.
Even now, *Christmas with the Trumans* sells a million copies each year.

Nevertheless, it is easy to get confused. It is easy to confuse him with President Johnson; they died two weeks apart. It is easy to confuse him with President Coolidge; they both pushed all the buttons on their desks. Bess, however, stands out in a way her weak-kneed husband never did. She was the brains behind the operation. Mama gave them the estate on the Hudson on condition that they never fuck again. Bess said Great. When they saw themselves in movies, in *The March of Time*, President Truman would bark enthusiastically. Bess would merely adjust her hat, and flash her scary teeth.

LET'S GO / FROM JOURNAL

(after Bernadette Mayer's reading)

Morning, and alive
again in the shower. The green shampoo. The
Harlow clip. The silver roots. This is your
academy award. It shines from the roots up.
Prickly scalp. Indians. Alive.

I used to think I wanted too much.
Now I think I want exactly the right amount.
Almost remembered—suddenly
                        I do, and don't
know how to proceed. The zebra plant. The
sunny day. The fitful sleep. The water bed.
People taking pictures in a station, then leaving
on different trains. They arrive very late.
There are no cabs. The buses stopped running.
They're tired and it's miles to home. This
tiny drama can barely be imagined up here.
Whom am I trying to impress. B was at least
as attractive as P. T, who has a hard
time fucking, wanted to fuck her. Outside,
car horns. Men shout, Bernie! Bernie!

We went to the bar, then went to your apt.
This time we didn't fuck. I was on
the water bed again. I hadn't expected
to be sleeping with you again. We
hugged the other way. Sure I could.
The candidates, all of them, were on your TV
in color.

Got call from M 1:30, said Meet me 3:15.
You leap out of shower like a lithe and amazing
animal. Beads drop from your fur, and
you yell, Let's Go!

AS IT IS

The poems: leaving.
The subject: gone.
The free zone: empty.
The real thing: in your trunk.

The sex life: seen by thousands.
The skyline: afloat.
The good advice: taken.
The animals: mildly amused.

The cottage: filthy.
The thatch: on fire.
Your beard: still growing.
Your car keys: numb.

Your father's hand: open.
Your weekends: blah.
The feeling: ambiguous.
The country: Japan.

The seashore: dark.
The cutting edge: notched.
The atmosphere: invisible.
Your lost beauty: always there.

WHERE I STAND

in your eyes

I mean: cool off
take the time

this is where I stand:
wanting you

wanting to
"be able"

to take a stand
& balance there

a surfboard in the blue cathedral
a washday miracle
the rising Tide of inexorable powder

tastes like salt
where I stand wanting
more, always "more"

your medicine
your strange ballet

where you stand
a different way

that is how I want to
do it, w/ that tough grace

my naked feet
the strong cool light

in your eyes

NOTE TO J.A.

The famous heroines
toddle up the ramp
burdened by their own
sad stories. This is

overwhelmingly real, but
our lives go on nonetheless.
Like wheelchair detectives
we reach for the sky

and come back with hands
full of energy. It
dissipates faster than
our eyes can record.

GREAT ART

for Donald Grace

Underneath your skin, your heart
moves. Your chest
rises at its touch. A small bump
appears, every
second. We watch for what appears
to be hours.

Our hands log the time: the soft
light, darkness
underneath your eyes. Our bodies
intersect like highways
with limitless access and perfect spans
of attention.

We pay for this later. I pay
for breakfast. We
can't stay long. We take off
to the museum
and watch the individual colors
as they surface

in the late works of Matisse.
They move the way
your heart moves, the way we breathe.
You draw your own
breath, then I draw mine. This is
truly great art.

THE PRESIDENT'S SON

The President's son wears a bracelet
in the Washington Post. A chip of hope
infects the body politic. The photograph
angers the powerful lobbies. The boy
will grow up to be even more beautiful.

I wash my car and think of you.
I visit the International House
of Pancakes and remember our lives
as important political figures:
the hats we wore.

        • • • •

Desperate for an afternoon shower,
the President's son looks into the sky.
The window-washer drops his tools and plummets
eighteen stories: one for each
year of the age he most wants to be.

JE SUIS EIN AMERICANO

Systematic problems demand systematic solutions.
A single system of meaning—the same words, the same
ideas for everyone—is the first step toward solving
the complex problems we share. How can you care about
your neighbor if you can't understand what he says?
When we use the neutral universal language, all fears
and hatred directed at members of other language groups
disappear. We break into smiles and a different era starts.

Werner Heisenberg. Jose knew she had entered the den
by the smell of gabardine. Serge Prokofiev. His
kleptomania increased in intensity. Now he couldn't
pass a drugstore without running in and emerging with
fan magazines. Alice James. His jockey shorts bulged
with the proof of his current hypothesis. People hate
fake intellectuals. Jane Bowles. Only a few things
matter. Marcel Proust. Marcel Proust.

Magda met Hop Sing in the refugee camp, and immediately
fell in love. This cowboy, he cook good, she thought
in broken English. Hop Sing, a cripple of some sort,
loved Gershwin. This proves what the foreign-born can do
in a land of opportunity. Magda was enormously fat. They
embarked on a thousand-mile joyride that included revo-
lutionary acts. Rent strike did not shift power web.
They named the spread Mazola, the mansion Il Ponderosa.

Marcel Proust. My sex life has included the following:
Great Hits of Famous Composers, palaces of dance, adzes.
My love life is twisting slowly in the wind. My night life,
she hokay, boss. My spiritual life nourishes hungry throngs.
My life on other planets has been pleasant, but now I must
return to my own people. My former life is on TV in 1955.
This is your life, somebody insists in a foreign language.
Then come noises. The room is full of strong air.

TAROT FOR MY HISTORY

(read at Somerville, Mass. by Ron Schreiber, 25/10/74)

My Attitude: The Seven of Pentacles

The stars are too ripe, and I just stand
and watch. They're going to drop if
I don't bring them in. Finally the big
one decides. It shudders and falls, quite
slowly, from the sky to the ground. As
it approaches, it assumes a significance
greater by far than its actual size. I

just stand and watch. It lands at my
feet. I poke at it with my harvesting
tool to see if it's safe to pick up. Then
everything is suddenly, terribly wrong, i.e.,
my real life starts, and I must live
beneath a hole in the sky from now on.

My Recent History: The Ten of Swords

I am on the ground face
down, and ten swords stick out
of my back. They are in there
pretty deep, and probably pin me
to the ground. My sharpest sensation
is embarrassment: this is a heavy
picture, and way too histrionic.
I would not watch this picture
on TV. I would not accept this
poem for publication. My face
cannot be seen, though; a little hope
in that. Also, this is happening
in the past, which is a relief.

My Direction: The Ten of Wands

I have drawn the ten swords
out of my back. I carry them
back to you, like a woodsman
carrying sticks. This is
what I call feeling. This
is how I draw meaning into
my life, another picture
out of the deck. I live
inside your hand. I burrow
there like scabies, and make you
wake up every time the bell
goes off. You pick up the
receiver and hear my voice.
You think, It is starting again.

My Personality: The Knight of Swords

I try too hard
I find love hard to
sustain   I love to
take off, move out
I want to move in
with everyone I sleep
beside   it hurts their
feelings when I say this
about the others   I want
it all, the simplest thing

that is why the clouds look
that way, my face moves
beneath them very fast

GREAT BOOKS OF THE 1950s

I Was a Communist for the FBI

You have joined the Communist Party to give inside information
to the FBI. No one is aware that you are really a loyal American.
Your mother dies thinking you're a Communist. Your younger
brother beats you up. Even when the Communists kill your
girlfriend, you can't do a thing. Finally you testify before
a Congressional committee, and triumphantly watch the faces
of the Communist leaders as you expose their secret plans.

The Old Man and the Sea

You write a symbolic novel about the eternal struggle between
the wills of strong men and the forces of nature. You select
a baseball star to function as a hero for two Spanish-surnamed
males. But they're the real heroes. You envision Spencer
Tracy in the movie version of your novel, and are totally
delighted when you learn that the Hollywood moguls have
picked him for the part.

Black Like Me

You want to know what it is like to be black, so you dye your
skin and head south. You have many strange experiences, several
of which are sexual in nature and involve sadistic white men.
When you tire of this, you drive home and write a book describing
your travels. The book shocks and enrages the white community,
and vaguely embarrasses Negro leaders. By the time your skin
returns to its original color, you have got a best seller on your
hands.

Profiles in Courage

During your recovery from a war-related injury, you collect information about members of the U.S. Senate who destroyed their political careers rather than abandon their principles. You find eight such men, and write a book about their fortitude. The year the book is published, you decide to run for President yourself. The magic returns to your marriage.

SOME

Some of the light comes through the glass.
Some of the noise leaks in.
Some of the cars keep moving.
Some of the drivers fall asleep.

Some of the words are meaningless.
Some of the clouds are full of rain.
Some of the lakes evaporate.
Some of the plants are dangerous to eat.

Some of the planes take off.
Some of the species grow extinct.
Some of the rooms have free TV.
Some of the films make you laugh.

Some of the books are never read.
Some of the relationships thrive.
Some of the friends move far away.
Some of the pictures fade.

Some of the girls are deadly.
Some of the men are bores.
Some of the songs have special meanings.
Some of the children give you a hard time.

Some of the pain is forgotten.
Some of the days are truly great.
Some of the sounds are music to your ears.
Some of the trees fall down.

Some of the dreams are frightening.
Some of the debts are paid.
Some of the show is over.
Some of the food is left untouched.

Some of the fears are groundless.
Some of the monks are deep in prayer.
Some of the sex is terrific.
Some of the pets escape.

Some of the tools are useless.
Some of the ink will not wash out.
Some of the instruments are out of tune.
Some of the socks are clean.

Some of the states forbid it.
Some of the students go to class.
Some of the snow accumulates.
Some of the situations are pretty strange.

Some of the stars are dead.
Some of the air is full of smoke.
Some of the land is covered by the sea.
Some of the time goes by.

STANZAS FOR MARTINA

1.

One minute you can be in
Baltimore, the next minute
you can be in Africa, riding
in the largest desert in the
world, on a bus 2 years ago:
that is nothing new

                   or even
interesting, Proust pushed it
so far into my consciousness
it's part of how I see things
every day, the way daily mass
used to be, or masturbation

I tell you this because I
called your office 5 minutes
ago & they said you Weren't There

2.

Smog alert. Way to head off
nuclear arms race. Beiderbecke.
Strange summer of '74.

New Ulster blueprint. Variety
of lifestyles. Separatist feelings.
Who ordered posters torn down?

Youths beat path to farm again.
Watergate wrongs didn't work.
America's great old resort hotels.
A century of Charles Ives.

Big wheels and deals.
Haiku-like perceptions.
Peek at a glittering age.
The older brother I never knew.

3.

These are the places I would
like to live: Santa Fe, New York,
Paris, N. Brookfield, Mesopotamia
Ohio (but not for too long), Florence,
Tangiers, Mexico City,

                 Provincetown
(off-season), Cuernavaca, Manchester
Vt. (I spent about 5 hours doing this
with Joe O'Hare in 1969, we turned our
deepest desires loose over 5 continents

& ended up back in the stairwell of
College Hall, sitting out an ice storm
the year we were depressed by Philadelphia)
the settings of my favorite novels

4.

I am hoping that these stanzas
will have a cumulative effect.
I am vaguely annoyed by the classic
sound of "a"s at the ends of words.
I deplore melodrama. I suspect
charisma. I am wary of change

in my living situation. Meanwhile
the sky is dark where it hits
the Post Office tower: years of accumulated
grime. I don't know if the clock works.
Twelve stories up you can feel the damp
of subway excavation, see the damp

good looks of the workers. No
revolution without them, please.

5.

Half of the flags are at halfmast.
The others are all the way up.
This indicates the death of
a moderately famous person.

I can't touch people I don't really know.
I mean, can't really touch them.
This is not an exclusively Catholic issue.

I want to be tough.
Okay, everyone has problems.
Life is hard, and most of us
have lots more to go through.

One smile on the street, though,
& I take off. The sun can be
so strong it makes your head ache.

6.

Each time you reach a clearing you see
bears, like the same bear over & over:
the look of surprise, the discontent.
Next to the road, 2 boys lie face down,
very still. They've been there a long time;
now they are perceived as landmarks, and books
have been written to explain their mysterious
pose. Above the woods the view is dim. When
you stop the car, your dept. chairman frolics
in the snow like an otter facing extinction.

You are afraid to go near the ravine.
You don't want to fall.
You suddenly understand why you are there.
A powerful sadness takes total control of your life.

7.

Midnight. Wake up (sleeping
since sunset). Don't turn
lamp on (Randy asleep).
Pad around apt. in search
of glasses. Thinking how much
tougher Alice Notley can be
than Bernadette Mayer, for instance.
Oranges green under kitchen light;
subject of important experiments.
Dick Powell movie on TV, followed
by Judy Holliday. They're both dead.

Want to call you up & say
Hi, the houseguests never arrived
& we didn't go out after all.

CLUBS I'VE JOINED

The Cub Scouts of America
The Boy Scouts of America
The Knights of the Altar
St. Dominic Savio Classroom Club
Connecticut Valley Catholic Vocation Club
The Charles Turner League (baseball for boys 8 to 10)
The James Mote League (baseball for boys 11 to 13)
The Birchland Park Junior High School Poetry Appreciation Club
The Birchland Park Junior High School Science Club
The Junior Great Books Program
The John Ashley Fan Club
The Guy Williams Fan Club
The Efrem Zimbalist, Jr., Fan Club
Youth for Goldwater-Miller
Young Americans for Freedom
The New England Anti-Vivisection Society
The Weekly Reader Book Club
The Catholic Youth Book Club
The Conservative Book Club
The Classics Club
The Junior Knights of Columbus
The Junior Holy Name Society
The O'Connell High School Social Studies Club
The O'Connell High School Debate Club
The O'Connell High School Student Council
The Catholic Youth Organization
Students for McCarthy
The Brothers of the Christian Schools
The Catonsville Nine Defense Committee
The Milwaukee Fourteen Defense Committee
The Camden Twenty-Eight Defense Committee
Philadelphia Resistance

The Herbert S. Weber Literary Society of LaSalle College
Lambda Iota Tau National English Honor Fraternity,
    LaSalle College Chapter
The St. Gabriel's Club ("Big Brothers") of LaSalle College
The Student Mobilization Committee
The Catholic Peace Fellowship
The LaSalle College Strike Committee (1970)
Dignity of Philadelphia
Philadelphia Gay Activists' Alliance
Students for Individual Rights of LaSalle College
LaSalle College Strike Committee (1972)
The National Student Association
The PBL After-hours Club, Philadelphia
LaSalle College Counseling Collective
The Poet/City Workshop
Some Of Us Press
Poets & Writers, Inc.
Committee to Stop Gino-cide
St. Matthew's Cathedral Parish
The Club Baths, Washington, DC

Light shines through the leaves
in front of window, and although
it's nothing new, it places me
in setting. Still life
persists, new shoots
push toward the great light.
The outer world is out
of sight mostly, except where
the pedestrians move. Sidewalk,
paved surfaces, leaves on other side
reaching up. It makes me high

too. I am not in love
with anyone this morning, I am
sleeping by myself. I am
calm. Lying on the couch
just now, I remembered being
so high on cocaine that I couldn't
move a muscle. I lay on Alfred's
couch in total fear. Now I wake up
at night and remember
that I am going to die. I am
a writer with no new work.

The day is full of noise and I am
grateful, it's full of grace
and light that takes me
up and out. I am serious
again, forsythia bloom early
this year, I am going to New York,
goodby. Intense

experience of pleasure has never
moved me as much as expectation
of an end to it. Seems real,
is real. Hello.

A FAST LIFE

Dedicated to the City of Brotherly Love

I thought I was incapable of love the year
I left the Brothers Novitiate   my father
thought that I should live at home   Alfred
thought he'd like to get to know me better
when he saw me walk across campus   my first
roommate thought that I was into heavy drugs
    Rob thought I was a hippie when I told him
I was living in a commune   my freshman
history and senior writing teachers thought
I was their finest student   everybody
thought that I should get my degree   my
academic counselor thought I had the wrong
priorities   the nun who taught me Renaissance
Painting thought I was a sensitive person
leading a fast life

Ken and I were probably the first people to smoke
dope at the Christian Brothers Scholasticate in Elkins
Park, Pa   Ken had been the first to grow a beard
at the Christian Brothers Novitiate   my first year
in Philadelphia, I "turned on" a lot of people, which
at the time meant to introduce them to dope   I never
dealt, however, and was very proud of that   Tom and I
got high each night before we went to bed   my favorite
album at the time was *Yellow Submarine*, and I liked
to fall asleep listening to "It's All Too Much"   *Abbey
Road* came out that fall   I joined the Purple Aces,
a group of 25 musicians and freaks who put on some strange
performances   we entered a talent show at Holy Family
Junior College, and caused a sensation   the audience
was totally unready for our act

Terry was a close friend of many people I knew
    she started a Resistance commune in a rowhouse
near Wayne Junction   I always wished I knew her
better   Mary Ellen and her cousin Toni tried
to start a Resistance coffeehouse   it was to be
funded by the CYO   the college chaplain joined
a group called the Hoover Vacuum Conspiracy,
who took responsibility for a draft file raid
in Elizabeth NJ   I went to DC on Moratorium Day
with some friends who lived in a house called the Hotel
Pel   we drove down in an old Corvair with a heater
that wouldn't work, walked around in the bitter cold
for hours, and drove back   we ended up at Bryn Mawr
College, drinking soup and trying to thaw out   Paul's
girlfriend lived there, in a dorm called Rockefeller Hall

the first and only time I dropped mescaline was
in the dorms at LaSalle in March 1970   a friend
told me it was like grass, only stronger
    it wasn't at all like grass   and although
I was able to ride the experience through
with manic joy in spots, I worried over
flashback possibilities for three whole
years   when I had a 4-day-long anxiety
attack in May 1970 I was sure the drug
was responsible, rather than my own sad pose
    I only smoked a few times after that   and
never forgot the one time I used drug lingo
in public, telling a self-righteous kid at
a Student Mobe meeting not to "push his
trip," then blushing at how dumb that sounded

Jimmie and I were tireless Catholic
activists   the Strike Committee wanted
us to get the Church involved in the
protest over Cambodia   we met for several
hours with a nun from the Cardinal's
Commission on Human Rights   later on
we learned she had called the Civil
Disobedience Squad as soon as we left
     after the rally, 5 big plainclothes
cops converged on Jimmie in the courtyard
of City Hall and roughed him up   Frank
McCarthy jumped off a tall building the
night after the Kent State murders   the
Strike Committee wanted to use his death
as ammunition for their cause

when Marty said he couldn't take me
seriously, I cried   he had studied
at the Institute of Man in Pittsburgh
before he became Director of Formation
     the Institute was popular with people
who were serious about their religious
lives   Marty was upset when I skipped
a night of recollection to attend a
memorial service for the Kent State
students   I found myself in trouble
when I introduced my girlfriend to
the whole community   it was whispered I was
really sleeping with men   after I came out
I left the Brothers expecting to feel a sense
of relief   but I didn't feel anything

I followed Jim O'Toole back to his dorm
after an Honors Dinner   in the recreation
room I met Patty   we started a conversation
that lasted all night, and watched the sun come
up from my apartment balcony   one week later
we slept together for the first time, both of us
wearing jeans and thick sweaters   Patty led
an active social life, and many other men were
attracted to her   some of them had strange
names, like Dusty and Bob The Shrink   this was
my first "romance" with a woman, and I thought
I was a lucky man   I was still a Brother at
the time, and I wanted to help redefine the
meaning of Religious Community   Patty wanted to
study in Switzerland more than anything else

I only was in Villanova once: on New Years
Eve with Patty when we got snowed in at
the apartment of her best friend and ex-
debate partner   I had a major crush on
the best friend's boyfriend   we smoked
a little dope and played a board game
called Group Therapy, which measures how
honest you are   I had to make an appropriate
gesture of affection to the person I found
most attractive in the room   when I kissed
Patty she knew I was lying   this was soon
before she told me Alfred was gay, a blatant
fact I chose to disbelieve for awhile   on
New Years Day we went to church with Patty's
parents   I wrote a poem I can't find anymore

I met Diana Rigg backstage after she
played Heloise to Keith Michell's Abelard
    she autographed my program   2 hours later,
I met Rob in a bar uptown   he invited me
to spend the night with him at the Plaza
Hotel, and I said Okay, not even knowing his
name   that was the most grace-filled moment
of my life   I met Richard Wilbur when he
read at LaSalle, and thought his work was over-
rated   he wore a tweed jacket with suede patches
on the sleeves, which I described as his "uniform"
    I almost met Ramsay Clark at a political
dinner once   I introduced myself to Ron Padgett
in 1970 at the Philadelphia Y, but was too shy
to start a conversation

Joe Kwazniak called himself the Grand
Duchess De La Salle   his friends called him
Kitty   John was known as the Empress   many
of their friends had what were called "drag
names," too   two weeks after I'd started
seeing Rob, I went to a party with most of
them in attendance   they called me Debbie,
the name of the woman my brother married
two years later   Jimmie, alias Olivia, planted
a tremendous kiss on my neck   it turned into
a bruise, which I tried to cover up with Caladryl
the next day when I visited Patty to tell her
the real reason I had stopped seeing her   I was
worried at the expectation of a painful scene
and the bruise made me even more nervous

one summer, I taught algebra and U.S.
History at my former high school   I
coached an intramural basketball team
and took 2 of my freshmen to a rock
concert in Atlantic City   I sought
and received psychiatric help another
summer   I worked in the Washington Navy
Yard and ate lunch every day in the CIA
cafeteria   the summer after that, I was
in love with Rob   I would leave work on
Friday, and not return from New York until
the following Wednesday   I am still
amazed that I could get away with that
     another year I had a job in Provincetown,
but came back after a week

I saw *Death in Venice* in New York, at
a theater near Carnegie Hall   by the end,
the audience was actually hissing, and I
was speechless at their lack of perception
and at the movie's beauty   outside, Rob
was waiting in the strong sunlight   he was
wearing a T-shirt and faded jeans   his
effortless beauty hit me hard when I saw him
there   I identified my feelings with Dirk
Bogarde's in the film, only thought that
I was more fortunate, since I could give my
feelings a name   that was the first time
I was really "in love" with another human
being   I was very fond of the idea of being
"in love in New York," too

I went to the Jersey shore on Primary
Day instead of working in the Green For
Mayor campaign as I'd promised   I asked
Sally to make the calls for me, an imposition
on her friendship I still regret   I regret
a lot about my friendship with Alfred, mostly
my lack of generosity   after I left LaSalle
I regretted having wasted my time there, but now
I'm not so sure   I wish that I had come out sooner
     I regret going to bed with Bob, which destroyed
our friendship, and not going to bed with Michael,
which would have cemented our friendship   for
a long time I said I had no regrets about anything
I'd done, just about the things I'd wanted to do
but hadn't   but that isn't true

Chateauneuf du Pape at La Terrasse each
winter   the deaths of Brothers David Darst
and David Ryan   Robert Lowell's confessional
poems (I wished he'd stopped at *For the Union
Dead*)   "after such knowledge, what forgiveness"
and a couple of other expressions   afternoons
at Smith's Bar or the Hideaway Lounge with Alfred
and Sree Rao   choosing to hear Ron Padgett instead
of Wystan Auden when they read the same night   the
novels of Jonathan Strong   the weak distinction
of never seeing a game in a basketball-happy
college   bourbon-and-cokes and rum Collinses,
neither of which I drink much anymore   and opening
my heart to the influence of the moment   all
used to mean more to me than they do now

when I was 21, I wanted to write
a novel about the year I was 20   it
would be called *The Last Revolving
Year*, after a Joni Mitchell song   in
the novel, I would move into my first
apartment with the man who was to be
my lifelong closest friend   I would have
my first love affair with a sensitive
woman   then fall in total love with
a beautiful boy   the novel was to end
on my 21st birthday, the climax of my
difficult transition from late adolescence
to adulthood   the story was based entirely
on facts   I hoped to write a series of
sequels describing my further growth

Alfred had his freshmen up for
sherry 2 or 3 times a week   I
disliked most of them   most of
all I disliked Tim   Alfred was
in love with him   Tim's fiancée
would visit him a lot   they'd met
at high school in Bel Air Maryland
      Tim liked to dominate the space
around himself   and so did I   one
year later, we finally made love
after joking about it for a long
time, on the floor of Alfred's office
while he was in class   we both felt
incredibly guilty over that   it was
the first of many times

when Bill came back from Europe, I was sure
I could seduce him   we had been good friends
our first year in college   now I thought
I knew what I wanted   I suspected Bill did
too   we listened to a Joni Mitchell album
on the dark third floor of my house, lying
on the rug within arm's reach   it was a
tender moment, and I wanted to lean across
the distance between us and touch him, to
show him that the distance between us was
not that great   just then Tim bounced into
the room   the water was off in the dorms
and he had come to take a shower   the mood
was broken   that week Bill met the girl
of his dreams   I never had another chance

in the house on Pulaski Avenue, Ken
sat in the third-floor window seat
drinking Cribari from the bottle and
crying over Joni Mitchell   Alfred's
brother lived with us during the week
     his wife accused me of sleeping with boys
but not to my face   Tom stayed over
when he could   I got my first case of
crabs, which I tried to cure with Lemon
Up   it didn't work   the president of
my high school class spent a weekend   we
ended up in bed, my most tender memory
of that year   Ken was in love with a gorgeous
but unapproachable swimmer   I slept with Tom
the night my cousin died

at our big Christmas party, Jimmie
followed one of Alfred's freshmen onto
the roof, where the boy had gone to take
a piss   I argued over some arcane
theological point with Sister Margaret
McKenna   later I found Tom, who at that
point was my lover, and Alfred, who was
my best friend, making out in Alfred's
bed   I stormed out of the house and walked
to Tim's room in the college dorm, where
I spent the night   when I went back the next
morning, I learned that Tom and Alfred had
spent their night in Alfred's car, searching
the expressway for me   they thought that
I would try to hitch a ride to New York

a kid I had been cruising for weeks finally
started a conversation one weekend   it was
one year after my coming-out, and I expected
something equally auspicious to occur   he
was a student at medical school, and asked me
home with him   the first thing that I saw
in his apartment was a photo on the mantel
that looked exactly like me, down to the
moustache and glasses   it was his former
lover, with whom he'd broken up the previous
week   I felt glad to be there   we stayed
awake all night, though neither of us came
    next morning was Palm Sunday   I walked
to the cathedral, where I met Alfred for High
Mass   the Cardinal walked in the procession

I joined the Philadelphia Resistance, and burned
my draft card on Moratorium Day   I did not tell
my draft board, because I thought a trial would
hurt my parents too much   I organized a Festival
of Life on the quad when the commandant of the Marine
Corps spoke in the Concert and Lecture Series   I
was press spokesman for the Defense Committee that
supported the college chaplain when he was fired
     I occupied the office of the Vice President For
Student Affairs and was placed on disciplinary
probation   I wrote poems for the yearbook   I was
president of Gay Lib   I subscribed to *The Catholic
Worker, After Dark,* and *The Paris Review*   I made
Who's Who In American Colleges & Universities   and
went to bed with some very beautiful people

I have a hard time writing about Michael, even though
I haven't seen him for a long time   when I heard
a song about "the love that I thought could save me"
a couple of days ago, his face flashed into my mind
     I felt that way about him, even though I didn't
(and don't) believe that love can save anything
outside the immediate moment   the night before he
left for Europe, we drove along the river   I didn't
say the same things I usually didn't say, and wondered
as usual what he was feeling   Michael had amazing
eyes, and I kept looking across the seat at him, taking
my eyes off the road   I remember every detail of that ride
     later on I wrote some poems for him, which like my
feelings were out of control   I still find it impossible
to say with any grace what his presence meant

even though we stayed pretty close, there were
difficult moments in my friendship with Tim

there was one dramatic scene in The Steps
when he handed me the keys to his car and said
he would see me tomorrow   I had expected us
to go home together   for some reason I have
forgotten, I was totally crushed, and thought
It's all over now   I drove around the city
with Ray until nearly dawn, babbling and
crying   it was a cold night, and neither
of us could locate the heater in Tim's VW

after nearly freezing, we found an all
night service station in Chestnut Hill   the
pump attendant thought we were playing a
joke on him when we asked for help

at 20th and Chestnut was a strange
antique store I can't find anymore
when Alfred and I went in one weekend
there were newspapers everywhere, and
one old lady who was talking to some
cats   the phone rang and the lady cleared
some papers off her desk, picked up the
receiver and said Welcome to Philadelphia,
the City of Brotherly Love and Sisterly
Affection   she then hung up and gave us
a tender smile   another store that later
burned was like that, run by another old
lady   it was on South Street, near Head
House Square   I never could figure out
exactly what was for sale

I saw *Sunday Bloody Sunday* 4 times, and said it was
my favorite movie   I always cried at the end when
Peter Finch as the homosexual doctor talks right into
the camera   I saw *Lady Caroline Lamb* at a theater
on Rittenhouse Square, and was hit with a tremendous
pain in my chest   I thought it was my first heart
attack   I watched *Star Trek* every afternoon in Tim's
room, sometimes smoking dope or having sex at the same
time   I saw *Jacques Brel Is Alive And Well* 3 times
in one academic year: at the Village Gate on my first
date with Rob, in a coffeehouse on Long Island, and at
the New Locust Theater, with Elly Stone recreating her
famous role   I saw one Marx Brothers movie, in which
Groucho stalks around in an academic gown, at least
10 times but can't remember its name

I got picked up at the after-hours
bar rather suddenly by somebody attractive
who was obviously stoned   we went to the
Savoy for coffee before going back to his
apartment, and I could see he was pretty
totally out of things   but I thought What
the hell   at his apartment, I lay in his
bed for what seemed like an hour while he
washed his dishes, folded laundry, etc.
    finally he climbed in beside me, gave
me a tentative kiss, and said Okay, now
you can fuck me   this made me laugh,
which he found pretty annoying   the next
day we walked through Center City together
    we both had a really good time

when the Reading trains passed beneath the
trestle next to Mama Lombardo's, the plastic
flowers on the ceiling swayed   her portions
were the largest in any Italian restaurant
I've ever seen   Apple Jack's was popular
for breakfast if you'd spent the night
in Center City   Dirty John's had okay
luncheon meats, but little else   C. K. Williams
hung out at Dirty Frank's, surrounded by
admirers   Dirty Edna's was the bar in Atlantic
City where I saw Spinner cry for the first time
     they made strong drinks   Imhof's of Germantown
floated veal scraps instead of real snapper
in their famous soup   both my roommates were
in love with the same waiter

Pat and I broke up after one stormy
Sunday when I took him to Lautrec
for breakfast and he walked out when
he learned they served caviar rather
than bacon and eggs   the same night
I met Spinner   that was my shortest
interval ever between relationships
     we danced to every slow song at the PBL
for 4 hours straight   "A Whiter Shade
Of Pale" played many times   I called him
every night that week   we had a date
for *Lady Sings the Blues* on Saturday
night   and acted like strangers when
we met at the speed line   neither of us
could remember how the other one looked

I made 4.0 my first semester at LaSalle
and received a notice of total scholarship
    3 years later my love life had caught up
with my intellectual growth and the money
stopped coming in   the Vice President For
Academic Affairs said I should be doing
better   I moved into a room on the top
floor of a decaying house, my first time
living alone   each morning I would make
a cup of strong coffee and sit in bed for
hours with a typewriter in my lap, writing
poems   most of them were not that great   I
dropped most of my courses in November   I said
school was a drain on my energy   I wanted
to concentrate on my writing

when the radical priest was fired I wanted
to help him pioneer an alternative ministry
    I wanted to unionize students in the state
of Pennsylvania   I wanted to do post-graduate
work at NYU in Twentieth Century Studies   at
Iowa in writing   and at the University of
Leeds in aesthetic theory   I wanted to be
living with Alfred when we both were very
old   I visualized our apartment, with many
books and records   I wanted to sleep with
Michael, but never did   I wanted to establish
The Poet/City Workshop in a storefront on
Germantown Avenue   I wanted to be living in
New York, near all the famous poets I admired
    I wanted to be famous myself   and still do

PRISONERS OF THE HEART

The refugee sits next to you on the plane.
You use his native language to describe the life
that awaits him in the country that you both
move toward. The refugee is inconsolable.

I walk into the bar where you are dancing
with my rival. I want to kill you both until
it dawns on me how totally predictable my feelings
can be. Then I feel predictably chagrined.

The person I slept next to last night drops in
to say Hello. I watch your expression crumble
like the beach carried off by an enormous body
of water that reminds us of some terrible scenes.

The celebrity enters the room. It is hard
to understand how such a tiny person can be
so famous. The awe-struck crowd grows silent.
You tenderly kiss the celebrity on her lips.

AT THE POINT

It is after midnight. Your fat friend
decides to go swimming. He takes off
all his clothes. The headlights of a car
flash, illuminate his body as he moves
down the road toward the beach.

The boy you are in love with lights
a joint. You both are at the end
of the boardwalk. Smoke rises into
the intense blue sky from his mouth.
His papers are covered with stars.

You actually ache with the desire to
touch the man in bed beside you. He is
on the college faculty, you are one of
his brightest students. It takes you
a long time to get back to sleep.

There are two houses. The big one is filled
with your friends who are going away.
There is a piano in the tiny house. You
walk into the empty parlor, sit down, and
play the only song you know by heart.

POPPERS

for Davi Det Hompson

In a bar in Philadelphia once, someone thrust a bottle of poppers underneath my nose at the foot of a flight of stairs. By the time I was halfway up, I had the sensation that my head was going up a much steeper staircase than the rest of my body, and faster, too. I thought that I was going to fall down backwards, and began to laugh with delight.

I was in bed with someone who had picked me up at the discotheque. We were doing the usual things, only I was totally bored. He reached beneath his pillow and produced a golden capsule, which he said was a popper. He broke it in half and smelled it for a long time, then held it out to me. It will make sex intense beyond your wildest dreams, he said.

Sam carries poppers everywhere. One night at the Pier, he took a hit and passed the bottle to Jim, who took a hit and passed it on to Tom. Tom and Randy also took hits, and Randy passed the bottle to me. For various reasons in my past, drugs make me nervous much of the time, so I politely refused to inhale and passed the bottle to Dave.

A friend of mine kept his poppers in his lover's Frigidaire for convenience. His lover is opposed to the use of poppers, so my friend didn't say what the bottle contained. The lover found the poppers one morning. He opened the bottle and sniffed, to discover what was inside. The rush from the poppers practically blew his head off.

POWDER PUFF

for Ann Darr

Her plane disappears in a famous and mysterious
accident in the Pacific. The Japanese army sees a flash
in the sky, and powder falls to the sea through some
puffs of cloud. In the collective memory, Amelia Earhart
strikes a jaunty pose in her leather cap. She puffs
one last time on her cigarette, and clambers
into the cockpit. She is behind the controls.
A cloud of powdery sand blows against her goggles.
She shakes her head and turns on the engine.
Exhaust puffs from the tail of her plane.
She taxis down the runway past two small girls in
party dresses from the 30s. The dresses resemble
traditional birthday cakes of powdered sugar. A puff
of wind lifts the plane off the ground. Now she is
airborne. She looks down on the towns of America
from her unique vantage point. She sees the powdered
snow on the great mountain peaks; she puffs from lack
of oxygen at these levels. She performs acrobatic feats
that take your breath away. She comes down slow,
in the delicate maneuver known as "powdering the baby."
A puff of smoke rises over region of domestic unrest.
Amelia takes a powder, crosses great lakes to get away.
She invents the Powder Puff Derby, a prominent airplane
race for women. The title is facetious, a reference to
the much-supposed weakness and vanity of lady pilots, as
opposed to their actual prowess. She advertises Wranglers
and Lucky Strikes, not bath oils or fragrant powders.
The press puffs her accomplishments. More than anything,
she wants to travel around the world through the air.

STRONG FEELINGS

I know the way to San Jose
I know the way to reach you: with my arms
stretched out in front of me to touch you
with my hands, make contact

between our palms and what they stand for
between us when I see you
again it is easier when we are
in the same place, it is hard

to reach across the distance
we are learning to explore
our bodies arriving at beautiful
new locations, and quickly departing

propelled by the strength of our feelings
into the future, where there are spaces
filled up with a powerful energy
the clear light in your eyes

POLES APART

Some photographs: white cross at top of rise in coast highway, Big Sur. Hermitage of Camaldolese: strictest order in the universal church. My father, looking very young and thin, bends over the inflatable pool. I am wearing white hat. My father smiles at photographer (probably my mother). It's 1952. Seals on rocks in fog, watched by diners in tourist trap on western shore of continent. After lunch, walk to beach in gusty breeze. Concrete steps lead down to sand from street. I realize I've dreamed this, and turn around to see if the persons I expect to see are actually there. They are: teenaged boys in thick jackets, high on drugs. I walk down street with Alfred in the perfect calm of noon atmospheric inversion on northern coast. People watch us from behind their curtains. I feel as though I'm in a western movie. Sign in gazebo on dock asks "Where have all the seagulls gone?" and there are no seagulls, although every other town in Maine is full of them. A famous writer lives here; we decide not to ring up. We make the foolish choice, we pick the wrong road, because that's all we think we can live with. Inhale fog; see breath in front of face when you exhale, and it's only August. It doesn't have to be too cold. The proof is locked in small room; it glows with an uncanny light when you are in that part of house. Someone's wife lives there, in perfect control. Assassinates your vision of the future. Letter torn, tossed into fireplace. This happens in American South. Western nights fuller of light than the bad dreams predicted. Campfires, stars: definitive life of each leaf, lovingly watered. The animals rest, the blankets are light and full of beautiful eyes. Decide to stop the music for awhile, and the blood moves through your body with impossible finality. The senses where it starts and ends. Deep light. The engineering triumph of grace.

FOR YEARS

I'm in bed in a room in the Plaza Hotel, New York. The guy
who picked me up is in the bathroom, and I'm wondering
what he'll want me to do, worrying that there's some secret
way of lovemaking between men that I've never heard of
and will look foolish not doing, because it's my first time
doing this consciously, saying It's a homosexual act! very
clearly in my head, and saying Okay to it anyway. When
guy who picked me up comes back into room (he's wearing
v-neck t-shirt, strange to see on person my age), I go into
bathroom. Soap is in a cardboard box, and has elaborate
design imprinted on side. I turn off light, walk out, and get
into bed. First thing I do is hold him very tight. I'm wrestling
in the dorm of the novitiate with my "particular friend,"
which is what a person you're too close to is called in the
religious life. He pins me, leans hard on top of me, breath
in my face. I come, hug him tight for quick sharp moment.
I don't know if he knows. I'm in my bedroom, parents'
house, making out with Patricia. We are going to Arena
Stage to see Lindfors as Mother Courage. Electric curlers on
bed, and I think I break the plastic cover when we roll onto
them. I come because I can't control it. I want to be inside
her. She takes off her blouse for the first time in her dorm
and I think of all the years I have waited. I kiss a man and

think how long I waited. My parents are in next room; what we are doing I perceive as exceptionally daring. I hear my father's hand on door and leap out of bed. Thank god my underwear is on. I open door a crack and slide out, blocking his view. Pascal leaps from my bed to the cot we have set up for appearances. My father is surprised at my agitation. My mother is surprised at my agitation when she asks me why I have started to associate with queens. I bring Richard home and we listen to his Beverly Sills collection in living room, to parents' consternation. In bed his chest has funny aftertaste. I drive with him to Philly and we sleep together for the first time. I sleep with Patricia for the first time on living room couch, wake up in middle of night, want to fuck. Tall boy follows me from snack bar into College Hall at night. He is a lonely freshman; I'm president of Gay Lib. I take him to my room and stroke his arm; he's trembling so hard his teeth are chattering. But he wants to. Alfred wants to sleep with me again, but I don't want to. Too much sex between us will screw up our friendship. In bed with him the first time, he touches my asshole and I jump as if touched with an electric wire. I am fucked for first time on my 21st birthday by black ballet star, and it's wonderful. I fuck Spinner constantly at start of relationship; he fucks me all the time at the end. At end of relationship with Tom, I take him to dinner for his 19th birthday. I ask him to apartment for coffee, and he wants to hold me. We start making love and both come at exactly the

same time, the first time that's happened with anyone. He's

sleeping with Italian kid from suburbs, and gives me crabs. I

get v.d. the first time I go to the baths. Jim has rash so we can't

go to bed. Carl has rash but we go to bed anyway. I'm not

supposed to touch him. Snow on street outside a foot deep.

Carl has been to bed with Allen Ginsberg. I walk with Jim

to riverbank in January. River full of melting snow. We kiss

but I'm afraid to do anything else, afraid we will be spotted

through the trees. He looks like my long lost twin. We get it

on on floor of Michael's bedroom while party is in progress

downstairs. He develops crush on Sheila. I develop crush on

Sheila too, and it all gets pretty confused. I develop crush on

blond bombshell who has stolen my lover away. I see them

at a party on Valentines Day. I see a boy in bar on Valentines

Day, and know we will be very close. I take dessert to Charles

Thanksgiving night, knowing he will be alone. We make

love on his couch, I have both my hands on his ass, it's great.

I take dessert to Kerry Christmas night, knowing he will

be alone. Mattress is on floor, and through window, foggy

light. Mattress is on floor in my dorm room, I pass a joint

to Cece, knowing I'm expected to make a pass, not wanting

to. I kiss her on our first date and it hurts her tongue. Prom

night is traditional for ending up in bed, but we never get it

on. Graduation night is traditional for goodbyes, but I meet

John, and we talk all night. He wants to be a Dominican; he's married now, we never get it on. Vernon wants to see the world; he joins the navy. I make slow love to him in American West. His body is entirely in my mouth, my body is entirely in his. That is how it feels. Electric chest. Electric chest of John against my mouth when we make love, my lover is in the same bed. I sleep with Kirk in same bed I make out in with Mary Ellen. Singer, bad teeth; he develops tiny crush. I develop tiny crush on Spinner, it turns into something else. The love I feel for Blaine turns into something else; I do not call for weeks and he does not forget. Danny's voice on phone after I haven't called for a long time: perfectly cold. We spend the night in someone else's bed, he fucks me, the most perfect sex I ever had. I spend the night on cot in Joe's apartment with David, who builds up to orgasm like a woman: I am in heaven. He calls me every week, then stops. I call Dennis after a long time; it's all over. I am in North Carolina on his living room floor, he's next to me. I crush his cigarettes. He lives in a trailer, we make love in trailer in Prince Georges County. He comes across my chest, sharp hug. Peter comes across my chest. He's a Congressman's son, lives in big house with autographed pictures. We sleep in his parents' double bed, and I listen all night for sound of car in driveway. We sleep in Richard's grandparents' bed and must be quiet so the neighbors don't think we're prowlers and call the cops.

Richard is one beautiful person, and we go to a friend's apartment to do it, I'm watering the plants in occupant's absence. I'm watering the plants when John arrives for brunch. He's even more attractive than his photo in the Freshman Register. We drink wine. I drink wine with Richard at Wolf Trap, Sills sings Donizetti. She autographs our program. I drink orange juice in Neil's apartment. He's a graduate student in psychology, studies and eats psychotropic drugs. It's foggy out the window; Walnut Street has been torn up. I tear up the letter my particular friend writes me when he leaves the community. I am not yet able to deal with that set of emotions. Tom is not able to deal with the emotions his attitude brings out in me. We go to bed, me drunk, him stoned; I don't know how to get him off. I shoot across his leg. It's the only time we'll ever be together like that. In the West I go to bed with lots of people I will probably not ever see again. I meet curly-headed kid whose name I can't remember in the dark back room of popular bar. We have sex right there, and it's great, something I have wanted to do for years.

SLEEP WITH PAUL

Film moves in front of eyes at breakneck speed.
It snaps: last frame involves four-poster bed
I wake up in and try to clear my head
and wonder who is sleeping next to me.

In seconds it comes back, and I am glad
I met him after so long, though I'm not
so glad I'm here without my car, and not
convinced he's the best sex I've ever had.

I try to sleep again but can't, so lean
across him for my glasses, walk across
to living room, and read a book called BOSS
about a great political machine

until alarm rings and he wakens. Then
I climb back into bed. We start again.

LUNCH WITH PAUL

"Bright sunny days and a starry clear night"
weather woman overwhelmed with joy
from high above the airport, she is watching as we walk
to lunch, but we do not acknowledge

her presence in our lives, though perhaps we can feel
her gaze in ways we have not yet begun
to understand, we are just too busy
watching sparks that happen when our eyes'

fields of energy collide, and we take mental note
of how they swerve and drift into the light
we want to remember every tiny event
that happens in the space of time we move

together in: the firetrucks speeding up the hill,
the dopey waiter slow to bring the check,
my loss of breath when our hands touch by accident in public,
the airplanes leaving trails across a dark blue sky.

SONNET

my nixon imitations cut across
the terrace of your cagney imitations
to the garden of my john wayne imitations
where bud the leaves of your diana ross
imitations, next to a deep pool of
goldfish mimicking my sylvia plath
imitations, from which a shiny path
leads to your proust imitations, you love
my dylan imitations most of all,
I die for kitty carlisle on the strength
of your kitty carlisle imitations, length
of time spent in imitations we call
"preparation" for the day when we
can imitate each great pose perfectly.

SONNET

for Richard Kain

a fast life   Roscoe's, 4 p.m.
with ten miles behind me and 10,000 more
where you want to go
through my eyes   I don't know
if freedom means a lot when you approach
my hero   Frank O'Hara: the magnificent OH
death will find me long before I tire

of watching you and swing me
where you want to go
I don't know   it's like a small
nest for me inside you
Port Richmond, 6 a.m.   Go
back to sleep   me too
in California where I used to live

DAY FOR PAUL

Home for lunch. Find bright light smeared on furniture
like red shoe polish. This happens every day when I'm
not here. Strength of sun through window makes me dizzy;
I can't eat cheese, drink milk or beer. Run hands beneath
cool water and wash my eyes. Check comics: Dagwood hangs
onto streetcar with both hands, moves down hill toward work
at high speed. He lives in one of the cities I love: San
Francisco, Boston, and one other. I live in political
capital, sniff out trouble spots. Smoke across the river
in another state. Boy with wire-rimmed glasses and moustache
smokes a joint in parents' house. Everybody else is asleep.
He lights up

       the sky is pink near horizon up hill from
tomb of unknown soldier, then turns brown as eyes travel
to the level of the roof across alley, it fades into soft
white, like fluorescent tube in gray room, then moves out
of sight above the line where window slips back into wall.
I don't move forward. I sit perfectly still. The only sound
in room is nib of pen as it moves across paper

                  it's me
five years ago. I am on the verge of big breakthrough
accompanied by pain. I have not read anything by Proust,
Dostoevsky, Rimbaud, or Frank O'Hara. I have not had sex
with the people I love and need most. I have not yet learned
to identify the people I love and need most. But I have
dreams about people who move like you, who make me feel so
full that waking up becomes a major letdown, and I want to
sleep all day and all night if it will make me feel that good
again, take me to the place inside my body where I can feel
you living all the time.

YOU ARE THERE

Wake to rain when phone rings, it's a man I went to bed with in another city, says parade was cancelled again. New year. Knives in throat from smoking dope for first time in a year at party last night. Smoke dope in Terry's apartment, listen: just because it's Dylan taking me out again doesn't mean that things can be the same. Oh no. Cry of tiny man who opens door to tiny room in my heart after a long vacation. The dust clears and the light is steady. Don't take this seriously.

You make me feel brand new. I watch you get fucked up, lose touch; you're gentle and you're beautiful, it's 1972. It's 1973 and I pick you up in a bookstore for ride home; you have to buy a scarf in Georgetown. Freezing day. I didn't mean to put this down so soon, I wanted to lead up to it, take the streetcar to the top of the hill, coast down to the intersection. Still too bad, too serious. It's tough they only give respect to straight-looking men. It's New Years in the little luncheonette.

I want you to know how fine you looked. I tell you things I haven't told anyone else. I am in your bedroom, I am learning to write. You open your   the photograph collection of your past can be limitless; the process is to slice each section of your history thinner and thinner until you are left with one fraction of a moment so clear—the raindrop halfway down the pane—that you can live through it again, so perfect in detail that you can watch your image breathe. Love and death meet here. Click of slide tray on the carousel. Love and death meet here.

Shine light through situation and the colors aren't right, like my father's first attempts in basement darkroom. Koda-color, 1954: toddler under arbor in the public park, facing bright green flowers. I never talked to flowers the way Ted Greenwald can.

On mescaline in 1970, I understood the trees for the first time, still do. The clumsiness of love, the slow awareness of where the roots are, of what the roots absorb. Naked hand palm up in air, no breeze. The sun bombards your skin with energy.

You are there, and the announcer with sad eyes, holding back the excitement in his voice, tells you You Are There, but the reinforcing wall inside his throat is too weak, his voice cracks and the pure excitement surges up into the hatchway of his face, the mouth, past white teeth in one strong current, straining toward the outer world it overflows into, coloring the waves of sound that break upon the ears of millions with the colors of the manic and totally new. And it is our history, yours and mine, that draws this out, that causes such a pressure in the throat of the man with sad eyes.

KNOWING IT

I open my eyes   you
kiss me, say It's dawn
I smile, don't even check
go back to sleep   you too

Buxtehude wakes us up
your roommate turned the stereo
on, which is o.k.   we kept him
up late w/ whatever we did

last night & I'm sorry
but not enough to have stopped
what he must consider the noise
we made   we call it something

else over here in the space
that our bodies fill up
w/ their action: coming
home & knowing it

SONG FROM DREAMS

department store manikins wear ritual garb
DUCHAMP spelt in gold above revolving door
night sea perfectly reflects night sky
murdering our concept of horizon

we live among Indians in Mexican hills
no hallucination! (purple haze first time)
Western beach: one unbelievable wave
the light escapes like priceless information

THE DEATH OF A PRESIDENT

In the spring of 1974, an Air Force enlisted man steals a helicopter in Fort Meade, Maryland, and flies it to the White House, a distance of twenty-two miles. He attempts to crash the helicopter into the Harry Truman porch, but is shot down by a quick-witted guard. I am amazed at both the serviceman's desperate attempt and the President's narrow escape. I write a poem for Peter Inman in which I mention this.

In the summer of 1974, I dream that my ex-girlfriend is the President's daughter and is living in the White House, where she drinks herself to sleep each night because she's bored with her life. In the dream, I go to the White House to try to convince her to get it together. But she's so far gone she doesn't even bother to get out of bed anymore, like Ann Margret in *Carnal Knowledge*.

In the spring of 1975, a man dressed as an Arab smashes his way through the White House gates in a car. He holds off the police for hours by pretending he has dynamite beneath his robes. He doesn't have any dynamite, the police are relieved to learn when they arrest him after three tense hours.

In the spring of 1975, I have a series of dreams which end with me running from the Ebbitt Grill through fog toward a park that turns out to be the White House grounds. Searchlights and alarms go off as soon as I get behind the wrought-iron gates.

In the early summer of 1975, I discover the secret telephone number of the President's daughter. I learn this through a process of trial and error: by dialing the White House exchange (456) plus different combinations of numbers. The President's daughter is a student at the junior college where I used to work. All the students there live in houses that have names as well as street numbers. "The White House, 1600 Pennsylvania Avenue" is one example of that. I get in the habit of calling the President's daughter late at night. When she answers the phone, I hang up.

In the summer of 1975, I go for drinks with Kenward Elmslie to the roof terrace of the Hotel Washington, where Al Pacino stayed in *The Godfather, Part II*. From the terrace, you can look down into what used to be called The President's Park. The Executive Mansion looks like a wedding cake set among fake trees. A light is burning on the "residential" floor, where the President really lives. It looks like a window in the bedroom of the President's son. I saw the inside of the room in *People* magazine. The President's son is a homosexual like me. He doesn't look as good as he used to. I plot the trajectory from where we are sitting to the window, thinking how vulnerable the powerful can be.

In the fall of 1975, the President is walking through a park in Sacramento. A woman in a long red robe aims a loaded pistol at him. The Secret Service quickly grabs the gun. The woman is part of an amateur group that made the first snuff movies, back in the Sixties.

In the fall of 1975, a woman squeezes off a shot at the President as he leaves a San Francisco hotel. The hotel has glass elevators, the kind that were used in the filming of *The Towering Inferno*. The aim of the woman with the gun is spoiled by a passing homosexual, who grabs her arm as she begins to fire.

In the winter of 1976, a black ex-mental patient scales the White House fence twice and walks around the grounds. The first time he does this he is kicked out by the Secret Service. The second time, he comes to within ten feet of the President's daughter. At about this time, I learn from my friend Jack O'Hara that the little gray boxes along the White House fence, which I thought were electronic devices to detect trespassers, are actually loudspeakers through which Walter Cronkite tells the story of the White House to tourists who wait in line on the adjacent sidewalk.

In the spring of 1976, I have the following dream: *I am walking south of the White House, near the Ellipse, when I see a black man in gray clothes scale the fence at the point where it is lowest. He runs into the park. I go across the fence after him, but lose him on the other side. I move into the White House grounds, expecting to be captured any minute. But nothing happens. I walk past the goldfish pond and find myself at the back door. The back door knob is gold and highly polished; I assume it's electrified. I touch it but don't get shocked. The door's unlocked; I walk inside. I find the kitchen stairway and walk up to the second floor. The carpets here are gold. The President and his wife are going to the movies; they're getting dressed. I am shocked to realize that the President is Ubu, and his wife is Mrs. Ubu. My nervousness turns to total contempt. I reach into my pocket for the gun. Mrs. Ubu sees me first; a look of surprise, then annoyance, crosses her face. But that's replaced by disbelief when she sees the pistol. She says Oh no. I say Shut up bitch, and push her against the wall. Ubu walks in drying his face with a golden towel. I kick him against the wall before he has a chance to call the guards. Both of them are quivering with fear. I slowly raise the pistol to the level of their faces. I aim it, hold it there and watch them squirm. I say Die fuckers as I slowly squeeze the trigger. At the last possible moment, I swing my arm to the left, put six bullets into the gold wallpaper. Ubu and his wife can't believe it. They don't know whether they're alive or dead. I think I am awake. I give them a contemptuous look, throw the gun out the window, and start to laugh. Then I turn and walk out of the room looking for a phone so I can call my homosexual friends and tell them what happened.*

SONNET

The river fills with shining rain, the way
your life fills up your body. When Rimbaud
walked out into the desert, there was no
cool stream for miles around. You have to pay
all night for what you do each day, in dreams
that teach you all the right decisions, which
you instantly forget each morning. Hitch
your wagon to a star. Each great hope seems
to melt away like snow beneath the force
of spring, the waking life again. Your eyes
grow heavy with desire, your strong will flies
out of your heart's cage, freedom-bound. Of course
it's far too late. The pistol smokes and jerks.
Rimbaud cries out, "Fuck you and all your works!"

WHITE PETALS

The Republic lies in the blossoms of Washington.
—Robert Bly

White petals
drop into the dark river.
Heedless of political significance,
they ride out to the sea like stars.

I'm the space explorer.
I travel to a planet
where there are no plants or animals.
Everyone lives in harmony.
I don't want to go home.

I'm the pioneer man and the pioneer woman,
both at the same time.
I build my house with my own hands,
and it's beautiful
with simple, perfect lines.

I'm the farmer waiting for the vegetables
to grow, so I can eat.
I'm the hunter aiming at the bear.
I don't want to shoot it, but my family needs meat.
The bear gives me a long dumb animal look.
We'll use his skin for blankets,
his fat to light our lamps.
Our cabin will stink all night.

I'm the cabin boy who graduates to captain.
Shipboard sex is rough, but it suits my taste.
I'm the man on the steps of the house
where the President's widow lives.
All night I wait for the stranger
to get out of his car
so I can flash my look of recognition.

I'm the cowpoke who sleeps with his horses.
I'm the man who loves dogs.
I'm the cranky President sneaking away
to swim in the Potomac.

I'm the black man.
I close my eyes
and it gets dark inside.

I feel the sun on my face.
I see the light through my eyelids.
It's bright, intelligent
free of all cares.

I'm the heir of a great American family.
My success is guaranteed.
Unexpected tragedy is all that can stop me.
I'm the popular senator teaching his son to shave.

2 FRAGMENTS FOR STEVE HAMILTON

Walk past dirty buildings
block after block
then a wide green park
before you hit
the mighty river.

So much to say,
so little time.
Then all of a sudden
nothing.

JET

for Kit Wienert

The concept "plane" is only
in your head. In the air
between two points, the fastest way
to travel is to trace
the great circle. Narrow lines
of smoke lace the sky,
golden threads upon a field
of blue. Where they start
they fade, spread out, a paradigm,
the moving fingers writing. Anselm said
"A bird flies in the window,
flies away, and you have no
idea of where it came from, of where
it will light." Sun moves behind
the jet stream, turning it black.
The man inside the Etch-a-Sketch
is graphing out his history
with both hands, on the face of the machine.

ENTRE NOUS
Poems by Tim Dlugos

MANHATTAN AND BROOKLYN

1976-1988

THOMAS MERTON LIVED
ON PERRY STREET

sky gets light
                "making the bed
is making the bed"

hot tea
thoughts of Ted
thoughts of all the money
I owe the government!

        got to go
        to work today

First Isaiah talks about
new moons, pagan rituals

            though their raison d'etre
            be not so strange

read office next to photographs
of Proust   "people
cry when they hear stories
of someone rising from the dead"

sun is out   no clouds   subway
moves beneath the house
it's noise

Great Spirit fills my body
a tiny light is all I need
the plants keep growing

                        I break
into a smile

my cultural and spiritual masters
as well as my political heroes
all lived in this world
and so do I!

NOTE TO MICHAEL

strange to see the river through the window
that lets the colors in behind me   it's real light
as opposed to artificial   it's real life
I'm in the middle of, I hope   where you are
is just as real (I also hope)   and
what we feel between us is a filament that bears
its own energy, glowing in ways too subtle
or too fast for the eye to pick up, a precious alloy
that puts us in the same place "on one level":
the level of the river and the light

TERMINAL DAYS

Coming round the mountain: Lazy Madge, Philip Glass Ensemble, NY Choral Society Featuring Belafonte (no more solo gigs, figgers they can buy his albums), Bella For Mayor. I don't smoke dope for the same reason Richard X digs opium. Lunch with Ian Young at the Terminal Restaurant: English military shackles, not to be confused with leg irons. "On for size." This year we are featuring the starving children of Senegal, Thailand and Bolivia in our kit. Ed Sullivan national chairman of UNICEF Day, reappearance causes splash. I write for magazines, spaces in which explosives are stored. Halifax Citadel, bright day: follow boy in school jacket down the long lawn, sun goes down. The Green Lantern Building. Head of Jeddore. In tourist cabin used by hunters, switch to All News Radio. Moynihan For Senate.

Photos of the Queen and Prince in living rooms all over North America. Photos of our apartment in DC. Somebody I know is in another country. Photos of my friend Mike Lally, whom I didn't meet until nobody called him that. Photographs of me that I have never seen.

The trees are green, then greenish, moving into frequencies of yellow-brown. It's a sign the season has arrived, as are many natural phenomena. Tennis bubble parked on Terminal roof comes down, in strange slow-motion. Inside, woman in white dress (suntan) watches as the tennis ball takes forever to drop. The hypothetical Second Assassin is shooting from the Con Ed smokestack, resting his gun on the anti-pollution device. Another puncture. Inside, tiny puffs of green as dumdums blitz the court. "Let's . . . get *out* of here!" It's *Black Sunday*, inside the blimp. "Bubble Collapse!" blares yellow press in snappily-written story.

Wheat germ, spinach and mushroom salad, Perrier. Miss you. Missed Philip Glass the first time, not again. Miss Collins is what some people still call my mother. She's been married for 31 years. In Springfield, my cousins say Hi to descendants of the kids my mother grew up with. In New York one is on one's own. Leaving Tudor City for the UN, things turn blue-green, cf. J. Schuyler. Blue sky, green light. Do what you want. Wherever you are, you're one in a million.

cool air in my chest   it's

"a fine day"   sharp-edged

buildings scrape against

"blue sky"

I am in your pants

they're white

and tight, in all

the "right" places

what right do I have

to wear them

couldn't fill your

heart, your shoes

what is left between us

is as empty as the sky

as fresh, and as impossible

to fill

I REMEMBER SPINNER

I remember that Spinner got his nickname in Philadelphia because of the way he danced. When he moved to DC, he decided everyone should call him that, instead of "Joe." I remember several resolute months of pointedly calling him "Joe," thinking his attraction to the nickname was just a phase.

I remember going roller-skating with Spinner and his mom and sister, at a rink in South Jersey, near Cherry Hill. I was totally embarrassed at being so clumsy on skates, when he was so good.

I remember seeing *Lady Sings the Blues* with Spinner when it opened in Philadelphia. He got so involved in Billie Holiday's plight he practically cried.

I remember Spinner had a chance to audition as a backup guitarist for Al Green, but didn't—he didn't want to live "on the road."

I remember Spinner's stories about jamming with B.B. King in '71 in Point Pleasant, NJ.

I remember Spinner's bedroom in NJ—done in an "Oriental" motif, with temple lamps and a statue of Buddha.

I remember the first dinner Spinner made in his first apartment—lasagna, at which he excelled.

I remember Spinner cooking an enormous pot of chili on a number of occasions.

I remember Spinner's affection for a wide variety of junk foods.

I remember Spinner's affection for a wide variety of animals.

I remember Spinner never used last names in referring to his friends. Since he constantly made new friends, many of whom had the same first name, that could be pretty confusing if you hadn't talked to him for awhile.

I remember thinking Spinner was literally incapable of consciously hurting anyone—and I was right.

I remember Spinner getting himself caught up in other people's problems.

I remember Spinner being so excited by a new song that he couldn't wait to play it for everyone. That happened many times.

I remember Spinner listening to "Monster Mash."

I remember Spinner's expertise about vampire movies.

I remember Spinner's expertise about the "death of Paul McCartney" scare.

I remember Spinner's attitude toward funerals—total abhorrence. He thought they were depressing, and absolutely refused to attend them.

I remember at least 3 times when Spinner decided to get totally serious about breeding tropical fish.

I remember Spinner as a bank teller, and how nervous he used to get about "closing out."

I remember Spinner as a disc jockey at a party on 18th Street, and later as a disc jockey in an M Street club. He took his duties as disc jockey very seriously.

I remember Spinner crying on a snowy January night, on the boardwalk in Atlantic City. I can't remember why he was crying.

I remember a perfect summer night, going to Wolf Trap Farm with Spinner to hear a Mahler symphony. When the music started, he lay back on a blanket and watched the stars move across the sky.

NEW HOPE

1.

part of me is growing
in the square beneath the dark
snow, the crocus
is somewhere under ground
growing in the bulb it has to split
to get where it is going:
into the heady air

part of it is staying
in the earth, to spread,
grow roots
as tiny anchors
another part is moving in
the wind, at some point in its future
(also *our* future)

even though we may not see it
part of us is staying here
to watch

2.

we ride out the waves
of rain the way we ride
to New Hope: warm
inside a moving space

our lives are becoming
tangled as the hair
of the wild boy hunters found

our lives are as golden
as his hair, as dark

our lives are entangled
with each other
forming strong braids

3.

when you touch me
there I move

part of me is growing
like the eye of the potato
my ancestors ate:
"eat and be strong"

part of me is never
changing; that is
the part you never see
can't touch

it is the part that registers
your light when my eyes close

it is the little room
where we have always lived

SONNET

The night he leaves, you find a shiny dime
from Canada. You eat the same beef stew
you always order, at Brigitte's. Now you
can do what takes your fancy, anytime

you want. You live alone. You take a walk
down Bank Street to the pier. Hoboken glows
with a rich light, and one green tugboat slows
and banks downriver. There's no need to talk

to anyone right now, as the dark blue
sky fills the water in between the streaks
of silver. In the breeze, the river reeks
a little less than usual. You're through

and want to ease the pain. You think your art
might do that, but you don't know where to start.

KEY STROKES

The wooden pier goes far out in the sea.
We dive and swim beneath it, snorkels up.
A dog swims past me, and I can't catch up.
I'm awkward in this element, and free
to pass through schools of fish without disguise.
Beneath the sea, a million fragile plants.
No sharks tonight, but always there's a chance . . .
Casa Marina looms before our eyes,
an empty shell where once dwelt Robert Frost
and Wallace Stevens. Here the air is bright
as yellow elder, and my mouth gets tight
before you loose it with your tongue. I'm lost
and drying out in unfamiliar light.
The sun, your chest, your dog's eyes are just right.

*   *   *

I take a dive. All that you have to give
is in your eyes. In dreams, I'm still alone,
washed by the rivers, blest by suns of home
in New York City where I used to live.
When I wake up, I taste my history:
the past in dreams, the future perfect, and
the present in your arms and mouth. Your hand
is scarred by fire. I'm awkward and I'm free.
I'm most free when there's all this time to kill
and you inside it with me. There are clouds
on the horizon, but they melt with loud
sighs when they hit the island. Take a pill
and walk out to the garden. Eerie fruit
grows here on funny trees with narrow roots.

* * *

Just think: your image lives inside of me,
though I'd prefer the "real you" any day;
and think, this heart, all evil shed away
is pumping under pressure from the sea
toward a new place, or new for me at least,
the old baptism symbol, only more
healthy and wise somehow, a metaphor
describing how one's life can be a feast
as on the day we barbecued the steaks
and knocked down mangoes from the tree beside
your bungalow for salad. When we tried
to say how great it was, we learned it takes
more than our words to capture times like that.
The image breaks. Your eyes are where I'm at.

SONNET

Fronds plummet from the treebelt to the street
Or hang on and turn yellow. If this light
Refracted makes my eyes smart, it's all right.
Each sunglass lens is flawed, to form a sweet,
Inaccurate and hazy image. Life,
Love, future matter less here. Money counts
Exactly as much as at home. I bounce
Eleven checks, but what the fuck. The strife
Not o'er, the battle not engaged, the gears
May slip for just five months. Then, with a roar,
You'll see me back in action. "There are more
Long lines in heaven and on earth, my dears . . ."
Each one is straining to be thought The Best.
Sweat it out of my system in Key West.

TO JB FROM KW

when I speak slowly, clearly
the tiny birds that haunt the edge of the sky
are pelicans and distant
whose own self-image might be worse by far
than ours: the big beaks
a prehistoric grace
they skim the edge of water with their mouths
and small fish are entrapped, with no
particular emotion

or might be a lot better,
who can say? but when I hear
you speak, I listen
and it's as though a bridge
were suddenly erected
across the impassable Gulf

CROSS DRESS

for Jan Morris

Shining on the green, and at very low tides, perhaps
a picnic lunch to a far corner of the lagoon, somebody is sure to
wave you goodbye, across the dark water of the side-canal,
a fourteenth-century housewife, or prying into a thane's back yard.

"But this Cardinal So-and-So, he was not at all like that,
he was always *cosi—urgh!*" And with this sharp guttural expletive
punt-loads of undergraduates, with parasols and gramophones,
suggesting in a laborious sonnet that Venice was divinely founded.

And they would eat with lofty frugality. One restaurant in the
recesses of the Basilica, glimmering and aromatic, all the divinities
are immensely long and exquisitely fine, flecked with grass.
A fizzy drink is awaiting you in its little red ice-box.

Grinding corn on a treadmill, or attending some crucial and
excruciating viva voce, it remains a queer and curdling place.
I went there once. Thousands of pigeons were released to carry
the news to every city. Make haste, it cannot last much longer.

IN LONDON

for Michael Chaplin

So-called patriotic organizations and stray busybodies
march up and down the room exasperated, one hand
made me chuckle to think of my lifelong soul-mate, the
smorgasbord kicked around by guys with a political stake.

A kookie set-up at home, yet I used to hang around the pad
dangling at the guy's belt, but he obviously didn't feel like
girls were in the running, Geraldine and this little blonde.
At school I shot some way-out lines.

In Scotland we did a lot of shooting. This was a new
Berkshire farm, now blossoming into a beautiful chick.
My father couldn't take his eyes off the big knife.
"Don't give me that jazz," I said, "I'm staying."

One night I got completely stoned and watched the
minutes. A lot of traffic was coming up toward us from the
friendship of hell-mates. We didn't take any problem
to the bathroom down the corridor, without waking me.

"I was in the gents. What do you expect me to do?"
Cain't afford shoes or a tie is to be pitied, I guess. But you
pushed. He has shown this time and again, often when he
"shall want to enjoy living in it first of all."

Let's go out with a water diviner and find them a
heritage for a mess of pottage. Has she no sense of
contrition. Why the hell didn't the goons move in and
father octopus, there must have been a time.

The armed forces of the only neutral country in Europe
became friendly with a couple of brothers of my own age.
My mother bit her lower lip. "It's too complicated." She
showered us with crumbs. In spite of her high principles.

BINDO ALTOVITI

Bindo Altoviti walks into the back yard letting the screen door slam. He slings his lanky torso into a webbed chair and pops a can of Miller High Life Beer. It's the champagne of bottled beers, the perfect drink to quench the thirst of a boy as effervescent as Bindo. The light in Bindo's eyes helps him see. He picks up Section C of the *Times* (Sports Monday) and idly scans the pages. He is looking for a picture of a man in whom the brilliant light that Bindo knows from personal experience has been captured and transformed into tensile strength. Long legs. Long afternoon. Bindo stretches, dances to avoid a pesky bee. He lights a skinny joint and settles back to get high. The world is like a big museum to Bindo and he's no famous artist. He's just a kid with long hands pinned against a white wall he doesn't know enough to call by its right name.

On campus, Bindo wears a purple smock. It covers his tight jeans. He wants people to like him for himself, not because he turns them on. He's an eccentric figure as he walks across the quad, his floppy garment a flag of revolution in a world of letter sweaters and alligator shirts. Bindo doesn't paint, he gets painted, and he sees that as a major difference between himself and the pustulated masses grubbing for advanced degrees. He separates himself from their tiny world by degrees: hoagies in bed instead of feeding at the common trough. But Bindo is too nice a person to remain aloof for long. He lazes in the grove of Academe, and feeds its wildest birds by hand.

What Bindo needs is someone to bring him out of himself, or, what Bindo needs is someone to force him to stay the same, keep him from moving, handcuff him to a metal frame and never let him go, grow, grow old, graduate. Gradually Bindo distills a plan. It's still inside the big room, cooled by the world's first air-conditioner that doesn't hum.

A painting is a window. Bindo looks inside. It's boring. Something deep inside him is boring its way to the surface. He leans against the marble columns with his thumbs hooked on his belt, waiting to see what will emerge. It's no emergency. It's an afternoon that lasts as long as you want it, sweet kid with a salty skin and long hands trying to be cool, air-conditioned building on a vaguely threatening street, muggy summer, strong and brilliant light.

TETRACYCLINE DAYS

grey haze over trees, as in
a pseudo-intellectual French movie

notice I said "movie" as in "just a movie"
not "film" as in "Film Industry in Crisis"

crisis of the day is in my mouth
it's dry, I cry, I don't
want to watch it

if only I could get enough
"sleep" as in "The Big Sleep"
not "rest" as in
"the rest of my life"

THE BEST OF GAUCHO

In Hartford today the biggest mass murderer
in Connecticut's history was sentenced to life in jail.
In New York today the biggest mass murderer
in Iran's history sat up in bed.

He fingered the remote control
the way he ruled his nation
—with an iron hand—
and scanned the channels

Love of Life . . . Three Stooges . . . How the West Was Won

until he saw the man with the bolero.

* * *

And now, folks . . . here's Gaucho!

The monologue, the polka
dot tie, the flesh
colored glasses, the big
cigar, the Studebaker
logo on the set, the dope
of an announcer, the foreign
language, the guests with dreams
of stardom, the clogs, the ethnic
slurs, the barracks raid, the *Granma*,
the history played out, the smell
of manure, the hat.

* * *

A gaucho is a cowboy like the Lone
Ranger, who never punched a cow, but worked
guarding a range (a *pampa*), a space
where history plays itself out. You play out
the rope (or *lariat*) and tie it in
a noose which can be twirled around your hat
(*chapeau*). When the cow meanders by, you
strike it like a snake and turn your horse
(*equus*) sharply to the right like a car
or the latest government. When the cow
falls, you fall upon it with a burning
rod, and brand it on its flesh (or *fleisch*).

The cow is called a doggie (*chien*); it doesn't have a personal name.
You are called Gaucho; you don't have a personal name.
Your horse has been spooked by the fierce activity; its personal
    name is
Silver. Don't cry for me, little Silver.

*   *   *

"Jane Alexander will star in Howard Sackler's 'Goodbye Fidel,'
which Edwin Sherin will direct and which will come to Broadway
early next March. The play is about upper-class Cubans who are
caught by the Castro revolution, and in its feeling, Mr. Sherin
says, it is something like 'The Cherry Orchard.' Mr. Sherin also
says it's a 'romantic drama' loosely based on fact, and full of 'love
and compassion.'"
          —*The New York Times*, November 30, 1979

*   *   *

THE LEGEND OF GAUCHO

Gaucho had three brothers:

Harpo, the Silent One, who honked his horn like a taxi
or a goose, his favorite gesture

Chico, who was never one of us

and Zeppo, the beautiful, who died old.

Gaucho wore a short bolero and a wide flat hat
like Señora Stanwyck wears
in *El Big Valley*

his weapon was a thong with three iron balls
State, Church and Family, the Trinity
that Gaucho loved

*   *   *

so we get a witch as President
and a renegade doctor killed by the CIA

and we get a dope as President
and a film in which the renegade doctor

is played by Jack Palance
the CIA is played by itself

and the witch is played on Broadway
by Patti LuPone (*the wolf*)

and the wolf stalks the pampas
and Gaucho doesn't sleep

* * *

walk out through the pampa door
and all you see in all directions
is grass, Señor

the cattle here are scrawny

I'm a cow-muchacho and I tell you
it is tough, the meat
the border war

toughened up the young men
lean meat, meester
heat my beans in pampa dusk

At night there are three colors in the sky.

Overhead, it's black as mud.
In the west, a faint glow from the Christ
of the Andes

further west, the Andes and the stars.

I want to be a gaucho star.
I want to be the man with the bolero
and the fake moustache.

When Basil Rathbone as Sherlock Holmes
figured out that Dr. Moriarty was about to steal
the crown jewels, a gaucho
was sent to murder Ida Lupino's brother
to throw the great detective off the scent.

The scent I like is on the pampas.
Damp grass, with a thousand miles
of air to breathe.

Here in the interior, the junta
is a thousand miles away.

I love a man in uniform. The uniform scent
of the pampas goes on for a thousand miles.

THE YOUNG POET

for Dennis Cooper

The young poet's work is sharp, stylish, and oddly moving.
The young poet's novel-in-progress is being written in collabora-
    tion with a National Book Award winning older poet.
The young poet takes off his shirt and poses for a drawing by
    David Hockney.
The young poet spends some time in L.A.
The young poet was Allen Ginsberg's secretary for a month.
The young poet cannot help that he is handsome enough to model.
The young poet got propositioned by Donald Barthelme in 1974.
The young poet goes to the Duchess and gets drunk.
The young poet goes to a gym and mounts a Nautilus.
The young poet buys an electric guitar, and dreams in Tier 3.
The young poet works in an office.
The young poet learns to rejoice that she is pregnant.
The young poet marries another young poet.
The young poets give their offspring unusual first names.
The young poet has bad teeth.
The young poet shops at Reminiscence.
The young poet lives on the Lower East Side.
The young poet applies for food stamps.
The young poet applies for a National Endowment grant.
The young poet applies for a job in a famous bookstore.
The young poet is a blatant imitator of Ashbery.
The young poet walks like Ted Berrigan.
The young poet used to flirt with Anne Waldman.
The young poet writes reviews.
The young poet stuffs envelopes at St. Mark's.
The young poet wonders if it's time for a haircut.
The young poet wears black.
The young poet knows the distinction between punk and New Wave.

The young poet sees the book as object.

The young poet is unabashedly ambitious.

The young poet starts to write fiction as a way of opening her language up.

The young poet changes her name to something more perky.

The young poet doesn't ask for autographs.

The young poet is a junkie.

The young poet is a fag.

The young poet is a cheerfully middle-class suburbanite set down in the middle of a self-consciously bohemian scene.

The young poet is a lush.

The young poet has a small press.

The young poet got published once in *Partisan Review*.

The young poet wants more than anything to have the first book published by Angel Hair, Viking, Z Press, Black Sparrow, or Lita Hornick's Kulchur Press.

The young poet gets quietly drunk at Lita Hornick's parties.

The young poet gets loudly drunk at Lita Hornick's parties and is asked to leave.

The young poet affects an English accent.

The young poet affects an Oriental religion.

The young poet drinks European beer.

The young poet deals grass.

The young poet is doomed by his career as an arts administrator.

The young poet studied under Kenneth Koch.

The young poet voted for Ed Koch.

The young poet takes himself or herself exceptionally seriously.

The young poet gets a little older, and his poetry matures.

THE STEVEN HAMILTON SESTINA

When people ask, I tell them that I'm gay.
But there are people who will say, "I'm *queer*,
not gay!," like my friend Steven Hamilton.
He says that the word "gay" defines a movement
of disco-crazed drag queens and Castro clones.
"Queer" doesn't imply the whole dumb sub-culture.

Now Steven and I both are queer for culture:
poetry, dance, opera, the gay
party circuit, the friends who'd think it queer
not to appear at functions. The Hamilton
Beach toaster pops up. With a cat-like movement
I grab my toast and bolt it. I'm a cyclone

of activity each morning. A clone
's a fingernail cell grown inside a culture
jar. Fuck that. Morning elements: a nosegay
in a small vase, gift of a handsome queer,
the favorite coffee of Margaret Hamilton
steaming in my mug, the rapid movement

of my eyes in sleep, the hasty movement
of my hands through my stubborn hair. It's Klon-
dike cold outside my little house. The Cultur-
al Council Foundation's in the mail. Ga-
len Williams sends me *Coda*. It's a queer
profession we are in, dear Hamilton.

When I see Alexander Hamilton
on money, it requires the furtive movement
of my hand to my teary eye. Steve's no clone,
but still there's a resemblance. In this culture,
if Dad's a politician, Sonny's gay,
cf. Jack Ford and Randy Agnew. Queer,

isn't it. And Steven says he's queer,
not gay. And he has never been to Hamilton
Bermuda. And the perfect languid movement
of his cigarette makes me half-think he's cloned
from a great actress, now-deceased. If Kulchur
Press puts out his book, will they call him gay

or queer? Neither. The movement of our culture
is away from dull gay Castro clones, and toward Steven Hamilton.

QUM

for Donald Britton

Saturday, Jan. 12: sky swarms
with microscopic particles. It's too warm
inside this bar, a grace note
to make you and my other friends assume I wrote
these words just now, before the reading.
That is an illusion. Needing
drastic forms of admiration is a virus.
Wanting people to desire us
we (meaning you and I) wear a bright veil
of language (meaning words) before which pale
the mundane elements of waking life.
"A poet." Fine. But sometimes I feel like the wife
of a demented mullah, in my thick chador,
two eyes peeping out, no body curves or
smile or sense of pity.
Marching through the streets of this holy city,
I can smell the slogans on my breath,
and my veil is Western journalism's symbol of the death
of reason and the triumph of some crazy throwback
to my suburban Moslem childhood. I can't go back
there any more. The keys won't
fit. Sometimes I don't
remember that this holy garb was of my choosing:
brilliant blue, like Mary's. God, I'm losing
my train of thought, awash in archetypal sentiment.
The words are microscopic particles, a sediment
of mirrored light, brilliant, filling the air
and piling up around us layer by layer.

"ONCE I LET A MAN BLOW ME"

Patty Astor, Jackie O, Klaus Nomi
half of New York wants to blow me
the other half could not care less
Woolworth-Woolco, Korvettes, J. Kress

Boning Up, South Orange Sonnets, Blocks
Michael Lally, Terry Winch, Ed Cox
Donald Britton, Bernie Welt, P and T
used to live in Washington, D.C.

Bobby Thompson, Michael Boodro, Ed Brzezinski
Nosferatu, vampire played by Klaus Kinski
politics of sucking blood
Jesse Helms, Ed Koch, Dan Flood

Coarse Grind, Drip, Electra-Perk
The Omen, The Fury, The Exorcist, The Jerk
The Long Island Four, The Heartbreak Kid
those I'd like to blow—and did

FLIPPER

postcard from Gardone where a fascist poet
is buried in a ship with his comrades from the war
I pull out of my driveway singing Mahler
Kindertotenlieder, though the kids aren't dead

me I am alive but wiser
older though no oldster, no wise man
God's little wiseacre inside a roadster
pausing for directions and another cola

bad knee acting up when I accelerate
miss my destination when I go too fast
slowing down my Alpine in the Alpine weather
light another Alpine, take a real slow drag

in the Negro opera, a brighter species
courses through the ocean singing Old World chants
you're there, like a dolphin in a cancelled series
leading divers safely back to summer camp

GONE WITH THE WIND

So this is what it feels like when the Civil War
moves inside for the winter: carnage
camouflaged by a native sense of politeness
and nervous concern for the furniture. The ironclad
ship is on the monitor (Cable Channel D)
and the doorman beats back stragglers.
All quiet around the West Village tonight, except
here and there a stray picket
gets blown away, kablooey, by a Puerto Rican youth
whose gray eyes do not constitute authentic revolution
but merely a regrettable throwback to the setting
of an earlier, more simple you.
He thinks he has discovered it, whatever "it" is.
He didn't arrive there first, but neither did you.

Then the deep civility of formal dress: the ball
wherein you looked resplendent
clad as a Zouave in regimental colors,
pastels mostly, dancing with the hoop-skirted tease.
A Moslem, they thought you were a Moslem,
when all along you were a courier,
bearing a tremendous secret.

The message is clear, though its application
less so. The clutter of period pieces has sparked
an appetite for the return to fundamental
values, and the heart is held hostage
in the clash of styles and mutually incompatible
futures, each of which already has grown fingers and toes
although it won't be born for many months.

Nurses tend the wounded, midwives deliver
squalling army brats, camp followers get knocked up.
But this is just a temporary highlight
in your personal history's inexorable movement
toward the next truce. Embassies
are made, phone calls placed on the long lines,
ships sail in and out of the world's
most perfect natural harbor.

Such groups of three seem naturally to form
around a common axis; it's normative, like God,
you'd say. Yet part of that traditional
formulation is breath, pure and simple;
how does that square with the carcasses in uniform
stuffed beneath your Queen Anne chairs?
The drawbacks of an armchair commission. Draw back
the venetians, and a world appears
which has nothing to do with your "chores."

PASTORALE

for Virgil Moore

The time the toddler crapped on the Urban Center floor
and we left it for the janitors to handle
you said it was a statement of the building's true
significance to the community; that, or just laughed.
Now you're dead five years, and I'm wondering
what you'd say was the significance of your presence
to those you "touched forever" (you'd laugh at that,
too). Update: Mary Ellen is a therapist in Center
City, John is a professional actor (so what else
is new, you'd say), Jack is married, Kevin
is divorced. I'm a writer living in New York.
Caught the upward mobility escalator
and live in a renovated building with a view
of the harbor, cheek-by-jowl with the poor
whose lives we thought would have improved by now
through self-determination and a brand new kind
of socialism, one which put down nobody.

I'm looking out the window at the water and the ships,
thinking of all you've missed. Reagan got elected
President! You shake with silent laughter and your eyes
are full of instant knowledge. *Right*, you'd say.
A few clouds hang against the blue; the water's patchy
where they block the light. You tried to swim at night,
you who were so frightened by the water, and went down
trying. Sometimes from this vantage point
it's 1960 again, the air can be so clear
it's like a dream of lost time, before the dope,
before the lost revolution. Your silence is as much a sign
as ever when I think of your laughter and the way you left:
going out by getting high and doing something impossible.

HOW I GOT MY BOOKS

from Section III: "The Cs"

I saw that purple book, Codrescu's first,
in *Paris Review* ten years ago, and rushed right out
to buy it. Next to it's his life story;
bought that at a discount when Terry Winch
was running Discount Books. The Coleridge
I got in college; its pages have turned brown.
Don't recall where any of the Clark
Coolidge came from; maybe Books & Co. when Burt
was there. I keep them next to a terrific
book by Calvin Coolidge, *Have Faith in Massachusetts*,
containing every speech he wrote as Governor.

THE RUBBER LADY

Opacity becomes her. Her mottled arm
is reaching from the far end of the terrace
to shake your hand: taut skin, stretched like gumbands
to the limit of endurance, the point at which pin-
points of light shine through like stars. She's glad
to see you, with none of the bewilderment
of others with her gift, e.g. Jimmy Olsen
who turns into Elastic Man against his will,
at inopportune times. She swears it's the turtle oil
that keeps her from wrinkling. She laughs heartily
and rises to the ceiling. "What you see is what you
get, only what you get gets longer."

Her mind's a blur. Sometimes she'll be athletic,
the medicine ball girls in gym clothes hoist.
More often she'll be mawkishly devout, like Alice
the Goon in the basilica, a single posy
rising from her pillbox hat and floating
'twixt priest and congregation. She's vulcanized
herself: pointed green ears, no heart.
She's vulgarized herself, a rubber shoe
endorsed by scores of sullen, unworthy hoopsters,
a sneaker sold in Shoe Town U.S.A.

She gets together with friends, and they bounce
ideas off each other. The ideas knock them down
but their leaded shoes right them. They're ready
to go on all night. Volcanic arguments ensue
with heavy fallout. The atmosphere finally clears
but the light is still vague.

She grew up in the tropics and would like to return.
This green shoot of a girl shot up and the needle
of remorse pierced her ego, deflating it,
deflecting her dreams. She's every man's dream:
breasts twice the size of Dolly's or as flat
as day-old beer. She's queer. They call her Doll-Face,
Doll-Face, and she adjusts her visage to comply.
It's raining in the city. She's a slicker:
bright, yellow, impervious to the drops.

as if Nantucket were Archangel, icebreakers
plow through the mushy Sound to carve a channel
I change the channel and I spend the day
like factory store chits received as pay

the joke that breaks the ice, the drink replenished
a spécialité de maison here
the raison d'être for another beer
your wordless presence to my nervous chatter

marooned in frost somewhere bereft of charm
for half the year, you manage to stiff-arm
oncomers with a fullback's thirst for depth and yardage
unchecked momentum as defenders gape

"appalled," their choice of adjective, while you
skirt grasslands chasing herbivores you swallow whole
and disdain mushy talk, and dream of tropics
as if Manhattan were the Hula Bowl

NERVES

Que sera, sirrah. I'm turning cyanotic
and you say goodbye in Japanese.
In the Misty Mountains, missed you,
Mister Right. Mysterious white
steamscapes pop up when the weather turns
toasty, whether you're there or not.
Oriental skyline sans sharp edges,
snipped out of the sky with blunt-edged
scissors, with kindergarten love. The nappy
Afro yawns, is blanketed with foggy kisses,
5 a.m. A yam. What? A yam.
The static on your telephone spells
trouble, so screw your concentration
to the sticking-place and, popeyed,
listen. I'm a man. M.A.N. And you're
my little export, a feather on a schedule
of impossibly unbalanced payments.

Hello, I'm Johnny Cash,
inventor of the first pay toilet,
the Johnny-Cash, which isn't my real name
at all, but the name of my original product.
I took it as my own when the powers-that-be
stole my great idea and made a killing.
They're sneaky bastards, the powers-that-be.
They're the guys who run things.
The President and all the heroes work for them,
and so did I.
They're the guys who make the wars,
who own the gold and land.
They're the ones who'll say this monologue
"sounds like a warmed-over Blitzstein libretto"
in the *Times* tomorrow. But I don't care
anymore, if I can sing my songs.

I wrote them all
myself. They're mostly about things
that I remember and people I knew.
I'm fortunate enough to have been personally present
at many historic scenes.
I was there when Judith Crist had her moments of doubt and pain.
I wrote a song, "Who Killed the Kennedys,"
and made a killing when it went gold.
And I was a guest on the old *Tonight* show
the night Jack Paar stormed off because the powers-that-be
scotched his famous reference to a certain "W.C."
They thought he was exposing how they purloined my invention,
when he merely was saying a secret hello
to his favorite poet in Rutherford, N.J.

This next song's going out to my favorite poet.
So the powers-that-be remain in the dark,
I won't use your initials, but
you live in New York, and you know who you are.

AMSTERDAM

mud in the Bishop's garden, a surprise
at St. John the Divine   Hungarian
pastries and a therapy appointment
on the warmest day of the year
so far, and a full moon   kids scuff
the thawed lawn beneath a steepled pulpit
must have looked the same way in Cologne
in Wells   in Bristol   cathedral cities
as it looks in Brueghel's sunny moments,
the stomping of an incoherent mob
transfixed, transformed into a lively dance
on the sunny court kids do the basketball dance
silent from the street jammed with the men
called "workers," "working class," when they had jobs
now they have an afternoon of dancing
down the sidewalk   doing the Trudge
the Strut   the Weave   the folk dance
of the folk of Amsterdam, whose wooden shoes
spawned the word "sabotage," an ultimately
useless form of protest   when you throw your shoes
in the machinery, you walk home with bare feet
I walk with scuffed loafers
past the old guys loafing on the stoop
of the conversion   the upper west side
of the cathedral towers would be washed by sun
if the cathedral towers had been built

THE ABSENCE OF LIGHT AND
A DRAWING BY EDWARD

boy with pale skin and hair black as the bottom
of the pool swims backward in flecked water

because he is a star he bears the weight
of hundreds of careers   it is a burden

that distorts his features, pulling back
his candor like a foreskin, till the chest is all

that places him here, now: it magnifies
his breathing through the muscles that rise

and fall with each breath in the shadowless
light, as if the light were everywhere

or nowhere, as if it were the act of breathing
that lights so evenly the parts that stay

when the eyes' light retracts and a foxy smile
replaces what they see with what they think

you want to see, as in the drawing by Edward
of Patrick Fox, who seems to be a fighter

drawn long ago by Bellows who has reappeared
from someplace else, a world where there are shadows

to sit in this uncanny, even light
and smile for an artist who cannot deny

his pale chest and black hair, who cannot fathom
the secrets of the star behind them

THE COST OF LIVING

for Douglas Crase

When you stop to think, it's quite the bargain:
the price of an Italian meal, a cramped
apartment, a job churning out speeches for some
butterball, the turkeys that you deal with
on the train or street. Think of it
as the price of an admission. We share this space
and dominate the settings we deplore
like Lurch the Butler, shaking his great head
and moaning in a voice impossibly deep. How's the view
from up there in your head? It's great. I see the Verrazano
Bridge, the mouth of the Gowanus where it hits
the bay, and three ships. But the jumble
of blocks and buildings baffles me, the borders
shift. South Brooklyn equals Cobble Hill
or Carroll Gardens, Red Hook's defined by storefront
industry, and the Heights are anywhere
west of Bedford-Stuy. The lingo of bait-and-switch
apartment ads spills into life, partitioning
the history of the view we saved like raw space
changed to living room, or lofty aspirations
converted to salable units. Suddenly
the alley's a self-conscious mews, and the Muse is off
to Yaddo. We live in a small room in our chests,
where language, that dwarf architect, may never find us,
though he designed this very retreat in obsessive
detail. We share his blueprints, even though our islands
are bounded by precision like a Gardol shield,
clear and impassable as the intensities
of sunlight as they divvy up our day.

SONG OF BERNADETTE

First me and my sister gathered sticks
Fuel for Daddy's hearth in France's armpit
Waiting for the voices, as in bedtime
Tales of Jeanne d'Arc, all we heard were clicks

Of castanets or locusts on the south wind
Blowing from Iberia through Smuggler's Heaven
All we smelt was wine and sour cheese
Blowing down from Bordeaux, factory *ville*

Then there was a lady in the grotto
Grotto, indentation in the muddy cliff
Standing on a pile of sticks
Standing on a globe of cold blue light

If I'd gone to college I'd have noted
'Lady on the globe atop the sticks' referred
To the world upon the shoulders
Of musclemen *en pointe* above a giant turtle

Instead I tried to change the channel
Looked for dials to spin but there were none in sight
Alice through the TV screen, the mirror
I knelt, said Do what thou wilt

You, you were the canny bishop
Watching through the telescope with half-closed eyes
Focused on a tableau you'd disparage
It takes you so long to apologize

When I shear my head and veil it
Peasant in a habit with accultured eyes
You'll be moved and I'll be moving
Soaring over tardily-improved fine tuning

ENTRE NOUS

I took a lot of guff about the team I coached
the intramural freshmen, entre nous
between the walls, not off them
sealing off their fate beneath a roof
of stars, sports illustrated
as in comic parodies of shooting hoops
a good day, shot a hundred (sky
darkened by the endless flocks of passenger
pigeons, children aim their 22s anywhere,
horizon to horizon)   it was the final season and
I took a lot of flak about the jackets we wore
me and the boys, we'd put on our jackets
and go out shooting, wild game, a game
of our invention   fouled out by the bum
of a referee, bummed out by the atmosphere
(invisible)   but buoyed up by the cheers
from the darkness just beyond the floodlights
that flooded our awareness with our fate
* YOU ARE LOVED *   I took a lot of pains
to get here, only to find myself a pigeon
a passenger on some fool's train
of jerkoff thoughts and blind desire   I broke
a finger when the ball was passed to me, and broke up,
flubbing the shot   but cheered up by the boy's
intensity, I lightened my burden as I lighted up
the joint and its dark atmosphere   I took a deep breath
of relief, and plunged back into the fray
my collar and my nerves were fraying, till
you came along, and opened up the floodgates
in my chest, the irrigation pumps
that fertilize the acreage entre nous

an empty space we've slated for development
which small birds you released fly over on their way
to nowhere   I fly across the floodplain
in a Piper Cub, on my way to the horizon
a cub scout to your pied piper, straight into
the endless Alp's dark atmosphere
I took a vow that when the door swung open
I'd enter to a choral * YOU ARE LOVED *
but broke the vow and headed through the ceiling,
sealing off my fantasies and breathing in
an atmosphere the stars of my invention never
punctuate, far beyond the pinspots,
buoyed up by a dense awareness that I am
a passenger shooting through my personal experience
on the way to Destination: Entre Nous
a famous space I still believe exists

THANKSGIVING SONNET

In Washington we made it at the baths
because you lived at home. In Jonestown, South
America, they all fell down. Your mouth
fell open at the pictures. Shiva laughs
and pours another flapjack in the pan.
It browns. Your ass is small and deep. I ate
deliciously and slowly. In this state
there's no such thing as "too" rich. In the can
the film gets longer. When you play it, whole
new episodes and characters appear.
It's all about the treasure Shiva stole.
You look about fourteen years old, my dear.
And when I lay you down and gently grease
your ass, a hungry nation rests in peace.

NEW YORK'S NUMBERS

David Samuel Menkes, Costume
and Decor   a Chelsea number
and a big cock   Gary Lauer
from New Jersey with his slouch
and his job   selling bargain
menswear in the arcade of the Empire
State Building   Timmy Scerba, editor,
Tobacco Institute News   he chainsmokes
and likes to fuck exclusively, unlike Henry
B., the artist with the finest dope
and sweetest eyes   he lives in a rooming
house, and raises his blond legs exposing
his blond ass   I eat out
with Michael B. at Pete's Place, Michael
whom I fucked, fell in love with
then out again quickly   Billy fucks me
quickly with his baby face and horse
cock I love to swallow   sex with Mark
is like sex on drugs, whether we're
on drugs or not   Sherwin with his drugs
and weird clothes   Randy with his accent
and weird book project   Edward
with his pose   Richard with his acid
comments:

Some would find it strange inside a dark room to reach
for another man's body, never knowing whether he's a Pulitzer
winner or simply some big jerk who works at Macy's.

I find it racy.

Some would say it's boring when some goon insists
you blow him, never caring whether you get off, or conversely,
goes down on you like an Accujac, never letting up until you shoot
without a kiss, a caress, or a chance to have some say in where
this sex event is headed.

I say forget it.

Some would say that numbers by their nature stretch
out into infinity, one by one, whetting a lust for one more
integer, an emotional breeder reactor turning out two units
of desire for every unit of satisfaction you feed it.

I say I need it.

NEGATIVE CREDIT

Decline in health, in reasoning
capacity, in looks, receding
hairline, threadbare chinos, Chinese
takeout (moo goo) every night at ten,
a sixpack from the geriatric deli
and *Our Mutual Friend* to drowse through
on the way to Nod and the recurring dream
of prison. I'm teaching other convicts
to write poems in a fieldstone classroom
through whose chinks the light appears
from outside. Some of these girls
are illiterate! exclaims Jean Harris,
who teaches reading in the women's pen.
She's there because of thwarted love, the same
machine that left these tiretracks on my bosom
next to the tattoo: "Flattered then Flattened."
Deflated hopes and pruned ambitions on the far
side of the river, the big Three Oh.
Who Do You Trust, that ungrammatical quiz show,
was Johnny Carson's vehicle when he was my age.
My vehicle is part of the rapid and rapidly
decaying transit system of a fabulous city.
My fables have no morals. My uniform is crisp
though drab. My lassitude amazes. My lust
instructs. You bore me more than I remember
was humanly possible. My heart's
as big as all outdoors.

CHEZ JANE

"I think it's fun to go to the prom
with a girl. I liked it." Your head
is in the clouds, like the observation deck
of the World Trade Center, and the clouds
are gray. "You know, you really look
like a woman." I'm writing off the top
of my head in your loft with its tropical
appointments: Cayo Hueso shorts, droopy
potted palms, complicated hash pipe
from Honduras, and a bright though eerie
bird perched on the petal of a huge
white orchid in your painting, the one
I admire. All this sounds "outlandish"
like the movie I hate, but it's not: it belongs
and illuminates, as unexpected and exotic
as the sailboat moored outside your window,
thirty feet offshore with people on its deck
and no way they could possibly have gotten there,
as if a mundane obstacle like transportation
had miraculously been solved, the way it's done
in movies: cut to the glamorous
soiree, and let the viewers fill in the intervening
action on their own. It's nice to drift through the history
of film within your view: a great ape
scaling the twin towers, Jessica Lange in tow;
Al Pacino swaggering in leather and chains,
four blocks to the south; and Laura Mars ensconced
in *New York Magazine*'s idea of luxury
where gay men sunbathe nude along the rotten
pier. But it can be just as swell to simply
follow the horizon with your eyes, the skyline

complicated, unfamiliar, from Bedloe's
(now known as Liberty) Island, past Hoboken
and the great green docks, up to where the giant cup
of Maxwell House is yielding its last drop. It's good
to have this vantage point, to fill in the river's
graduated silvers with your eyes, and watch the gray
of sky and street diverge to gold and misty blue,
like the eyes of a mariner. "I feel like one, too."

SUNDAY, BROOKLYN HEIGHTS

drop a quarter
in the box & listen
to the gospel
of Saint John Lennon

THE CONFESSIONS OF ZENO

for Cheri Fein

It was nearly midnight on a relatively peaceful
night, and the contest was almost ready to start.
We'd had a pretty good dinner, fair cigars,
and a rather long stroll through the maze.
The topiary may have needed trimming, and the shaggy
yew and you made it a practically magical scene.
"Having an okay time, honey?" I queried.
"I guess so," you dreamily replied. Then
the starter's whistle faintly blew. We moseyed
to the gate, which hung by one hinge, and were handed
application blanks by a balding half-wit. My pen
was nearly out of ink, so I yanked a Mongol
pencil from the semi-conscious jerk, and mulled:

> "Let's see . . . to participate you need a name.
> The one I use is close to the one I was born with.
> Education . . . almost graduated from college. I live
> as close to Manhattan as you can get without being there.
> Credit rating . . . I see my way clear to pay off
> most of my debts, though I'm always on the brink
> of bankruptcy. My relationship with my roommate
> is nearly over, the one with my steady is about to end
> or move into high gear, I don't know which. Last night,
> in a state approaching total drunkenness, I came
> within a hair of getting killed by a cab that fairly sped
> out of the semi-darkness. I'm a tepid Catholic, living
> in what Baptists call "the latter days"; the Resurrection's
> happened and the Final Judgement's coming any day.
> In California last week, I thought the final earthquake
> might take place, but I'm still waiting."

We finished filling out our forms at almost exactly the same
time, and turned them in. Our answers were nearly identical,
we were pretty amazed to learn, since our personal histories
had been totally different, with a few exceptions. We could
almost feel the tension mount. I turned to half-face you.
Our hands almost touched. "Are you partial to me?" I breathed.
You started to redden, then thought better of it. Your lips
had nearly formed your answer when word reached us from officialdom.
We'd qualified. Too suddenly, the contest began.

GRIST

Seated one day at the organ,
at West Point, you watched the ushers
gather their composure, walk down
the chapel aisle, tap your mother on the shoulder
and ask her to step outside. You saw it
in a mirror strung above the keys. The concert
(Couperin) went on. They hit you with the bad
news at the intermission. Think of it as a toll-
booth where the uniformed attendant
hands you a ticket with small square holes
punched through its surface in what seems to be
a random pattern. It's not, of course;
the data is all there, and the information
you'll need for the rest of the drive
through these sere parts. But the card is
obsolete, grist for a computer
which has not been used for generations. Clip it
to the visor and take off past the blasted
oaks, dusted with cocoons of the gypsy
moth. There's a grove to stop in,
a resting place, where every leaf's been stripped.
They resembled springs, the ones that make
a typewriter carriage return, only made of wool.
Then they threw their white scrims up
and settled in. New growth is expected on the hard-
woods; the softwoods and the evergreens are not
so lucky. Luck means less when it's circumscribed
by travel time and route of preference
to journey's end. The variables
thin out, which is not to say
that crazy things can't happen. Looking

for the Moby Dick Motel, you ask a pump attendant
for directions and he sends you to the Moby
Dick Gift Shoppe, in another town.
There can be explosions too, though these
days they are mostly caused by laughter.
But much of the time, things proceed
apace, at their own pace. You leave
and you arrive, taking breaks to clear
your head. You wash up and you sit down
to eat. It gets brighter, then shady
as you outpace the moths. The dark
arrives in concentrations that gradually
strengthen, and the porch lights go on.

FROM JOURNAL

Picking up background material for a copy assignment at Sanky's, I pass a desk and there's Terry, S.'s former assistant, whom I haven't seen in years. Terry! It's been years! Tim! she exclaims, and we reminisce about our first meeting, my first New York employment interview, at Planned Parenthood for Sanky's old job. It must be ten years ago, Terry says, and when I correct her (five) she doesn't believe me, possibly because she thinks I look ten years older says my intrusive vanity. Terry doesn't look a day older. She's been out of the industry; she and her husband retired to their dream house in Front Royal, Virginia, two years ago. What's she doing back in New York? Well, she falters, I lost my husband five months ago . . . I'm sorry, and tell her so; tell her also about my father's death two weeks ago, my mother's loss similar to hers: husband passing too short a time after they'd reached their retirement destination, miles from friends and familiar landscapes. Terry's back in town scouting possible jobs and Staten Island apartments. She might move back and share a place with her sister, but there's a snag: What'll I do with my furniture? It's all valuable antiques. She alternately glares and looks at me imploringly as she ticks off the pieces. A marble-topped coffee table! A beautiful mahogany dining-room set! Twin beds made extra-long especially (my husband was six-feet-two, eyes tearing up)! A combination bench and coat rack with the original mirror! The classic sideboard! She's starting to get worked up. Then the trouble of moving it all! The week they moved to Virginia, she broke her arm, her husband almost had a second heart attack, and the cat developed cancer. When they arrived in Front Royal, she had to locate an orthopedist, a cardiologist, and a vet. The husband and the cat died. They sold their house in Cobble Hill, occupied for five years by a couple of young men who called Terry "Ma" (she pauses to see if I get the idea), so she can't go back to Brooklyn. It's a dilemma, and she wants to know how my mother is facing what she perceives to be a similar crisis. By staying put for awhile, I say, and Terry agrees that the first months alone are the hardest, no time to make a big decision. She asks how my father died, and when I tell her (the sudden massive heart attack, the coma that looked as though it would last for months, and the quiet, equally unexpected death), she tells me, it's better than his being a vegetable. He had a vegetable *garden*, I want to say, but instead reply that I don't know how impaired he would have been, but he was a grumpy patient even when he had a cold (she nods; *men*, she thinks), so a long serious illness would have been awful for him, thereby setting up an opposition between death and discomfort, choosing the former, though neither I nor more importantly my father believed in that sort of glibness, and it's his life we're discussing, six stories over Times Square this gorgeous afternoon.

HARBOR LIGHTS

Kokoschka sky with thicker clouds
"South American Kokoschka sky"

under it, the girders   the gables
the cables   containers and the working ships
stock-still on the bay

I rise at dawn and write because it's
clear, though it's cloudy
this a.m., the sky approaching
purple, like language in an awful poem
making me anticipate an awful day

but light falls on the hilltops
of Staten Island, so let me revise
that forecast: it's a mammoth harbor
big enough for tons of weather

COLUMBIA LIVIA

In the latest field guide, they don't rate
a map. Their range is worldwide,
though one needn't like it. "Familiar
to city dwellers," Peterson writes,
maybe adding "all too" in a whisper,
though his illustration's great: the grays
with sharp black trim a perfect
urban statement, and the startling
nape of purple and electric green
a combination oddly artificial, even
in nature. It flies above its English
title, Rock Dove, a name suggesting period
politics and music, or a ghastly marriage
of mineral and bird, disconcerting as
doubling up the names of species can be:
the chicken hawk, for instance, or the liger
in the zoo out west we read about as children,
almost regal in its bleached-out stripes,
a lone mulatto in a world which granted it
no quarter, the kingdom of the animals.

FOO DOG BLUES

So many dynasties, so little time:
the slogan on a T-shirt I could buy
in Heaven, if someone in a uniform
would spell me from my duties at the gate.
Heaven's a boutique out here, like Greetings,
Design Observations, and All American
Boy back home, a member of the nouveau
mercantile class: shops that sound
like elements of waking life, posture,
form and aspiration. Meanwhile, cousins
Fortitude and Patience languish where the steel
bands play calypso music and the dope
smoke wafts through rotting incunabula.
I'm glad that my commission is divine,
albeit impossible. It makes the borders
clear, sets my cap and large incisors
on edge, cutting through the day's detritus,
the piling up of detail in a wooly rug
I wear around my neck like the lion
I was: an ancient teacher's cub scout,
trained to watch and wait with eager paw
clutching a small pearl atop a silken
pillow, a ladies magazine's idea of grit
and purpose, the synthesis of price and pride.
Atlantic and Pacific, they know the terrific
power of the sentry, and his burden.
I've been around for years, and am almost
invisible, like the guardian angels. A ring
of fire is how they first appeared, worlds away from
the consumptive blonds with pastel bathrobes
and wings who populate the wayside chapel
windows: a down-to-earth caricature of life

unknown among the sensible, the purely
spiritual being. When gods come down
to earth they appear as nondescript travelers
whose every gesture is a test. Sit awhile
and stroke my mane beneath this banyan. Babe
the Blue Ox strolls by, lowing for his patron,
exemplar of the brawn that built this country,
strange as that may seem. I meander
over to the bridge, and nuzzle Marco Polo
as he stares into the river, surrounded by dogs.
He's something never seen before in these parts.
In the water, he can see the goldfish dart
beneath the stones, and on the muddy bank
rabbits with the fungus of longevity
between their paws, under a full moon.
They nibble when they eat. And I've outlived them
all, fierce as ever, though I've put a groove
in my paw where the pearl fits; can't lose that.
The halcyon days of puppyhood with sticks
of incense in my mouth, the smoke ribbons
curling like a halo—good dog!—around my ears;
all the years of smiling or sneering, they never
knew which; and now the humdrum stream
of traffic past the phony oriental
gates, palm trees on the dusty street,
rumble of the good earth far below. Tarzana
is a far cry from nirvana, and for an illusion,
maya stings. I've never caught a rabbit;
that's not my job. And you're right, I've never
been a friend of yours. I have been selected
for a special task, a destiny unique in history.
To the impious, it sounds like a Disney
short: The Cat Who Thought He Was A Dog.
But for robbers, and floods, and fires, and even

the eventual earthquake, I mean business:
a guardian set in stone by a forgotten artist
commissioned by the emperor who brought us floods
and fires and the eventual earthquake.
He wanted the moon, and tried to reach it
via firecracker; you probably have heard the rest.
I want to close my mouth and rest with the moon
in my face, facing a stream of travelers
who pass me single file on their way to the interior
and touch me as they pass, for good luck;
and join the other dogs, the real ones,
on the explorer's bridge waiting for the stranger
for whom the mundane happenings of these parts
are a great adventure, something to drive him on.

EAST LONGMEADOW

Endicott Peabody was the governor.

Dick Hickey, Jerry Pellegrini and Frederick Wheeler were the selectmen.

Richard Clark was the town clerk.

Father John Wolohan was the parish priest.

Clyde Walb was the scoutmaster.

Donald Emerson (blond, crewcut) was the sixth-grade teacher.

Officer Craven was the police sergeant.

Miss Eseldra Glynn was the other sixth-grade teacher.

Mr. Francis was the only Negro teacher.

James Latourelle was the plumber and Little League manager.

John Quinn was the doctor.

James Brown was the dentist.

Robert Bean was the grocer.

Sanford Nooney owned the hardware store.

Ed Pratt ran the Esso station.

Frank O'Hearn was the real estate agent.

W. Harley Rudkin wrote the humor column for the *Sunday Republican*.

Stuart Crapser was the principal of Birchland Park Junior High School.

Angelo Correale ("Gorilla") was the assistant principal of Birchland Park Junior High School.

Kenneth Battige was the leader of the hoods.

The Brega twins were the wild kids on the street.

Father Hugh Crean was the assistant parish priest.

Charles Bowler was the town Democratic chairman.

Helen Hayward was the town nurse.

Lois Lopes was the librarian.

Mrs. Jones, a Negro, was the Avon lady.

Alonzo "Dennis" Jones was the school basketball star.

Wescott Clarke (blond, crewcut) was the handsomest boy in school.

Nancy Dalessio was the prettiest girl in school.

John Quill was the TV weatherman.
William L. Putnam owned the TV station, WWLP.
Jimmy Fiore was the grocer for the Italians.
Walter Uhlman was the town engineer.
Hiram Moody was the town eccentric.
Mr. Teed was the Congregational minister.
Brian Crosby was retarded.
Mary Gregory was the president of the Catholic Women's Club.
Billy Barrett was the head altar boy.
Cookie Bates was the leader of a Dixieland band, and wore a goatee.
Ruth McMullen taught art, and wore a smock.
Allen Pash (blond, crewcut) was the boys' gym teacher.
Dorothy Gladden was the moderator of the Poetry
    Appreciation Club.
Laurie Richmond was the girl whose mother had shot her in her
    bed before committing suicide.
John Brusnicki was the pharmacist.
Vincent Panetta was the divorce lawyer.
Mrs. Blake was the richest woman in town.
Marion Cooley was the piano teacher.
William Twohig was the postmaster.
Archie Rintoul ran the Community Feed Store.
Fred Geoffrion Senior had a nervous tic he got in the war.
Helen Geoffrion was a practical nurse.
Harvey Cadwell was the guidance counselor.
Genevieve Crosby was the mother of three who introduced the
    sack dress to town.
Diane Johnson eloped at age 14 to Elkton, Maryland.
David Lyons had cerebral palsy.
Paul Ollari was the paper boy.
Jeanette Goodlatte wrote the "East Longmeadow News" column
    for the *Union*.
Wilton Hayes had a wooden leg.

Joe Siano was the barber.

Babe Meacham was known as "The Mayor of Maple Street."

Ann Dunbar owned the ladies clothing store.

Mrs. Baldwin ran the Busy Bee Kindergarten.

Raymond Drury was the disc jockey for WTYM, *"Time* for Beautiful Music."

Stephen Brega was brain-damaged after he tried to hang himself.

Elwin Doubleday was the high school principal.

Nora Braylee was the leader of Youth for Christ.

Jimmy Walb was the president of Demolay.

Fred Lindner was the man who sharpened lawnmower blades.

Dolores McDonald was Mary Gregory's sidekick.

Tom Williams was an executive at Package Machinery.

David Bowe had a speech impediment.

John Hird was president of the Harvard Club.

Howard Frykberg owned a restaurant on Route 20 that failed when the Turnpike opened.

Bob Latourelle was the captain of the Little League team.

Eddie Lombard was the milkman.

Robert Drumheller owned a German shepherd that always chased my bike.

REGO PARK

You thought that it would be a piece
of cake, but it turned out to be a slice
of life, and now even the crumbs
have disappeared into the cracks in the linoleum,
borne away by smirking ants. They march
in lockstep. Last night you could hear them
practicing behind the plasterboard
where the smell of curry is locked in
forever, however ants conceive
of forever. What must be the grimmest marriage ever
of form and function gave birth to this boxy
sward, whose only stretch of green
hovers yards above us, reflected in the blue
tile walls of Ohrbach's, where the jeans
have names (someone else's) imprinted on their seats.
It's someone else's neighborhood. You watch
as from a height, and the walls fall away
to show the ants at work. The New Bombay
Cinema is featuring escapist nonsense. The Untouchables
are on TV in apartment 3G, and manic groups
of swarthy men drive battered Chevrolets
nowhere in particular, as in the rest
of this developing world. It spreads
across the access ramps, as many for the lame
and halt as for the hordes on the expressway.
They're going to the beach, and think it dumb
we new Americans aren't. One has to
agree, but with reservations. There's nothing
like an empty beach, in Mozambique, say—empty
for a reason, like the next cell down the drab
green hallway, smudged the color of the sea

when the wind brings water from the west,
where the sludge is. Live with it
and you forget it's there, as with a dull ache.
You wear a form-fit duncecap, watching whitecaps break
like someone from another planet, perfectly
all right except for the way you speak
and the shape of your head, which wants to be a steeple
in a place of boring buildings and exotic people.

THERE'S SOMETHING ABOUT THE DYING

light that impersonates a welcome to the new
(for those without a memory) state of affairs
in which the air that brushes past our temples
lightens perceptibly as darkness strikes
the township, and the only lamps left burning
are the ones the year-round residents kept up
when the tax cut lowered expectations like a shade
to keep the outer shade from entering
the kitchen with its knotty sideboard crafted
in a basement workshop, and commemorative
plates against the walls. In the coming
of the night where scrub forests separate
the sky's striations from the heavy thicket,
there is a giddy vigor that can last
for hours past the final light, a textual
concordance that speaks volumes when compared to
its original, the day and what goes on.

PHILIP'S RAZOR

Joan Armatrading sings, "We had fun
while it lasted" as I wildly
pogo in my living room, a Merit
dangling from my mouth, wearing nothing
but the super-baggy shorts you gave me
on my birthday. I must look ridiculous,
something I remember when I think
of you. I cried last Sunday when
I saw you, a ridiculous thing to do.
It's ridiculous, too, how the feelings
never go away and how I'm insanely
happy to sit down next to you
not having to say a word, the rush
of old devotion overwhelming all the more
recent bitterness and pain. I never
thought I looked ridiculous when we were
together. No matter how unfocused
I became, your sense of proper visuals
salvaged the tableau: you and me on Astor
Place. Now among the drunken Negroes
on the subway and the hordes on Fifth,
the option of ridiculous behavior's
gone for me. The holographic keenness
of your critical sense, a razor, as in
the medieval argument from visuals (what you see
is how it works), at my poor posture's
throat has been withdrawn, and I am alive
in an outer borough, where this sudden
untoward keenness makes me feel like crying
again, but not ridiculous. Browsing
as I bounce through a great collection

of originals: your painting on my bedroom
wall, your grace and perfect gestures
of affection, your cutting words and deep
exasperation, and my feelings so sharp
I could have been a high school senior seeing it
all in my mind as it happened, every second
a neo-classic tableau of exquisite beauty
fucked up by ridiculous feelings when I had
a hard time making the leap from godlike
contemplation into a life whose elements
of style included everything I wanted most,
and everything I hated. These uncompleted actions
persist and grow more tangled in the Twentieth,
Greatest of Centuries. The universe is whole,
not holistic, and there is a place for you
inside it, next to my feelings, though no longer
by my side. It is meet and just. Just right.
"Oh babe, I miss you" (Kim Carnes) even though
the argument from visuals places you across
the river, out of sight.

IF I WERE BERTOLT BRECHT

I'd take a bath, first of all;
then I'd throw away those drab and ratty
suits I'm always photographed wearing.
Buy some new threads; and while I'm at it,
get myself in shape at the nearest Holiday
Health Spa. Next I'd trim the fat
off my plays, getting rid of the didactic
boring passages that make me such a German
artist. I'd develop a modest sense of humor
and a sense of modesty, and treat the ladies
better—they're people, too. If I hated
California as much as I say, I'd leave and go
somewhere I liked better; but I love California,
so that would eliminate a lot of grief.
I'd shave the silly moustache, get a tan,
and turn my life into a sane and happy one,
all before I went out for my sauerkraut
and knockwurst, into the Weimar night.

JANET'S REPENTANCE

The half-completed chore meets the half-remembered
song over cocktails in a musty pub,
"The Wagon Overthrown." Trust these yokels
to raise the beery standard of a slow
day's breaking story: one upended Dumpster
on the interstate, reported by the Shadow
Traffic team. Dictators galore have toppled
with no saloon to celebrate their fall. Harvest
when the leaves turn, plant when mud sucks boots:
that's it, wisdom-wise, out here. There is no sense
of politics among the folk of yon breathtaking
vista. They're like the grazing sheep, unable
to add up two and two, unlike we past masters
of the abacus, whose problem lies in multiplying,
which the natives have down pat. The calculus
of change is down the road a piece, lying in wait
to hijack the consumptive parson and steal his clothes.
Looks good in black. I pour another tumbler-
ful of mead, and mix it with the local
ditchwater beer. It's dull inside the taproom
when the clouds change shape so fast and the shadows
pile up. The antique radio collection,
the antique decoy collection, the German mug
collection, the popeyed keep: artifacts
of an interior eaten away by the forgetful
spirit, where it lives. Cut the team
loose and let the gig coast down to the Dutch
door, past which lies the life of drink: a fruitful
meditation on the power of change, the next cloud
on the program, the exile that the ruler
deserved so well, the rest of the task, and
the last line of the refrain.

TIM DLUGOS, YOUNG REPUBLICAN

There used to be a better reason
than pure perversity, but I have a hard
time remembering what it was. When I was
a kid it stood for incorruptible
disinterested and uninteresting public
service: Herbert Hoover swearing
"I'm a statesman, not a politician."
He was a very great statesman
and a lousy politician. Then there were
the Henry Cabot Lodges, with the younger's
global perspective a new generation's
improvement on his Grandpa's narrow view.
Grandpa was an old Republican, Henry and his
first son George (who lost to Teddy
Kennedy in '62) were the new Republicans.
There were others, too: John Anderson
and brave Bill Scranton battling
the pinheads, Goldwater and other obvious
fools who run the show, these days. Now
to be a young Republican means to serve
the sharks of Big Oil and the heartless
vampires who want to drink the poor man's
final drop of blood, except when I apply
the term to myself, when it means what
it used to mean (a genuine Republican
way of choosing sides).

OBSCURE DESTINATIONS

There is a wealth of corn within the checkerboard
five miles beneath this dark industrial wall-
to-wall. I like the way the rectangles an hour
out of Newark give way to less conventional
swatches of grain about the time that "Midnight
Blue" drones through the headset for the third
time straight. One becomes a critic
at this level, the dumb benevolence of an above-
it-all mood heightened by the complimentary
beverage served with unexpected promptness by a man
who will slip you his address before you disembark.
Merci buckets. Leapfrogging the continent
is more fun every jump. I like to readjust
my time in stages, once a zone. The trip proceeds
like basic education: the fields of plenty increasingly
knotty geometry problems, then the booby-
trapped hurdle of the High Sierra, something
to get over. At this joyride's end will come
our destination. Ah, but where are we *really* going?
Further, one supposes. The pilot edits points
of interest according to no-nonsense standards
and points out the survivors: Grand Canyon, Si,
Donner Pass, No. Below's the place where men in service
uniforms and clear-eyed Baptist women make
the things that make them great. Beside each cluster
of adobe huts, an obscure landing
strip whose wind-sock is the only sound for miles
when our drone fades. Encapsulated in the jumbo
plane, I want to get over them fast, and reach
a port of call obscured by green
mist on the precipice, to live there

in the customary style, both feet
on the edge where the ground meets water
by the ton, which rushes in from what
for a little while will seem the wrong direction
when the mirror's yanked away.

THE GLORIOUS MYSTERIES

for Gerrit Henry

I shall arise and go now. It's late
and the bars close early in this state,

the product, doubtless, of the dusty Blue
Laws, and history's inexorable hand. You

make one think you know a lot about
that subject. Just a decade back, your clout

was heavy, as you expertly ascended the slope
of byline recognition. Any dope

who opened an arts journal saw your name,
and songwriting, you hoped, would help extend your fame

but something suddenly came over you
and burned the raw ambition out of you

refining it to something with a bit more merit
to make your work somehow express the Authentic Gerrit

and in this higher state you found you could
assume nothing about the relative good

or bad points of your craft. You simply did it
and turned it into something special. Now admit it,

though you don't wear the crown of Laureate
and publishers aren't battering your door yet

it's glorious to proceed, to take the next long
step. To simply go on is the best song.

TO BE YOUNG, GIFTED AND BLACK

Calculate the exact percentage
of times the Nerf ball reached you via lateral pass
when you held out for a slide-rule or the new
translation of *À la recherche*, hurting and confusing
the sleepy dusty delta day's perception of What
Gives. The times you looked the gift
horse in the mouth were the crucial
moments, although it was "just" a mule.
"Forty acres, metric-scale: let's see . . ." and the red
caliche formed lumps of concentration, mirroring
your slow ascent into the cream of the regional
crop, to hover at the top of an unshaken glass
of milk and absent-mindedly pick bolls
surrounding the rough-hewn bench where basic
learning happens in the words thrown out
and caught across a distance measured by conventions
of advancement, to the next rung of a ladder
that turns out to be a road transversed
by equidistant crosswalks, thousands of them
shimmering on the tarmac from your level
of achievement all the way to the horizon
with its phony pool of water, which maintains
a discrete though immeasurable distance
however many triumphs you chalk up. The race
may be unwinnable, but you're a credit
to it. The debits are the ones in red.

DESIRE UNDER THE PINES

I like to wake up early by myself
and walk out to the forest which divides
the beach from bay side of the island, like
the line of hair that starts at breastbone, hides

the navel and descends into the thatch
beneath the tan line of a boy I saw
a picture of once, in a magazine.
He isn't in the woods this morning. Raw

desire al fresco isn't quite my speed
these months. I like to scout for vireos
and robins almost as much as for guys.
An ashtray from the Hotel Timeo

in Taormina, a signed lithograph
by the late Tony Smith, and a shelf packed
with great books of our time: the souvenirs
of my hosts' histories. I left mine back

along the trail, like interesting litter
thrown out of Conestogas on the long
trek west. The drivers knew that "We can use it
in Oregon" was a completely wrong

criterion. They had to get there first,
and lightening the load was the only way.
Beside the path, the wren that lights in brush
sounds like a footstep in the gathering day.

BRIAN AND TIM

New York	Massachusetts
D.C.	New York
the mountains	the ocean
St. Bonny's	LaSalle
graduate degree	college dropout
ceramics	poetry
Paris	Dakar
Denver	L.A.
Chinese	French
ex-Catholic	bad Catholic
waiter	copywriter
Rehoboth Beach	Fire Island Pines
bridge	TV
Montaigne	Frank O'Hara
Rascals	The Ninth Circle
sleeping with someone	sleeping alone
going home with someone on the second date	going home with someone on the first meeting
introducing self before having sex	having sex before introducing self
young men	boys
The Dry Look	The Wet Look
Moet	Heineken
a townhouse	a highrise
red	blue
twenty-eight	thirty-one
twenty-six	twenty
ratatouille	paella
an altar boy	a priest
A Confederacy of Dunces	*Our Mutual Friend*
conservative Republican	Sixties liberal

Jockey briefs	boxer shorts
overwork	indolence
psilocybin	mescaline
cocaine	cocaine
Lacoste	Lacoste
Proust	Proust

THE LIONS OF ST. MARK'S

for Edmund White

1.

It is partly a matter of light.
Mornings, one feels it gathering
the strength it needs to melt the unabsorbed
dew between the shoulder blades, from last
night's steam. The process
is guaranteed to be in satisfactory order
hours down the pike. There's time
to fill a few more reams before the map of Florida's
spread across a corner of Tar Beach, making us
honorary Sun People, though the clouds
and shadows that obscure the eyes of some
galoot are endlessly more magic.
Strange to think the pristine air controls
the somber damp that muffles all the bells
of the Basilica. In the little Polish
parish down the street, it's time
to light a candle, partly from devotion
but mostly for the image it provokes:
nostalgic you as supplicant, mantilla bobbing,
kneeling on the slab before a saint whose up-
turned eyes are hidden by a cloud of smoke.
He has been expunged from the calendar
like a wasted day, though we like to think
that no day's truly wasted. Rising late
and raising the venetian blinds, one quick glimpse
of sun in the piazza and the grazing herds
of pigeons marks the scene indelibly
as laundry. Then back to the rumpled sheets.

Later there'll be time to hit the Gem
Spa for Camels, but for now the wisps
of vapor left over from last night are
enough to make the well-tuned habit purr.
This is familiar music.

2.

The Venetians, till then under the care
of the obscure St. Theodore and his crocodile,
urgently needed the particular care
of some more eminent divine. They were weary
of the tennis shirts, mostly; alligator
tears over the death of style expressed in pastel
blousons, each emblazoned with the saint's
particular emblem: no dice. This street needed
scouring when the gentry moved in more, perhaps,
than in the unself-conscious days when Ukies
passed long hours strumming native instruments
on the stoops beneath a broiling sun, as pallid
in Hawaiian shirts and leis as ever in the hell-
hole of the kitchen at the Kiev. Arthur Godfrey's
voice trailed out the window like a string
of sputum waiting for some arriviste
to fall for the illusion of the light and try
to slip the pearls on one by one, scattering
the unself-conscious products of the Great South Bay
like so much litter. When the water
rises, the stones in the piazza
seem to be a crop of shellfish. It's why
they gave the lions wings—to fly away from here
and never get their feet wet. Slogging through
the Arsenal last night, we thought
they had the right idea.

3.

The arched bridge turns the canals into highways.
Let's take a ride in the speedboat!
There's no way to get lost; the Campanile's
calm demarcations of the light's
intensities will penetrate our lazy skulls
even in the panicky minutes when its mass is
hidden by the spray from other joycraft.
Did I tell you about my wonderful ride
down the Grand Canal with Peggy Guggenheim? We talked
about the literary lions, and I wish
that I could imitate the way she flew
from anecdote to anecdote. There was a terrific
story of Auden on his first acid trip. He walked
out to the street and saw the mailman smile
three blocks away. Apart from that, it was
a normal day. Post-nap, pre-tea: the normal
constitutional. She had her fluffy
dogs with her, and they sent up quite a row
when we sped under bridges where the cats
crowded the parapets. This is a metropolis
of cats. They lounge among the houseplants
in the windows of converted slums, the better
ones of which have Peggy Guggenheim's autobiography,
Out of This Century, on the coffee table next to Volume
One of the new Proust and the obligatory
crop of cat cartoons.

4.

When the Basilica was burnt, and the precious body lost,
a special miracle was devised, a form of replacement
borrowing the pagan notion of the soul's

migration. They found another body, looking
like the first. And the crowds rejoiced, sending
pigeons skyward. I had an identical dinner (chicken,
Pinot Grigio, and a salad with ambitious
dressing) last night in a place around the corner.
Mostly, I'm off beef; crowds of meaty
lookalikes have turned me from the whole
experience. They line up at the Saint's
front door as the lions glower and the lamps
snap on. There's something heady in his patronage
that made our city's troops invincible beneath
the pennant of a great evangelist. It's a team I'm proud
to have played on, but now I think there must be
more to life, although it's way too early
for fleshing out exactly what. Have a pastry
at a table in the colonnade. A fizzy drink
awaits you in its little red icebox.

5.

Sometimes in a brutal winter night, you may hear
the distant roar. And sometimes you may hear the slap
of hand on thigh that indicates a merry joke
among the mute, because you don't hear laughter.
Thank the stars tonight's not one of them.
You ramble past the dark cabanas on the Lido
and watch the lions sport in mid-air, under the last
full moon of a summer when the stifling wind
has kept its distance. This old slug-a-bed
wants a little fresh air to clear his head
before being swept away by sleep. The candle
in the lantern smokes too much, clouding
your eyes as water laps your Weejuns. A Parisian
novelist spent time here, kept a journal; and a German

liederdichter died here, partly from devotion
to an image that provoked. Mr. Lewes fell into the Grand
Canal, while Miss Evans and the other lions
roared. A land requiring sealegs is a dark
and perverse place, until the light comes back,
sending all the little mammals scurrying
and you across the street (barefoot, with trousers
rolled) to buy more cigarettes, this time
the Canadian brand with a Victorian
sailor on the packet. There should be a cathedral
of addiction on the corner where the bialy man
hangs out, full of shrines to the tobacco emblems
and Ah Men catalogs of yore, as well as to great
moments in the histories of Sun People: the first
trip to Florida, the birthday party
where you met the leading lights, the glint
at noon on lions' golden wings, and the Lido
afternoon when we whipped up a pitcher
of vodka and Campari and placed bets
on which would be the first to sink,
the city or the sun.

A WAY OF LIFE

Fogbound on the screened porch with the sound
of muffled breakers where the street
ends, ended yesterday, and crackling

noise from passing pickups: Breaker! Breaker!
as crackers with Delmarva twangs
screech into mikes. They're talking

to each other, a good thing. Up here, it's Margaret
Mead among the bridge players, testing jargon:
"Should have played the heart trick!" She's in

above her head, where the cloud hovers,
though the beauties never tire of hearing her
mispronounce their language. Contract is

a way of life, like the quick vacation,
and archetypal porches do a lot to add
to the illusion, if that's what it is. You're in

a chillier-than-usual resort, holed up at the Beach
House or the Casa Blanca, boning up
on precedence of trumps or screeching

Muggins all night at a beautiful opponent
who fails to take advantage of the lower-than-usual
ceiling and a streak of flawless hands.

THREE WISHES FOR
THE MURDERED SISTERS

I wish the fascist mouthpieces were right;
that you'd had guns.
If you had to go out, I wish
you could have done it like Camilo
Torres, taking a troop of them
with you to the ditch instead of ending up
like murdered women anywhere, under the West
Side trestles as in the revolution. I wish
that Haig and Duarte had been there when they dragged
you from the earth, and that a subterranean
river of blood had caused the ground
to sink beneath them, swallowing the lies
they try to feed the people you loved.

A BIRTHDAY NOTE TO KAREN

Hand in hand with another young and celebrated
Actor, you're captured in the act—
"Pastrami Central, Wolf's 6th Avenue Deli"
Patrol cars squawk, as fleetfooted
Young *Post* reporters run to log the fact.

But once upon another time,
In DC, the deli was the Fairfax, where we'd all
Run out for beer and Pepsi when the poets
Took a breather from some brilliant or godawful rhyme.
How long ago that seems! It was the fall,

Date forgotten, when we met
At Michael's place on N Street, where the topics
You were most likely to run into much of
The time had been suspended, and what we'd get
Over and over was the news of someone from the tropics

Young, attractive, talented, who'd dwelt
Of all things, on a European houseboat, and
(Unless my memory's wrong) who'd spent time in some jungle.
"Karen." You sounded quite impressive, I recall I felt,
Although you were approachable when we shook hands.

Recollecting, too, your poems (do you still write?)
Exotic in their setting and extremely clear.
Next, your stint as Modern Dancer, and your La Boheme
Lean-to in the WPA loft, a makeshift white
Oversized tent to screen you from the people passing near.

Very strange to think of, from tonight's perspective; history
    can be so
Elementary for all its knots. One takes the next step, come
    what may.
Three Oh (dare I say it) is a great age;
I've been there; I should know.
My fondest wishes for a super day.

SODOM

The Mineshaft, Friday night:
"Just Men"

if I can find ten
I'll spare this city

WHORES DE COMMERCE

Redundancy is in the air, a stack
of congruent flat clouds as visitation
of abstract form whose brain waves
bring us perfect pancakes, the kind beneath the smiling
portrait of Aunt J., once in a blue moon. The blue
breaks through, and then the clouds are merely
similar, like an altered brownstone
whose pediment was torn down to distinguish
our house from the others, in the salad
years before the Landmarks Officers had cut
their teeth. Johnny burned a sign
in wood shop, "The Modern Stone-Age Family."
It's weathered silver, and holds up the base
of the crack that appeared when the classical
departed our facade. The harbor gods
are angry, and the sacred foghorns
cease to blast, a blest
relief. Self-sufficient merchants built
this street, these dikes. They came from Holland,
itching to rev up their scary cult.
Duplication, with its hints of conflict, was the first
to go, go further. Three became the holy
number, and the space we shared began to shake,
to change irredeemably. There was you, then me,
then the thing between us, resonating like a bosun's
whistle through our nine-square grid: places
we can sleep, and eat, and watch the tromp
l'oeil vista through our 3D windows; places
we can fuck in, listening to music with our ears
between the phones; places whose profusion
dulls our appetites, whose extrapolations

break down, finally, out there where the clouds
have joined in common cause and snow begins
to intercept the light we thought was meant for us.

SOLIDARITY

for Jane DeLynn

As a white male Republican
who grew up in a middle middle class
environment and went to private schools,
I cherish my impediments: Polish, college
dropout, queer, which make me individual
but don't make me a victim

I have cousins I don't even know
facing down the tanks (or so
I like to think) in Poland where the air's
as white with snow as here
I care about them not as individuals
but as victims of the things we never faced
as individuals

        maybe that's why you can say
that you don't give a fuck about the Polacks
that when the Jews your people were marched off
into the winter, it was Polacks
my people who held the bayonets
for centuries, so why
should you give a fuck

I don't know what it's like to be a Jew,
but I know what it's like not to be one:
in my Viking hat and foreskin, washing down
my mastodon steak with milk while outnumbered
humanists, scholars of God's word, huddle
on their island of civility every time I belch

that is an illusion   another
is that my life or yours is normal
if these are normal times we should retire the word
for total action   we are on an outlaw island
privileged to speak sincerely
and be loud about it, our necks
aren't on the block

a privilege purchased with the sweat
of other individuals, our forebears   till the day
he died, my father called his childhood buddies Jewboys
they called him a Polack   they'd grown up
in the Bottom, wooden houses
crammed between the river and the railroad tracks
in Middletown   my father's sister's
sharpest memory of childhood's of her mother
looking out the attic window toward the river
where her sons and their friends
the Jewboys were stranded on a raft, halfway
to Portland, with stormclouds blowing down
the Connecticut, the dull reports
of thunder growing louder

there is no safety from the storm in huddling
with illusions that our privilege is anything
other than a raft
people facing tanks are victims
and the tanks are driven by average Joes
saving the world for normality

you're my kind of person   and it's your individual
traits that provoke my fondness, even when you
piss me off   but I feel responsible,

able to respond, when the cousins I don't even
know dodge the lightning   I have cousins
I don't even like, like you do
it's easier to take them when they're part
of a whole, a people, but that's not what I mean
by Solidarity—I mean that I can feel
responsible even when they're not my cousins
but yours, and that it's a right I assume,
unpurchased by another individual's
sweat   if we are to make
a history, we must be the source
not a cork that bobs on the ancestral stream
I choose solidarity with them and you
though I'm not a Jew, but a Polack

when the Ghetto Fighters rose up
in '43, Jew and Pole fought side by side
until they were mowed down by the tanks
that leveled the city they shared

when we share this city we are
friends, not victims   history's an impediment
only when I can't shed tears   when I see
red on the sidewalk I cannot recognize
whose blood it is from the color   the normal
weather buries it   where we are
it's snowing heavily

TWENTY-FOUR HOUR MASSAGE

"Mr. President, the Soviet Union is invading Western Europe!"

"Well, I guess we'll just have to (a little lower and to the left) implement a pre-emptive nuclear strike."

"Mr. President, New York is being torn apart by rioters!"

"Well, I guess we'll just have to (higher, higher) mobilize the National Guard."

"Mr. President, California has been totally destroyed by earthquakes!"

"Well, I guess we'll just have to (right there, ahhh, that feels great) call the Red Cross into the picture."

"Mr. President, the polls show that you'll lose the next election by an unprecedented margin!"

"Oh, no! Does that mean no more twenty-four hour massage?"

FOR DENNIS FROM DELIRIUM

On a brownstone street, in a brown study,
I worry both my thumbnails bloody.
My cuticles are ripped to shreds,
and dreadful dreams are in my head:

some gorgeous boy's disdainful look
at the grim photo on my book—
will he discern pomposity
where I intended levity?

Or will the lack of *accent grave*
or *aigu* queer th' appeal I have
(or hope to) for *Les Mandarins*,
J. Merrill and his Merry Men?

Perhaps the blurbs are too self-serving
or the sex scenes too unnerving.
Should "fuck" have been replaced by "heck"?
Will childhood comrades wring my neck?

Attacked by people I admire
as a poseur, or knave, or liar,
perceived as dry, or shrill, or bored,
or (worst of all) roundly ignored:

such is the substance of my fears,
provoking moans and wails and tears
and making me feel so alone
I call you from the nearest phone

to gnash my teeth transcontinentally.
It must seem I'm unbalanced mentally,
but honestly, it's "just a phase,"
and so I want to sing your praise:

You did a great job on my book.
I like the way the poems look.
Your protean labors are stupendous.
Entre nous, dear, you're tremendous.

EPITHALAMIUM

for the wedding of Penelope Milford to Michael Lally
February 14, 1982

we come to seal a contract
a solemn agreement in which the party
of the first part doth agree
to live up to the binding vows
he makes in public to the party
of the second part   who shoots the same
vows back in his direction, according to
the law

        according to the calendar it's
February, day before the feast of Februata
Juno   the day when Roman swains
and maidens pledged their love in sweet
billets, to honor the goddess

                    in the days
before the priests changed the act, naming
the feast after one of their own, a victim
beaten with clubs

                    they canonized his death
to make it legal, the way a wedding places
true love on the official map   a map on which
the unofficial sites are never marked   but
now your blood and names are in the records
in the same manila file

                    we come to tell you, we
who love you both   it's not as though we buy
the city line on a day the church cleaned up
it doesn't start today, it started
on the day your eyes met, and it grew, kept
growing   as we watched you, knowing
it was sweet, electric, all the other
words used to describe this thing
called love, as inexpressible
as names of gods before the priests
and poets moved in

                    this wedding means
we celebrate the things you share   and
share with us today, as in the past
and possible future   and honor that
which binds you, and you to us:
not what is beginning, but what goes on.

SOMETIMES I THINK

I'm a blond trapped in a dark-haired body.
I'm a boy trapped in a man's body.
I'm a sensitive straight man trapped in a homosexual habit.
I'm a monk with a burning desire to sleep with as many
    people as possible.
I'm a Yankee locked in a Catholic tradition.
I'm a wolf in sheep's clothing.
I'm a mystic who wants to be loved.
I'm an angry man disarmed by a sense of humor.
I'm a promising writer disarmed by my life as a dilettante.
I've got champagne tastes and a beer budget.
I'm a fatalist who pursues each avenue of escape.
I'm a saint in a temporary state of mortal sin.
I've missed the boat.
I'm lucky to have missed the boat.
I'm on the cutting edge.
I'll live forever.
I'll die soon.
I'm powerless in the face of imminent nuclear destruction.
I hear the bombers overhead.
I've been here in a past life.
This has all happened before.
I'm a woman trapped in a man's body.
I don't like the men or the women.
I'd be a great actor.
I'd be a good father.
I'd have been a great composer.
I could have had a V-8.
I should have gone to a better college.
I bought their sick lies hook, line and sinker, and I'm still
    buying them.

It's not too late to change.
I can't get enough.
I've had enough.
I can't take it another minute.
I need a change of scenery.
God is dead.
Marxism is dead.
Allende was too soft on the middle class.
I ought to be a painter.
I want it all.
I've been spoiled.
I'll never overcome my male ego.
I'm glad to be a man.
I want to run for political office.
I'm a potential Presidential assassin.
I'm crazy for living in New York.
This is the most beautiful city on earth.
I'd like to live on the Cape.
I'm a great big phony.
I've been incredibly lucky.
Luck is the quality the third-rate attribute to the genuinely talented.
I'm a vampire of other people's emotions.
I'm a vampire.
My relatives are beyond the pale.
My relatives are the normal ones.
I fall apart too easily.
Bishop Sheen was right.
I should go to confession.
I've made nothing but sacrilegious communions since I learned
    to jerk off twenty years ago.
I'd like to live in a developing country.
It's my fault that I broke up with my last lover.
I'm a latent alcoholic.

I'm an alcoholic.

I'm in perfect control of my drinking.

If I'm worried about it, I'm probably a potential alcoholic at least.

I try too hard.

It's not worth having if it doesn't fall into my lap.

It requires a grand gesture.

I need a drink.

It's time for a nap.

It's time for sex with another total stranger.

I hate sex.

Nothing whatsoever is wrong with liking pornography.

I'd like speed.

I'd like heroin.

I'd like Paris.

I don't like any of my old friends anymore.

I'm an elitist.

I'm a snob.

I'm "broadminded" in the most annoying liberal way.

It's my right to know the Third Fatima Secret.

My palm shows that I'm bitter.

I'm a paragon of mental health compared to lots of the people
    I know.

I'll end up in jail.

I'll die in jail.

I'll die a suicide.

I'm free to do what I want.

I know what I want.

FILM

Buildup of the sudden snow on nested ships
Obscured by the wet snow blowing horizontal
Faster when it's closer, slower at the plane
Where it fades into undistinguished film
Illustrating theories of physics or the best
Of background animation, early Disney as opposed
To cheapo imitations from Japan   My Task:
To flesh out the cartoon of the morning,
My white walls, blank stare   Eno's
Film Music extricated from white jacket
Think of Melville as it fills the air

FROM JOURNAL

The Apparition at La Salette to the children: "The farmers cursed my Son, so he made their crops fail as a sign that they should repent, but now (long sigh) they curse Him more than ever." Well what the hell did she expect? Ham-handed louts beating their children, their livestock, their wives in inarticulate rage . . . the peasant is more eternal, perhaps, than his Divinity.

The spate of Marian apparitions to peasant youngsters started early in the nineteenth century in France, in the most desperate pockets of under-development. Lourdes—the pits. They seem to me to be a clear response (divine or hallucinatory) to one of the revolutions, Industrial or French. The romantic notion is that heavenly visitations happen only to the lowly as a sign of divine contempt for worldly ideas of success. But why do they only happen in the country? There's no Lady of East Baltimore or Harlem (though in the Fifties there was an apparition of Mary in Fairmount Park in Philadelphia, in a tree to which believers pinned several hundred dollars in currency. The Parks Department took the money away; rumor has it that it's still collecting interest in a bank account nobody knows what to do with.) That Knock or La Salette or Fatima was picked because of the gullibility of the inhabitants is an ineluctable (though snotty) conclusion.

The disdain of American religious for Mary's recent encores is as deep-seated as the average parishioner's unshakable faith in them. The Mother holding back the arm of her pissed-off Son, "Don't hurl those lightning bolts, Honey!" is an unforgettable image. And we *are* so guilty. In Fatima the sun danced, and the Holy Family appeared in the clouds as if projected by a giant Carousel. After nineteen centuries, it was reassuring to have some visible sign of divine presence, even if it came across as more characteristic of Disney than of God.

Holy girls on the verge of puberty are prime material for apparitions, e.g. Bernadette. Ripe for the plucking: stringed instruments hung up on the branches in which the virginal globe appears like Glinda the Good Witch in *The Wizard of Oz*.

In New Hampshire there's a shrine of La Salette maintained by the religious order the apparition spawned: granite statues of the Virgin, the children, the sheep, statues of every other apparition, a big wooden crucifix at the top of a flight of wooden stairs built into the side of a New Hampshire mountain, which devout tourists ascend step by step on their knees. A scandal, no doubt, among the more traditional New Hampshiremen, the Yankees: "Dja see them wops goin up the stayahs on their knees?" There's a prayer for each step, a Hail Mary.

Sister Lucia, to whom Mary appeared at Fatima, expressed concern when Pope John did not reveal Our Lady's third secret in 1960, as per her instructions. The rumor among Catholic diplomats at the time was that the message talked about inescapable nuclear destruction, and that it was too scary for the average Catholic to hear. The rumor among liberal seminarians at the time was that the message consisted of two words: "Just kidding!"

STEVE REICH AND MUSICIANS

Mandalay bazaar ——→ women with baskets
on their heads taking long strides sideways
——→ sidewalks, 1952 ——→ the Maxwell
House percolator ——→ reveille ——→
strange birds, as in cartoons but with dignity
——→ rain so soft you laugh with relief
——→ path cut into cliff above cascading
brook (Tibet approach) ——→ bike-a-thon
——→ the wayfarer in "Valderi Valdera"
——→ a series of transparent Lucite panes,
some with water running down their surfaces
——→ a dog transported by it all ——→
all clear after the air raid.

NOT STRAVINSKY

Dark-eyed boy in tight designer jeans and sneakers on your way
from basketball practice at Bishop Somebody High, I

don't know what you're playing on your Walkman but it probably is
not Stravinsky.

MAY RAIN

It's gray, and grayer Bruckner fills the room.
The chill is on the outside, but the gray
lives in my chest, a ghost. My heart's its tomb.
"I don't expect to see you in the day,"
a man I see at night in shadows laughs
on 23rd Street, when our daytime paths

at random overlap. Trick, not a friend.
A jerkoff phonecall with a college boy,
accounting major, something new, from N.
Y.U. (why not?), which isn't. He's the toy
that keeps me from my work. The Bronx Frontier
and Black Survival beckon. I'm not here

but leave a message and I might return
your call if I come back. It's time to dial
the weather, then a friend. I want to learn
important secrets now, like why I smile
when what I feel is terror. A dumb grin
contorts my mouth, and thunderheads move in.

THE BAR

hanging light
hanging low
hanging out
pinball glow

Pac-Man fever
TV screen
chimpanzee
men in jeans

Man o' War
man oh man
get a drink
get a tan

take a ride
take a piss
shoot some pool
blow a kiss

blow a god
suck a dork
new gay man
old New York

Talking Heads
darkened room
light a joint
va-va-voom

J. J. Mitchell
Steven A.
Peter Hujar
where's Rene?

East Fourth Street &
Second Ave
not great, just
the best *we* have

PSALM

Each year I forget the simple fact
that spring's new leaves are of a sickly
hue, Lord; not at all the strong dark
green in Wallace Nutting silver-prints
of my youth. You remember: the country
lane a dozen miles from Boston running
past a field where the amazing pink
of dogwood and white of apple blossom posed
against high summer verdure, dark and beckoning.
Not so the oak by yonder carriage-house.
Call that green? It's half yellow, and its bark
is gray, not brown—no, silver today.
Clouds behind the clouds behind the yellow
clouds upstage, and behind them all a vast
emptiness, if the naked eye can be
believed. It can't, as You and science teach.
Teenaged children throw a ball around the street,
speed it on its way with expletives, while pre-
schoolers with their stately gait have their
ball, too, this one phosphorescent in a tiny
hand, a place to focus in the changing light,
which doesn't fade, but shifts perspective,
like the slim retarded girl in the gray or silver
make-believe fur who waits each afternoon
on the stoop or corner for the kids who play ball
to walk past and smile. I'm waiting, too.
Like a Doberman longs for an enormous field
big enough to run across as hard and as far
as it can; like Mr. Ahmed longs for a prospective
buyer to walk in so he can unload the Arabia
Felix Restaurant and happily return to the stony

village whose photograph adorns his menu; like
a bourgeois idealist longs to see the world
through Wallace Nutting's eyes, in which
the chlorophyll does its job right; so my soul
longs for You, Lord, for the vast amused amazement
of your grace, in this your Strong (and holy) Place.

FROM JOURNAL

On most perfect sunny morning of the year, most perfect that could be imagined, walk down Strong Place to my landlady's cheeriest greeting. This is my neighborhood, and elitist gripes about living "so far away" seem dumb now. Look at those trees, those shadows (and their absence)—not that I have anything against the elite.

At St. Peter and Paul's Church ("the oldest free-standing steeple in Brooklyn") the doors are wide open. A funeral inside. No procession, just the line of limos that always makes me think of the Mafia or the Vice-President until I see the hearse. Codger on the corner shouts affectionately, "Well hello, Mary," and a potato-faced woman in her seventies says, "Hiya." Brooklyn is the home of thousands of Marys—used to have to be the middle name at least of every Catholic girl, my mother (Mary) tells me, unless they were hifalutin or Canadian in which case Marie was permissible. What knocks me out when I think of it is the overwhelming presumption of the working class, as well as their matter-of-fact faith. The girls who grow up beautiful and slender with what's known as "every opportunity" in the East 70s or in spiffy Soho lofts have trivial monickers, like Brooke or Kimberly; but hordes of poor dumpy overweight moms in housecoats and carcoats in Brooklyn name their daughters (who'll end up looking just like them) after the Mother of God. Not a bad idea, really; despite the jejune artistic renderings, there's nothing to suggest that the Virgin Mother herself wasn't fat and dumpy in some Galilean version of a housecoat after what theologians, sounding like General Haig, call the "Christ-event." I like the idea: peasant woman with a throaty voice, deep lines, deep laugh like Magnani or a healthier Viveca Lindfors; or maybe just a chubby pale old lady with bad eyesight saying "Hiya" to old friends at a funeral, decades after her co-starring role in Salvation History.

CLOSE

for Brad Gooch

Spring peaks: the third of May, the feast of Love.
Cherry flowers old, magnolias new.
Peahens chase tots in the cathedral close.
We share a therapist, up there three stories.
I'm here to recollect, and recollect I shall,
but first let me get over this amazing blue

of sky above new green of leaves and blue
of polyester running shoes. I love
to think it's something absolutely new,
this light and weather, like my summer clothes,
but they predate us both, say histories.
Pretending it's the first time is a shell

game. Can't beat Demon Time, they say, though Shel-
ley disagreed. The rains came, the winds blew
and swamped his tiny boat. I'm not in love
with impiety, just with youth. The new
world is a-comin', old draws to a close,
a row of vignettes pasted on a story-

board by young go-getters with success stories
and salable today, beneath the shel-
tering deciduous to kids in blue-
jeans, teenaged like the leaves, amazed by love
that sprouts like sudden flowers on their new
embarrassed shapes. Their childhood's at a close,

a time they thought the doors would never close
behind them or before them, as in stories
on *Time Tunnel* or *Twilight Zone*. They shall
learn differently. It used to make me blue
to think of it, but now it makes me love
great days like this one with a giddy new

intensity. It *is* completely new,
this light, that five-year-old with his fat close-
mouthed nurse, that row of petals three long stories
above my head, where you are. And they shall
never be quite the same again; the blue
sky either, or you, or I. That's why love

"makes all things new." Beats history. This bloo-
ming close opens my shell to Love, to you.

WALL STREET SAUNA

"Isn't your name Dag?" I ask the beauty
"Walter," he replies, agrees we've met before,
Though he didn't let on when he let me
Chase him through this sweaty maze an hour or more

Ending up in talk, not action
Where fat brokers who have never seen a gym
Stumble through the penthouse of a narrow tower
Narrow as his waist, wait for the likes of him

To emerge from steam, emerge from darkness
I emerge into the street, and walk uptown
To the park where Walter's presence
Stays with me until I gulp a Pepsi down

Loll beneath th' explicit basket
Of the statue that makes Nathan Hale too pretty
Hanged first day of autumn, as a rebel spy
When he was discovered in this very city

Wonder if the chill of morning
Cooled the air enough for him to see his breath
Hanging like the clouds in steamrooms
Sign of young life as he walked to meet his death

SONG

Early summer sunlight and the wise guys whistle
(Squad car down the block) to let the dealers know
Under brims of cocoanut and baku
By the subway steps old men play dominoes

Salsa in the shade, the junk trees verdant
Empty lots that suddenly are full
Of city flora, as if broken glass were mulch
Pollen and the bus fumes make my own eyes swell

Underneath the footfalls, trains go uptown, downtown
Nothing out of place here, not a note or hair
Doesn't take a seer to spot a sucker
Cotton suit and boater in the shimmering air

ON THIS TRAIN ARE PEOPLE
WHO RESEMBLE

Allen Ginsberg
President Carter
Lynne Dreyer
Geraldine Fitzgerald
a monkey
Brian Epstein
Don Bachardy
the son on "Sanford and Son"
Rose Lesniak
Mrs. Sanders (neighbor, 1966)
Erin Clermont
Sid Caesar in drag
Terry Bartek (wrestling partner, high school gym class)
"Dad" on "Dennis the Menace"—in fact, I think it *is* Dad, "Henry
                    Mitchell," grayer and with deep
                    lines in his face but the same
                    receding chin and purse-mouthed but
                    benevolent expression, in a summer
                    suit that's old but neatly pressed
                    and clunky black shoes. He wears
                    a sad expression, too, and I wonder
                    if life has been unkind to him,
                    thinking how awful it would be to
                    have a third-rate sitcom as the
                    crowning achievement of your artistic
                    career, to be reduced to taking the
                    subway and having people recognize
                    you (if you're lucky) for the wimp
                    you played, maybe remembering the name
                    of the smirking brat who played your son

(Jay North) but never yours or any of
the program's other grownups, who by now
are dead (Mr. Wilson, R.I.P.) or grayheads
like you. I'd look sad too, I think, as
he walks out of the car at Penn Station.

JUNE 25TH

Governor Cuomo is recovering
from alcoholism
which is why he doesn't want
to be Vice President

in the same dream
his wife doesn't know
any of the secrets
he confides to me

Don't know why
there's a cloud up in the sky
and I'm trembling here at my
"machine"

it skips, like me
out of class without permission
I don't even give myself
permission, but here I am

FAILED PILOT

The Hardy Boys Mysteries, starring Kip Noll as Frank Hardy
and Jeremy Scott as Joe Hardy.

SUMMER, SOUTH BROOKLYN

gusher in the street where bald men with cigars
watch as boys in gym shorts and no shirts
crack the hydrant, rinsing yet another car
a daily ritual, these street-wide spurts

of city water over rich brown and deep white
of ranch wagon and arrogant sedan
whose "opera windows" seem less *arriviste* than trite
they shake the water from their hair, shake hands

with neighbors passing, passing generations
I watch and am not part of, for the block is theirs
by family and tradition, and I'm no relation
an opera drowned by disco beat, draw stares

from big boys with big radios that might outlast them
brace myself for insults I recall
forgetting the adult they see when I stride past them
until I realize they're kids, that's all

MY DEATH

when I no longer
feel it breathing down
my neck it's just around
the corner (hi neighbor)

HARDING'S BEACH

The families, the summer
visitors in sporty cars,
the bars, the short-lived
culture of the rays: peel them away
and it all boils down to colors.
To paint them is to lose them. Half
an hour from the dropping of the sun behind
the clouds, or haze, or smoke from a faraway
tragedy above the solid cottages that punctuate
the scrub due west, and almanac sunset.
In that interval, the wheel slows or perception
speeds up with the circling terns.
The train brakes at the dark green
suburbs of blue, and continues through
to the shadows on the other side. Grass
brushed back like a kewpie's forelock,
miles of it, and an impossible tangle
of kelp that describes the interval from moss
to brown, life to garbage. It's a simple
world for a gangly plant with big cells.
A boy fishes; then he goes away
to rest. A father and a son
stroll past the abandoned lighthouse
whose lamp room has been sheared off
with surgical skill. The boosters call it
"local color," but for now old stories
of seagods' bowler hats with razor brims
and architecture are an insubstantial gloss
on depths of fading light. Consolidates
then goes away, but leaves a scar.

The nests of terns are scratches in the sand,
no more. They flee at any sign of danger
and leave their eggs to boil, a vanishing race.
The cracking of a shell beneath a shoe, the beach
that used to be a billion shells, the shell
shaped like an ear trumpet locked inside
its strongbox for the night, and still
you hear the ocean.

IF WE'RE SO FUCKING SMART
WHY AREN'T WE RICH

for Michael Lally

in the world (the world,
remember? we live there, you
in LA, me in NYC, like
the bookends of the continent
if the continent were made of
books, but) there's no place
made of books

NEW MUSIC

The lovemaking grows more intense, not less.
Ten million men and women out of work
The price of a sound currency. Tim Page
Brings us "The New, The Old, The Unexpected,"
Two hours of new music every day,
Six hours of sleep, eight of work, and art
Simmers on the back burner with desire
For Fame, for Fortune. Rules: choose one, not both.

The reasons for not moving grow more lame.
Ten million stories in this naked city
And one of them is ours. I'm like Tim Miller
Spraying my name in paint upon my chest,
Reminding me of who I am. A man
By any other name's a refugee.
I shall not back away, but take my stand
Where love and honesty are one, not both.

It gets more complicated with the years
And less so. There must be ten million ways
Of making love, but all I need are three:
The new, the old, the unexpected. Grace
Is like New Music hitting with the force
Of tidal waves, or like the atmosphere
So clear these mornings we forget it's how
We've always lived and breathed as one, not both.

I touch you on the eyes, and chest, and wrist.
Ten million dollars wouldn't change a thing,
The price of a sound mind. "Tim Dlugos knows,"
Voice-over from an old-time radio
Reminding me of where I used to be.
I'm here, and so are you. To make it art
Is easy when you're musical as we.
Live it or live with it: choose one, not both.

MYRON AND MILTON'S CAPRICE

The sky shifts, even when you cease
to notice. On the forest
trails and up the beach, pairs
of model-quality (their bodies, at least)
youths, one limping, lean together heavily
and lurch from the Pavilion to the panorama
of blue tones as seen from the porch of the blue-
jean manufacturer's house. The only thing
between me and their Calvins is Calvin
and the air, cool this morning in a way
to which they can aspire. An aspiring architect
left with an aspiring violinist on the final
boat last night. I'm halfway through
a novel in which some aspiring Nazi-hunters
capture the senescent Fuehrer in a rain-
forest, and transport him on a litter
through a thousand-mile swamp to answer
for his crimes. When one drives the evil
from the source of the Amazon, one hopes
what emerges is a better place to live.
This one's uninhabitable, and its former
denizens, though horrors, have to stay somewhere.
An inbred hospitality (*their* concept) too
often leads them to your own front door.
Underneath the moral is the illness, underneath
the illness is the real, a Reichian
notion. Underneath the ocean is the litter:
driftwood, clumps of weed, the antique bottle-
glass effect of a jellyfish duplicated hundreds
of times in the short distance from the dune
crossing where the pairs of footprints commence

to meander or dodge through the obstacle course
to their destination, a single sneaker,
spit up by the tunnel-vision slice
of spectrum that links the gnawed-at
beach to the horizon. Clues out there
past Natasha's cottage and bottle-tree, all
the evidence we'll ever need.

TO CLEAR THINGS UP, SCOTT

McKenzie was the flower
power singer with the long
tresses and love beads
who sang John Phillips'
"San Francisco" in '67, reaching
the top of the charts, and Scott
McKinley is the poet with great
eyes and a particularly
graceful way of expressing
tenderness asleep in the bed
I just left to write this down

COLUMBUS DAY

(A collaboration with David Trinidad)

I.

I was dancing at the Paradise Garage and there were
all these Negroes. The mirrored globe slowly
cast bits of light across our faces, black
light, faces colored by their expressions.
Though ebony and ivory go together, ebony
has fabulous half-tones. "White notes"
equal "vanilla pudding." Are you hungry?
Yes. A meatball sandwich and a Bud
would be terrific. Maybe Nino's is still
open, though maybe not, this being
Columbus Day. There was a parade
awash in politicians. The most off-putting
thing about Mario Cuomo is his mom's
first name: Immaculata. The kitchen
hasn't been immaculate in ages! Oh unwashed
dishes of politicos! Easy to put off
the housework and simply concentrate on having
a good time with the native language.
You can lead a hortatory, but you can't
make her vote Conservative. Courtney
Kennedy mugging for her father (TV
campaign spot in '64) is not
the same thing as Courtney Kennedy
mugging her father. Some language,
that marches past with music and confusing flags.

II.

Free video games at Beefsteak Charlie's on Sunday
night. Spinach quiche at the Lion's Head. "Tell
the little idiot he just missed meeting
America's most famous schizophrenic."
"Quadrophenia" by the Who is blasting, and my
pretentious host is furious. "E. Schwartzkopf"
equals "Betty Blackhead." Edith Head had
short, neatly cropped black hair, enormous
glasses, and seven erect Oscars on the mantel
of her Beverly Hills living room. She gave
good costume like I hope to give good poem,
up here on the podium at church. You can
lead the Pope to Sartre but you can't
make him think. I think of you often,
here in New York City. I miss your attentive
gaze, your simple ways, and the waves
of your slightly-mussed punk hairdo.

III.

It's like exploring a New World, it's like
getting out and *using* the limp God gave you.
"Time to stretch your legs," said Torquemada
as he gently placed your body on the rack.
A Rolling Rock in the early afternoon
at Cafe Orlin on St. Mark's Place
equals a terrific headache at sunset
on the Promenade. If Colombo
(his real name) had sailed into the planet's
safest harbor, he could have docked and eaten

a bowl of the delicious yogurt that bears his name.
You can lead a horse to Pasteur but you can't
make it purify your milk. The human kindness
drops into your veins like Milkbottle-H.
I have a talent for one thing only;
I'll show you sometime.

NO SYMPATHY

For David Salle, who believes
a canvas by its nature
is "dead space," whose art
plays with that fact in post-
painting paintings, whose technique
combines the worst of Seventies
conceptual theory and Eighties art-
as-investment-commodity hype;

For Peter, who stormed away
when I told him that David has
a marketing strategy where his
aesthetic should be, a paraphrase
of something the painter himself
told his longtime roommate, my friend
Jane Sheffield, a fact I never got around
to telling Peter, because he stormed
back shouting that my observation
was "stupid and Midwestern," though
I've never even been to the Midwest, while
Peter himself hails from North Dakota;

For Brooke, who's amazed that old friends
try to manipulate her good will to find
work in Hollywood as writers or actors,
when she never even said a simple Thank You
to the old friend who introduced her
to a famous director, an act of kindness
that led to her landing that first big role
and made her famous enough to resent
the aspirations of people with less
success than she has now, but
the same amount of manners.

SONNET

Joe Jackson walks into the Ninth Circle
Guess you didn't recognize who that was
I'm on this earth for one reason: "Because"
The world is round, which used to be enough

To turn me on, but now it often takes
Higher prices, greater values, coats
Of many colors, tangerine and purple
Excluded, and cuffed pants of tweed

To top things off, a black beret, looks tough
On Village kids today, and me a seedy
Generation back   my Fate hag gloats
Staying her snip until I paint more fakes

Like this one, which like me will never last
Dress formal as Joe Jackson's, talk fast

SONNET

Stevie Nicks walks into the Parisian weather
in Brooklyn where the "heat wave"'s mild
December 3rd and waiting for the Child
who's born and laid upon the oxen's plate

of straw again, bound up again in swaddling
clothes in Health-Tex patterns, and projecting
good vibes the way Matt Dillon looks onscreen
shirt off and washboard stomach   when I'm waddling

home I think of him   the Teenage Fates
in chorus chant, "You wish"   I do, rejecting
sagacity in favor of new leather
and what's inside, a-tremble at the clean

wet silver sky and street   the natives tout it,
cool light, slim trees   there's something French about it

SPY OF LOVE

New numbers in your address book (I looked).
Let's not go, gentle, into that. Good night,
I'll call you in the morning, though you might
be sleeping now with someone else . . . I'm hooked

on jealousy and speed, high on my list
of dark emotions. Took a walk at ten
this evening where the sulfur lamps pretend
they're sunlight, though their quirky waves have missed

the vitamins we store up in our eyes.
Depletion and allowance bring me here
to Brooklyn and to poverty. It's clear
that something's got to give. Perhaps "tith I,"

though rats alone live in my granary.
The spy of love feeds on chicanery.

THE NINETEENTH CENTURY IS
183 YEARS OLD

for Keith Milow

It creaks, that Saint-
Saens piece for the piano, grand
in its way, for its century,
which never seems to end: Camille,
1835 to eternity. In the icetray
of musical notation, Saint-Saens is
the cube with the favor frozen inside,
a scarab labeled "Hope" or "Despair," the invasion
of dinner by a horde of Euclidean forms.
They leave their laundry everywhere: their melody,
their progressive politics and chords, their timing
and their sense of time, their long line
to the bathroom and their dark forebodings
for this Administration and the next one,
dumped on the linoleum. A finger
pointed ceilingward for emphasis
can be pure gesture, but the vectors
proceeding from its tip are boring
a tunnel through your upstairs neighbor's
floor. Quiet down and listen to my gossip
about the dead. Saint-Saens liked to dress up
in women's clothes, that time-worn combination
of defiance and anxiety, evening gown and beard.
The bearded pianist Paul Jacobs told me that story.
He's dying of cancer, while the music
of this endless century persists.

GREEN ACRES

Doo-doo da dum-dum, "Fresh air!"
Doo-doo da dum-dum, "Times Square!"
but today is one of those in which such inimical
models overlap: on 43rd the sky's
as blue as if the *Days of Heaven* sequel were
about to start a years-long run, and the air
I breathe repels the fumes (*defense de fumer*)
of Darth Vader buses, seemly in their bright
white armor for a change instead of resembling
the refugee props from a bad Japanese science fiction
(a redundancy) movie they can be   today
I'm Eva Gabor telling Oliver, "Ve can
go *home*, dolling," drawing up the plans
to turn that patch of feed corn on the balcony
into a spread that will make Park Avenue's
traffic isles a cornucopia for hungry
mouths   today, a single farmer feeds
nineteen Americans, and I want to help
my husband do his share, though he's far away
straw hat, straw bag, straw between my Thomas
A. Dewey front teeth   grab straw from the drink
behind my blooper ("I'm sorry, sir, we don't serve Coke;
we *do* serve HoJo Cola") and rush out to those fields
of plenty where the ground's too hard to plow
but the bums sing field songs anyway
"Water Boy, where are you hiding?"
"In the background of a dynamite rerun, or
between the lines within your Book of Days."

A SENSE

of time present, in colors of the stone
and mortar of the houses built by times-
past generations on the street that I'm
traversing. I have made them each my own

in borrowed light of a midwinter sky,
midafternoon, as classes end and shouts
in timeless modes roll down the hill and out
into the harbor where they fade and die.

From my position, that's the way it seems,
Joralemon and Clinton, where St. Ann's
pink stone confection looks delicious, and
the eyes of wayward children fill my dreams

like crumbs for starlings threatened by the frost.
On their way homeward, watch them flick an ash,
the joint that hangs beneath a down moustache
a vehicle for downhill rides, to Lost

from Confident and Callow. It's a trip
I've taken, rider on a bumpy sledge
whose mileage makes me think I have an edge,
"experience" that lets me let 'er rip

but don't—not even when compared to these,
the unbruised, unexamined of the day
who light up, deeply draw and drift away.
Each, walking past, provokes a little breeze

that fades like memories of being driven
by elders to the treeless city where
a "permanent" was something done to hair
and light the sum of all the time we're given.

FOOT GEAR

Slogging through the New
York city streets I wish
I owned a pair of LL Bean
shoes with rubber wraparound
soles, ducks I believe
they're called, and that I was
in bed again with Kenneth Elliott
who wore a pair of them back
to my place last night.

THE INFLUENCE OF ALCOHOL
UPON HISTORY

The Last Puritan, a photograph
of Astor Place in 1952
by Rudy Burckhardt, a 17-year-old
blond hustler from the hills
of Oklahoma, a ticket to Rome,
a hundred dinners at the finest
eateries in Greenwich Village,
and a thousand cocktails for the new
acquaintance du jour—what I've bought
when I got drunk.

THE MORNING

The vitamin-charged slush of Total cereal,
momentum of an early start,
the Breviary's poetry, a flash
of insight from the TV preacher who's dressed
in ever more appalling polyester suits . . .
I shun them. It's the morning,
all I care to know for its duration.
Dream of, of, of . . . can't recall, but
the night before I dreamt I was in bed with someone
I was gaga about. Woke up and there he was,
gaga in his sleep, moans, thrashing.
My nervous clients think I need a thrashing
—"On the stick, you!"—and they're right,
on one level, theirs. A story up, I see
an old woman whose arms seem filled with slush
shouting from her window, like Molly Goldberg
on Fifties TV, and I wonder the same thing
I wondered as a tot about the home tube stars:
I see them through a glass, can they see me?
Appropriately darkly. Through the speakers
I learn what Pierre Boulez was getting at
in *Le Marteau sans Maitre*. Un question, Monsieur:
did your hammer demand emancipation
or had it always been a freelance tool?
I risk playing the fool
because this is a world I am creating,
not "text" or "slice of life," and old contexts
don't hold. "Water, water!" A parched prospector
crawls downhill toward the container port.
He plops into the harbor like a grizzled seal,
treads water and surveys the scene.

Stage left: bridges, helicopters overhead.
Stage right: the islands Puerto Rican couples
with tots and prams survey from Bay Ridge Park.
This world's finest anchorage is filled with freighters
which themselves are filled with freight
from everywhere. Drop it here. Then
back through the Narrows to the endless sea.

PRETTY CONVINCING

Talking to my friend Emily, whose drinking
patterns and extravagance of personal
feeling are a lot like mine, I'm pretty
convinced when she explains the things we do
while drinking (a cocktail to celebrate the new
account turns into a party that lasts till 3
a.m. and a terrific hangover) indicate
a problem of a sort I'd not considered.
I've been worried about how I metabolize
the sauce for four years, since my second bout
of hepatitis, when I kissed all the girls
at Christmas dinner and turned bright yellow
Christmas night, but never about whether
I could handle it. It's been more of a given,
the stage set for my life as an artistic queer,
as much of a tradition in these New York circles
as incense for Catholics or German
shepherds for the blind. We re-enact
the rituals, and our faces, like smoky icons
in a certain light, seem to learn nothing
but understand all. It comforts me
yet isn't all that pleasant, like drinking
Ripple to remember high school. A friend
of mine has been drinking in the same bar for decades,
talking to the same types, but progressively
fewer blonds. Joe LeSueur says he's glad
to have been a young man in the Fifties with his
Tab Hunter good looks, because that was the image
men desired; now it's the Puerto Rican
angel with great eyes and a fierce fidelity
that springs out of machismo, rather than a moral

choice. His argument is pretty convincing, too,
except lots of the pretty blonds I've known
default by dying young, leaving the field
to the swarthy. Cameron Burke, the dancer
and waiter at Magoo's, killed on his way home from
the Pines when a car hit his bike on the Sunrise Highway.
Henry Post dead of AIDS, a man I thought would be around
forever, surprising me by his mortality the way
I was surprised when I heard he was not
the grandson of Emily Post at all, just pretending,
like the friend he wrote about in *Playgirl*, Blair Meehan,
was faking when he crashed every A List party for a year
by pretending to be Kay Meehan's son, a masquerade
that ended when a hostess told him "Your mother's here"
and led him by the hand to the dowager—Woman, behold
thy son—underneath a darkening conviction that all,
if not wrong, was not right. By now Henry may have faced
the same embarrassment at some cocktail party in the sky.
Stay as outrageously nasty as you were. And Patrick
Mack, locked into my memory as he held court in the Anvil
by the downstairs pinball machine, and writhing
as he danced in Lita Hornick's parlor when the Stimulators
played her party, dead last week of causes I don't know,
as if the cause and not the effect were the problem.
My blond friend Chuck Shaw refers to the Bone-
crusher in the Sky, and I'm starting to
imagine a road to his castle lit by radiant
heads of blonds on poles as streetlamps for the gods,
flickering on at twilight as I used to do
in the years when I crashed more parties and acted
more outrageously and met more beauties and made
more enemies than ever before or ever again, I pray.
It's spring and there's another crop of kids

with haircuts from my childhood and inflated self-esteem
from my arrival in New York, who plug into the history
of prettiness, convincing to themselves and the devout.
We who are about to catch the eye of someone
new salute as the cotillion passes, led by blonds
and followed by the rest of us, a formal march
to the dark edge of the ballroom where we step out
onto the terrace and the buds of the forsythia
that hides the trash sprout magically
at our approach. I toast it
as memorial to dreams as fragile and persistent
as a blond in love. My clothes smell like the smoky
bar, but the sweetness of the April air's
delicious when I step outside and fill
my lungs, leaning my head back
in a first-class seat on the shuttle
between the rowdy celebration of great deeds
to come and an enormous Irish wake in which
the corpses change but the party goes on forever.

MUSIC THAT MAKES ME CRY

"Someone in a Tree" from *Pacific Overtures*
Samuel Barber's "Adagio for Strings"
"What a Day That Was" and "Big Blue Plymouth" by David Byrne
Paul Robeson singing "Balm in Gilead"
"Oh You Who I Often and Silently Come" and a couple of other
    Whitman songs by Ned Rorem
"Who'll Prop Me Up in the Rain" by Kenward Elmslie
"Action Camera Lights and You" by Tom Steele and Chuck Ortleb
The Marschallin's monologue from *Rosenkavalier* (a flood of tears)
Joni Mitchell's early albums, up to *Blue*
Side one of Joan Armatrading's first album
Nina Simone singing "Little Girl Blue" and "Don't Smoke in Bed"
Judy Collins' song about Che Guevara
The chorus of the dead in Stravinsky's "Persephone"
"Fourth of July, Asbury Park" by Springsteen
The "Our Father" trope from Leonard Bernstein's *Mass*
The "Flaming Angel" theme in Prokofiev's Third Symphony
"Solitaire" by Neil Sedaka
The Goethe songs that Michael Bilunas dedicated to me
"Another You," as sung by Steven Christopher Abbott

ANOTHER YOU

Second Scotch at three
in the morning. I just wrote
a note to tell Tom Weigel he's wrong
about Elizabeth the First. I watched
Columbo, *The Twilight Zone*, and a Channel 13
version of an Ursula LeGuin tale, *Lathe
of Heaven*, which starred Bruce
Davison, whom I've thought was sexy
since he dropped his trunks and had his
way with Cathy Burns twelve years ago
last summer, in *Last Summer*. Earlier
than that I was in bed with someone
you don't know, a new friend (named David)
who makes me want to slow down, buy a dog,
move to some more reasonable city with the seasoned
veterans of my generation, the children of the Sixties
who haven't gone professional or lost their ability
to feel. We were making love the way
new friends do, tentative but hungry
and exuberant, when "Leaving on a Jet Plane"
came on the radio (John Denver wrote it,
did you know?) and my sense of wonder at a new
simpatico body dissolved to the ache
of wondering where you were at the moment,
and what I was doing "in the arms" (the armpit,
actually) of somebody who wasn't you.
I wonder, too, why I just called it
"making love" when I reserve that term
for what I do with you exclusively. We shall
make new friends and "temporary neighbors" (a Frank
O'Hara phrase), but "There will never be
another you," I want to hear you softly
sing right now.

TONIGHT

Barry Davison is finishing *Remembrance of Things Past*.
A hustler's hair and eyes blow Dennis Cooper away.
Bo Huston comes into his inheritance.
John Craig seems pretty stoned.
Lanny Richman's working overtime.

Sam Cross and Janet Campbell watch "The Thorn Birds."
Cheri Fein is getting ready for her wedding.
Steve Hamilton goes to the poetry reading.
Mark Butler is waiting for a phone call from New York.
Michael Szceziak isn't home.

Steven Abbott's somewhere in the Moslem world.
Michael Friedman's torn between two lovers.
Emily McKoane has dreams of empire.
Joe Brainard feels the dope kick in.
Rob Dickerson is getting used to living on his own.

Diane Ward rehearses her performance.
A shopclerk's hair and eyes blow Donald Britton away.
Morris Golde goes to the ballet.
Darragh Park drinks Perrier.
Doug Milford isn't home.

Brian Foster's living in the world of fashion.
Philip Monaghan thinks he'll go to bed with a friend.
Bobby Thompson stands behind the front desk.
Chris Lemmerhirt feels the dope kick in.
Alex Vachon's working on his resume.

Randy Russell hits the books.
Mary Spring is getting ready for her wedding.
Christopher Cox goes to the opera.
Charles Shockley seems pretty stoned.
Edmund Sutton isn't home.

Michael Lally and Dennis Christopher rehearse their play.
The Changing Light at Sandover blows Tim Dlugos away.
Jane DeLynn goes to est.
Teddy Dawson drinks a Lite beer.
John Bernd isn't home.

Frank Holliday paints.
Michael Bilunas eats out with a man who has a famous last name.
David Craig's not part of the picture yet.
Henry Spring is dying of emphysema.
Kenward Elmslie's working on his musical.

Kevin Bacon's onstage in *Slab Boys* for the final time.
Edmund White is on a "boy's night out."
Brad Gooch makes copies.
David Hinchman feels the dope kick in.
Keith Milow isn't home.

Dianne Benson's living in the world of fashion.
A sequence of strong drinks blows Ed Brzezinski away.
Tor Seidler goes to the ballet.
Eileen Myles is on the wagon.
Patrick Fox is getting used to living on his own.

May 12, 1983

WEEK

No
copy, copy
deadlines long past

all that I've been
doing's, being
in love with a boy

THIS MUCH FUN

> *Heaven is a place where nothing ever happens.*
> —David Byrne

Poised as if to fly, the sea-
bird arches what will be its haunches
in a million years. The cable
flashes 'cross the Great Atlantic
and turns my chest to mush. No
birds on the cables of the Brooklyn
Bridge—too noisy—but the view
I step into like blocking someone's telescope,
the dime-a-peep variety, 's as sweeping
as a Cinerama travelogue or diorama
battlefield or episode from Mormon history.
"Like a movie on TV" is how the boy
who saw his teacher shoot himself in class
described it. The cycles of these days
and nights reflected in the *TV Guide*'s
a kind of Daily Office: Matins,
I Love Lucy; *Dream House*, Lauds;
Love Boat as the liturgy for noon, then *Gilligan's
Island* speeds us toward the vesper light.
Something in the air that shimmers in the dawn's
damp blue seems kind by sunset; pathetic
and fallacious, too, but with all the best
intentions. There are ways of blocking out
the sound, and Collects for the major feasts:
the Birth of Little Ricky, or the loud arrival
from heaven of an astronaut, confused among
these puny castaways. I cast away my fear
of walking down the street with headphones
and tune in. "Good Friday Spell" from *Parsifal*

informs the G.E. Building's sunlit
spire, and "Fanfare for the Common Man"'s
a sweet reminder of revolutions lost on C.P.S.
To be this young and having this much
fun's a situation that makes me
nothing if not grateful. Some choice.
But glimmering in the distance is the forge
where somebody somebody used to love turns youth
into a weapon. I want to be nowhere
in that vicinity, a place that doesn't
exist because the qualities that put it on the map
of language come together only once, for all
of time, anonymous as the light
and secret as the air that it impregnates
in the smuggler's harbor. What's inside
the carton marked "Bananas" is the captain's
beeswax, not yours. But what's inside
the history of something over which you exercise
complete control. What's inside the feeling
is a range of permutations comfy by now,
the carburetor settings for the formal play
of light on architecture. Surfaces abound, but
translate into energy when you add a drop of language.
Things fall away, in other words, like scales
from the sides of fish who find their patch
of green-gray lousy with chemistry, though
one must admit it's an impressive river.
They wash up at our feet, lavabo
towels in fins. We thought they had to
swim, but they aspire to fly away the way
birds have to. I'm waiting for the milky
patches in my history to dry, sprout
feathers. I'm gonna love that man
till I die, a hypothetical

event beyond my ken. It happens
every day on the detective show
at twilight: a murder in the first
five minutes, a second halfway down
the plot line, to shut up a villain
pestered by scruples. It broadcasts
afternoons like clockwork, the kind
you never need to bother winding. When I feel
rundown, I think of daily horrors like that,
soothing not because of their dramatic
tension, but as demarcations of the antinomic
light that's always new, always familiar.
It's the same time it was yesterday
at this time, which makes me think of heaven,
and hell, too, both of which may boil
down to the same thing finally: a place
filled up with more than you can know
or handle, whose limits are your own
and whose events are functions of those limits;
I'm half-blind. There's no getting out of it,
anymore than out of this frenetic day,
whose edges have been planed by the triumphal
music, a perfect reason for tuning it in,
but not for writing it down or thinking
it can really help. Nothing can. But nothing's
all I pack these days on long trips
through the daylight, as new as forms that we
extrapolate then shatter, as empty
as the forms to come and the amazing energy
that shoots through and illuminates their most
apparent qualities. It keeps me going
in circles that constitute a tour
of the horizon, as far as I can see
or ever will, when "ever" means "today."

LIT

As if the light contained an outer room
and secret inner chamber which initiates
could enter through the door of the grandfather
clock's dark case, lowering the weights
and pendulum to work the silent
gears and swing a boy-sized square
of wainscoting aside, exposing the hatch
to the hideaway of the richest man
in America, which overlaps the setting
of your life the way competing theories
of light complete each other's mysteries,
by cancelling the possibility that either could be
wholly right, or like the surface of the bay
on a particular breezy day, the one in which
you scarred your thigh on the towline, taking you
off skis, out of the sun. When you came
to the city, you wished you had a deeper tan.
I'm here to help you lower that desire
from your bike to the Sheep Meadow's waves,
perceptible from just one angle, of crewcut
green so uniform it might have been applied
in a single stroke with the broadest brush,
or for another reason.

SPINNER

If Plato's right, my "you" is a reflection
of years-ago phenomena, the way I felt
when faced with your unquenchable erection
and well of nervous energy, that let you belt

the latest songs and dance till sunrise,
high as a kite whose string I held. You were as sweet
as your nightly two desserts, as unwise
as I, and just as loath to meet

unpleasantness head-on, as when you told me
that we were through. "Impossible," I said,
a disbelief that still enfolds me
when I wake and remember that you're dead.

I'm writing to your shadow, which recedes
with youth we shared and spent, to fill
the absence of your voice, my dull need.
Ghost of a ghost, this puts you farther still.

OCTAVIAN

I had a point to make. Then I forgot it.
These days, to be "on" or "in" my mind's
a useless definition of a deep
half-truth. I was choked with rage. Then
I went to the seashore. Through the smoked
and non-prescription lenses, the stack of washed-
out primary tints shimmering with other-worldly
clarity from the parking lot beside the chowder
hut's a blowup of a science textbook graph,
"Alluvial Deposits": soft green of the beach
grass, toughest plant in America, laid beneath
the steel blue, then sea blue, then blue-
green of the ocean on the other side of which
you gambol, stripped into the composition
under a majolica sky. Colors from a Freilicher
or Porter, though I couldn't gauge the depth,
overlaid like drippings on the straw of a Chianti
bottle, the brand drunk exclusively by art school
sweethearts. At low tide, cast for sections
of our history to dredge up and resent, then
walked along the beach toward Wellfleet, practicing
my monologue. "I well remember the day
I thought it so unfair of you to gallivant
with young tarts on the further side of these
marine phenomena. It was yesterday, and as the last
light of evening found me on a spit between a tidal
swamp and the parapet of dunes that shields
the Herring Cove for spooners, I thought
you would deserve it if I turned to your bosom
friend, the one you made me promise never
under any circumstances to romance, and kissed him.

The fucking mosquitoes were impossible."
The newfound and regrettable tendency to turn
my life into an opera was washed out
by the colors for a blessed while. All that air
and a fluffy cloud that blocked the sun for half
an hour, as pettish as your coltish love
made me. I walked beneath the shadow of a deep
regret that such devout and histrionic passion
provoked no grand-scale tragedy, merely the usual
smorgasbord of bitterness and fantasies of murder
and revenge. Then the shadow lifted. I was on the quay
and you were on the packet leaving Illyria, clutching
the telegram that told you of your great-uncle's demise
and your whopping legacy. The wind blew your bangs back,
and the grimace never left your face as yell
after Confederate yell escaped your throat, progressively
overlaid by the thwack of waves as you shrank
to a speck above the boatwales, then disappeared.
There were postcards for awhile: "The Queen of the Nile
has a nice asp, har har. Miss you, X." That stripe.
After a delirious evening, I walked out with a roll
of silver to call you from the corner. It was snowing,
and the operator couldn't believe I had my forty
drachmas ready. Force-fed, the payphones in a five-
block radius died. Your voice had changed. I stopped
loving you and began to love the impossible, an image
of the two of us together. Then the libretto
shifted as the ingenue arrived onstage, and you
and I became a subplot in a farce of ancient
origin, though the music was ours. Eight
days a week, you know I really care. But gradually
one learns the impossibility of forcefeeding the time
that starts in pain as a tunnel, but opens

like a Chinese fingertrap with lack of strain
to reveal itself as the corkboard
on which the light one loves more than a lover
is tacked. I can spend all day here.
Then I'm going home to sleep. That's something
permanent, a concept more advanced than "final,"
which breaks down under the pressure
of knowing that it ends when you do, if
you do. The ocean shares the possibility as you
go deeper, until the dark line just below the sky
widens to another hue, one which can only
be imagined from here. There may be more,
and though there's not a drop to drink
in any of it, that's not why I came. I'm here
so the progressive fields of color are everything
between us. It was off the mark to call the fickle
boy Octavian, after the undergrad who changed
his name and filled his world with power.
And it was wrong to have given him a silver
rose, though it was an artful stratagem.
I wagered I could wrap the mutable
in immutable foil, but all I forged
was a gewgaw, fit for a suburban shelf
of Hummel figurines and family pix.
Today I picked a beach rose, which shriveled
at my touch. Then I pinned it to my bodice,
a spot of operatic sentiment to set against
the tempera of sea and sky, as packed
with light as ever, the greatest colors
for the emptiest parts of the world.

ARMAGNAC

A night of bitter dreams, a Quiet Day
in Advent led by both the local vicars
for both their flocks, so few they couldn't play
a football game. The Anglicana flickers

in votive lights beside the polished shrines,
each lovingly described in the brochure
whipped up for tourists. Take your place in line
to ogle. I am what I am, as pure

as driven slush, and cold as melted ice
inside my drink in the piano bar
last even. Song and smoke cease to entice
entirely after snifter and cigar

are drained and snuffed. A candle with a black
pinspotted shade, this sky. I see them all,
He sees each, names them "stars." In Armagnac
a cask of brandy; here, a *cage aux folles*.

CAPE AND ISLANDS

Little birdie footprints. Then a rush
of gray surf ridden by the yellow smut
of brine or soapsuds flushed by visitors
from off-island, down to the sea. It bastes
the sand in preparation for a meal
the ocean takes in small bites, pecking
like a bird. The surgical acuity of morning
light's sharp angle dapples fish
who opened wide to feast on visitors
from neighboring dominions, and were yanked
from theirs. The birds race the waves back out,
scouting dross for something edible. Whoosh.
There go their footprints again. The edges of a time
make birds and sea take turns, the way the edges
of a space stove in the bottom
of my ship and keep me from traversing
that stretch of sea. "Web of life" and "fabric
of time" denote a single skein: the third
dimension of the dotted line on the map
between your life and theirs. You can't
get there from here; what seems like a wall
of windows is the net itself.
No place is not an island or a detail
of one: not this frangible
ping-pong ball of a planet, its lagoon-
before-the-electric-storm watercolors ridden
by white smut, disassembling
and reforming in patterns of a delicacy
and votive or other scientific significance
that might be intentional, a signal
we have not yet grasped; not the mass

of land, no longer continent, coloring
the ocean twenty miles away with sludge;
not the lonely town, whose lights are less
a scalpel in the night than a suspension
which becomes a sediment the closer to
the cottage it gets. Places at the bottom
of the sky, a continuum
like human skin, no less surrounded
because one can never find the edge one needs
for peeling off the mudpack or harvesting
the morning crop of beard. The Razor-
backs, the Jets, the Terrapins, the Knights:
armies 'neath the lights
whose ignorance is bald or receding like the dunes
of Coast Guard Beach, the gums of America. The Crimson
Tide swoops into the bay and sticks around like smut,
crusting and intoxicating clams. There is a blight
in the affairs of men, as tangible
as gooseflesh to the blind, who provoke it
through no fault of their own. They're alone
in a world of perpetual darkness. Across
the border is another state, from which the sound
of foreign words in delicate incomprehensible
patterns caroms back. They're playing
ping-pong over there, having a wonderful time.
Together we have formed a union, though drastically alop
to visitors with the rudest social sense: "The Heiress
and the Waiter," "The Shiftless Boy and the Adoring
Priest." We're looking for a sort of stability
which depends on absence. The blind lead the mapless,
and though they're sure of foot along
the causeway through the bog, there's no way
they can know the charm and endless

pain and entertainment of the disconnected
sectors of the city where their voyage ends.
From the plane, a sky the optimistic
color of the UN flag gives way to shades
of green, green smut. They're near the airport.
All it takes to bridge the physical
distance is a little hop across the weather
or its absence, but to stitch the sense
of placement in the center of a field
of vision to the rattletrap conventions
out of which you live as from a weekend bag
requires a vehicle: a football
that rotates on its axis, shaking off
the cartoon fleas as it heads for your solar
plexus at the speed of sound. Someone
threw that thing at you, and wants you
to run with it, not fumble; but to where?
Even the biggest voice across the widest stage
booming out to the largest audience
in history can't solve the problem
of what to do with all that space
between the words, the proof that there is more
to come, something that you haven't heard
which will teach you more about the place
you see or the places you have learned about
from previous communiqués. They require an answer.
I have a hard time sometimes thinking
I am really here. The lady in the bar
with the wig teased into a ski-slope
ending at a precipice of forehead and a massive
chin could not be Ethel Merman, no matter
how alike they looked. Maybe I thought
it was impossible because it was me

this was happening to. Now that she's dead,
I'd think it was especially impossible, but maybe
there's a place where it could still be Ethel
Merman at the bar. Maybe my perception of the boundary
around this island is as weak as it was
that night, and the range of communiqués
is greater than I'd ever dream. At the foot
of the street is a river. You'd never dream
a tunnel with a train was far beneath it
unless you knew, a knowledge that depends
on people other than you. Once across the river,
another foot of another street dead-ends
at another, larger river, under which
a train runs, too. Hey. Hey, it's me.
It's what you want to shout into the sky
when the last sad traces of pastel
fade into the twilight zone of steeples
and green docks on the far side of the water.
In the Lower Bay, what appears a mothball fleet
has people on its decks when seen through Dad's
binoculars. They're playing ping-pong
or football in an easy give-and-take,
the principle behind their action not unlike
the way you breathe, or have to figure out
what something someone says really means.
The air turns frigid instantly, and it's time
to go beneath the water on a train
and run into the people whom you say
you know while doubting it, although
you never can be sure they're not exactly
what you think they are, the way the woman
in the bar turned out to be Ethel Merman.
She opened her mouth and in an unmistakable

voice said, "Vodka and orange juice, Eddie,"
a sentiment I've echoed hundreds of times
in the intervening years. A votive
current runs beneath the pleasantries.
You watch it as it turns into a sewer
of the histories, yours and the ones
you catch, like viruses or lower forms
of sealife to voracious birds. I'm nesting here
in the remnants of the gifts that washed up
after the storm. I cannot be anything
but grateful, though I aspire to be,
the way that burly seamen round the Horn
and aspire to home, a cozy port that starts
to exist when they lose sight of land.
I'd never been that far away before, and I needed
something to connect me to the places
that I knew, a rope or language. We're going
to sell what we have, then we're going
to buy new things, and we'll be back before
you know it, to bring them to your little nests.
I can see the harbor beacon now,
and the pelicans, the gargoyle
guardians of the green pier's uprights.
We stepped ashore at sunset, to the cheers
of a throng in motley: bongo
drummers, the Iguana Man, a clutch
of Ethel Merman lookalikes, and boys
whose skins seemed burnished, then buffed.
Every man should have an adventure like that.
They mistook our "hallos" for "aloes,"
a plant of strong medicinal
properties they grow. With delicate
incomprehensible gestures they led us

down a causeway to the aloe bogs,
past shabby bungalows, each rooftop crowned
with wheels for nesting storks.
We learned through observation that the crowd
of well-wishers at our sloop's arrival
had turned out not to greet us, but to say
Goodbye to the sun, and that they gathered
thus each afternoon. In my years among them,
I learned many secrets: skin care, bongo
drumming, and darker ones of which I may not speak.
I met a burnished maiden there, and married her.
She is your mother. But something alien
persisted, even in the heat
of sex in the horse latitudes or trying to speak
the inutterable in a tongue
I barely understood. A subtext
lay beneath the coral and the sand
like a water table when the kitchen tap
is clogged. Millions live that way, trudging miles
up mountainsides on stony paths to springs,
to lug back dippersful in tall ceramic
jars their culture's lost the knack of making,
relics from the days before the well
their grandfathers dug ran dry.
We're getting farther from the source
of our predicament, which led us to the birth
of narrative. But sequence is as much
an artifice as the perfectly preserved
seaside village where you brought your family
on your return. Those people are nothing
like their forebears; rather, there's no way you can know.
I thought I knew this person, and that we
were friends; then he did something

terrible, incredibly mean. Maybe
I never knew him. Maybe he was not the same
person I knew. I told him
all my secrets, even the dark ones.
Now the knowledge lies behind
his gestures, as familiar as the light
that floods the shed where we put up preserves.
What he does with it's his own
business. The ball's in his court.
I'm getting thirsty waiting for the serve.
It's one of those spaces, where the sluggish
pace slows down the asymptotic
progress of the game. There's just the light
and the knowledge of your own heart
at work, not the things that fill it
but the way it moves. A Valentine
is etched upon a chamber wall. The millrace
of your blood washes it away. Whoosh.
The shards are off on an excursion
down your body's highways, to return unrecognizable.
I was afraid you wouldn't recognize me,
so I tried to stay the same, but pressure
built up like a boil that festered
despite my expertise in skin care, an oubliette
of smut churned up by history
I tried to trap. That's when I went to the beach.
The air looks non-existent here, though
I feel it on my skin. The sandpipers' strategy
vis-à-vis the waves persists: quick bite,
quick flight, repeated as the day
grows logy and the shadows corpulent.
I have a hard time sometimes remembering
I'm part of the largest audience watching

as the largest stage in history is trod
by those unfolding a sequence that at first
seems tawdry. The nightclub owner and his fleshy
love walk out along the moonlit seawall.
The song they sing in their loudest voices
is kitsch, and their lines predictable. Yet
the clumsy hand of one barely encircles
the other's waist at the end
of the number, as if frightened
by what it will or won't discover.
In a dream, the gesture stopped the show;
like falling down a stairwell or an empty
shaft of light, the incompletion
and its resultant terror woke you up.
A motion out of time, and a voice to say
it's time and you're almost out of it. But
gradually that shipwrecked feeling yields
to a nascent certitude, the edges of which
won't take shape, like batter that resists
the form you need for breakfast, spreading out
to form a layer of porous comprehension
across the horizonless stretch
of darkness when the noises of the waves
blot out the thoughts you live by, or try to.
It's not that something's missing; it's simply
that the colors haven't filled the spaces
in yet. It's a project, like fishing,
to stitch a half-completed history
out of whole cloth. I stayed in Key West
for awhile. Then I went to Broadway to audition
for a leading role. I fell in with the nephew
of a famous writer, then split for Mykonos
to cool it out. Once there, I rooted

for my favorite teams: the Bright Eyes, the Poltroons,
the Vipers with the Best Intentions, and the white
stucco walls of individual
houses which have stood in the same place
forever, islands in the muddy
tidal flat of time on an island
where all the time in the world is receding
like the dream which, for once,
gave you all the clues you needed
to plug the hull and plot the course
back to your island home.

Fame the insatiable cousin
And Claim his termagant wife
Fashion the eyes of a dummy
Pare the soft wood with a knife

Day is a talented liar
Night a delirious fool
Lifetimes of utter devotion
Spill and discolor the pool

Perfume can give me a headache
Beauty can give me a pain
No one will give me the right time
Stand with a straw in the rain

Stand with a colorful sweater
Sweat in the colorful air
Air your regrets to a stranger
Lock up your life in a stare

THE FRUIT STREETS

There's a little cottage in the back
of a composed facade. I want
to live there. There's a little
composition I can doodle on the keys
in basic chords. The man with an electric
speaker where his voice should be
in corduroy is sweeping down
the Fruit Streets, as a lady
inside my cloudy memory of other lives
or movies sweeps the cobblestones
with her train. She's on her way
to Pilgrim Church, where Beecher thunders.
Rain sweeps in from the bay.
I wonder how much good a sermon
can do, though they were once as popular
as cautionary soaps about the rich
to rubes today. Within the stiffness
of a form and collar let me touch
your eyes, take your hand. I'll lead you
to a land of colors—Cranberry, Pineapple,
Orange and the spurious Joralemon—and thrilling
tastes. The rawness of the wind is softened
by a blast of citrus, as the view
from the Heights gains pigment with a flick
of the Tint dial. It's a new world
out there, as if a box of Trix
had spilled across the harbor where the grays
and silvers played beneath a sky they perfectly
resembled. In the glow of an ass-backwards
native lore, Paradise could be as sudden
as a bite of fruit, or death

to the congregants. Protestants
find both "forbidden," though the preacher
whose words moved a government himself
may have brewed the metaphor while doodling
with a colleague's wife. The life
of the flesh is lived inside a sack
of flesh, but the life of the memory
is spun out in the names by which
we know the streets. It was here
I smoked a joint with John before he left
to turn into a rock star on the Coast
and watched the fireworks.
They lit up the sky,
Cranberry red, Pineapple yellow,
Orange orange, against the electric
blue-engorged horizon, radiant scrim
you can point to any twilight on your way
to drinks with friends, silly rabbits.
Pellets of our histories have piled up
in my mind, the Nation's Attic,
a nation carried onward by the names
of streets and Protestants like Carrie Nation,
where hatchets that remain unburied
reduce saloons to slivers. There's a beam
of pale light playing on a chink between
the landmark's bricks, a sliver of decay.
It's colorless, a paradigm of how I want to look
to let you see through what I say to find
the cottage with the patch of lawn where I live,
a dooryard in the patchwork of a city
you know about because you've heard it
in my voice, as if by faith.

FOUR ORGANS

after Steve Reich

give the mind its head
in a choirloft when the spare beginnings
accordion and the harmonic
purr of a blower overlays the hit
or miss of a perfectionist on methedrine
which becomes a symphony of increments
unfollowable
but knowable in portions as the source
of pleasure as the wine flows
up the corkscrew
a process of intoxicating space
that grows to accommodate a wingspread
igniting the maracas
causing the whole to turn

WORDS FOR SIMONE WEIL

attention, it is a poem
but uncomposed, the way a fearsome sky
shakes out its skirts attempting to decide
to rain on them, handing the pathos back

the fallacy: desire exists outside
the closed world of a chest whose ardent heaves
don't rustle its own lining of dead leaves
a Petri dish, a common meal, a bone

one thing to chew on, something else to know
it's yours to eat before you eat it   best
to save it, not a torture, not a test
a tension, like a poem you can watch

obedient to the movement and the whole
of a vast midland, all you ever see
the brown and yellow clouds mean history
for now, for then, for when you heed them both

TRINIDAD

The black
republic can be fiercely
gay, David. Deep in the heart
it's Carnevale time,
the way it once was Greenwich
Mean or Miller Time, a shot
of fiercely single-minded
energy beneath the skin
so sharp you'd never know
you'd missed the vein entirely,
whose ore you've started learning
how to mine. Mind your heart.
It's beating like Caribbean drums
whose music fuels the national
dance. You have the whole day
to join in.

CHRISTOPHER ISHERWOOD

I want my writing to be
like Christopher Isherwood:

clear as his eyes
and short as his height.

HEALING THE WORLD
FROM BATTERY PARK

Om Tara
Tu Tara
Ture Svaha
—Tibetan Mantra

Draw a deep breath. Hold it. Let it go.
That's the smell of the ocean.
Our forebears hailed from out there. There's a stele
to mark the spot where Minuit exchanged
a mess of beads and trinkets for this island.
He may have thought it proof he was
a clever trader, although if the sky
were sky-blue as today, the sunlight's flash
through bright glass would have been magnificent,
and that might have had tremendous value
in another culture. In another language,
"minuit"'s a division of the day.
I've divided my days among a host
of places near the sea. I get a lot
of comfort when I walk a beach, or through
the narrow streets among a crush of traders.
Sand in my shoes, sand of the Castle
Clinton courtyard where all of New York
turned out of yore to see the Jacksons,
Andrew and his wife. He'd whipped the bloody
British in the town of New Orleans
and massacred the Creeks. His steely eyes,
as blue as Western skies, saw the space I see.
He breathed the same air. There's a little part
of him in me, that wants to drive away

the savages who populate the dark
expanse beyond the porch light's reach.
It takes a Trail of Tears to teach
that neighborhood improvement's not the point.
May the breath I draw become a balm
to soothe the exiled people of all times
and lands: the Cherokee, the Jew,
the people of Tibet whose loss brought us
abundant wisdom, the kulak and the Sioux,
the lover I abandoned and the friends
I drove away, the difficult and friendless
kicked out by their family, their school,
their church, their boss, their spouse, who found them too
impossible to put up with for one more minute.
In this park, their refuge, I divide my time
and feed it to the world when I exhale
like bread for ducks. It's not a fantasy
of power, and it's not about the rediscovery
of arcane treasure from a better place,
quieter and more romantic, like Tara
in the days of kings or in the antebellum
South. It's about the light that permeates
the sky above the boathouse where the sloop-
for-hire is moored. One romantic night,
it sailed across the harbor with my love
and me aboard. We drank champagne, and trailed
our fingers through the surface of the oil-
and-water stew that buoyed us. When we grew
apart, the two halves of a single wake
that break on banks across the dark expanse
of river from each other, I chose rage
to hold my sorrow's head beneath the waves
until I couldn't feel it anymore,

though somewhere under driftwood-littered slips
or in the trash-strewn slime a fathom down,
I knew that it was hiding. May the breath
I draw become a healing touch
to ease the pain I caused him, and to speed
the light that passed between and through us on
to its next stop. Here I divide my heart
among the teenaged couples and the shy
or clandestine romantics from the big
law firms who nuzzle on a bench, and queens
in stained Quiana shirts who cruise between
the slabs of stone with names of boys who died
in World War II. May it soothe my father,
who couldn't say how very much he loved
his wife, and all the tongue-tied men. And may
it heal the women, too; millions
like my mother who are left behind
when what they love about a man is wrenched
out of his body, hidden in another place.
In another language, "Tara" is the name
of a she-god sprung out of a human tear.
She heals all wounds and brings the world a sense
of peace. On this island where the gods
would outnumber the humans in a week if such
a mode of birth became habitual,
I beg her presence as I feel my breath
flying like a jet from Newark
out into the world. There's a quantity
of tenderness I feel sometimes
that drops into my chest precipitous
and golden as the sun into Fort Lee.
I couldn't tell you where it comes from, but
I'm learning where it hides. It's in the nectarine

you ate for breakfast, or the thing
you're doing now, not in what you think
you should do or in what comes next.
And it's not in what you think "God" means;
the only certainty is that you're wrong.
Draw a deep breath. Thank you, mother.
Hold the light inside and let it find
the ragged spots, a gentle tongue to probe
for caries. Then expire.
A little part of you is in the wind now,
a trace of pain or coffee in the scent
of brine that clasps you like a lover,
closer and more faithful than a lover.
Bless me, father. This is my first
confession: I'm living in the light
at the bottom of a sea of air,
everything I need in a place I share
with everyone. It's in your hands.

JULY

The foot should never go where the eye has already been.
—Capability Brown

I knew the place had capabilities
the moment that I saw it. How the house
stands sideways, for one thing; the front porch view
is of the lowland garden and the swamp,
not Mecox Road. I had them bring a crane
two years ago and excavate a pond.
There's no place you can stand and see the whole
of it, a trick that Brown used when he built
the lake at Stowe. The prospect from the knoll
where the house sits is very much like Stowe
sans folly and tempietto, though the plants
are all indigenous. Along the path
that winds down to the swamp, I've placed the reds:
bayberry in clumps, and trumpet-vines
on higher ground. I planted the tall reeds
myself, in hipboots, clearing out a years-
old jungle which is growing back so fast
I'll have to stock with Chinese grass carp, which
can grow to twenty pounds, a sort of Sumo
minnow that feeds on waterweeds. I hope
they don't eat lilypads. On the steep slope
beyond the pond's a sea of chicory;
it all goes blue next month. I've put some blue
lobelia there, too; off-blue, towards red.
The sequence of their blooming makes the view
change every week all summer. Light. Dark. Light.

It keeps the eye engaged with every step,
whether you want some inspiration or
a tussy-mussy (it's a word of Vita
Sackville-West's, means "wildflower bouquet."
I spent some hours making one today).
The path you can't see, over by the shed,
is verged by ailanthus; in a year
or three, the branches will have overgrown
to form a shady tunnel. At its end
I'll place another garden, which will block
the sight of houses going up like weeds
from here to Job's Lane Beach. At the high point
of their influence, Brown and Repton moved
whole villages whose jumble interfered
with one long view. *That's* capability.
Behind the ailanthus, in the woods,
I'll put in a spring garden by-and-by,
lady's slipper and jack-in-the-pulpit.
When you're heading down the hill or through
the meadow, there's no way you can tell, but
all the paths are spokes which lead you back
to one place, the lawn with the butternut
as hub, a spreading Tree of Life, as in
the *Roman de la Rose* or Genesis.
I wanted something right there for the eye
to focus on. Then I remembered Fairfield
Porter's painting called "July," with those
white Adirondack chairs. They're perfect there.
See how the white turns pale blue as the night
creeps in, full of mosquitoes and fireflies.
And don't be frightened by the strangled cries
from the swamp; those are peepers bellowing,
not *Psycho III*. The sounds and smells grow dense

this time of evening. The mock-tympanum
lugubriously beaten by the waves
a mile away sounds muffled in its quilt
of fog. The cooling air is redolent
of linden by the porch; its flowerets
will burst next week. I'll celebrate with friends,
throw a festival. The lurcher comes inside
and dampness clambers uphill from the pond
or blows in from the beachfront. There's a spot
of cloud against the night sky. Dark. Light. Dark.
It blossoms downward, filling up the yard.
Pretty soon your hand before your face
will be the farthest prospect you can see,
delight in. It's familiar by now,
the rote procession into night, and oddly
comforting, like music I recall:
a blues lament that all the things you loved
have disappeared, and you might as well be
anywhere, underlaid by gentle drums
that let you know you're near the ocean.

KING OF THE WOOD

Know you not
your father's house and name?
We were driving up Mulholland,
my Dad and I, a month or so
ago, in the big white Ford
with which I'd passed my road test.
Speedometers back then went up as far
as one-eighty, two hundred even,
even though anything out of Detroit
would fall apart if driven half that fast.
I asked my Dad, "What is it like to die?"
He paused, gave me a withering look,
and said, "It's not *like* anything."

Later we were separated. Always
it's that way near the end of the dream:
a landslide blocks the trail down which I've walked
for gasoline in an old-fashioned can;
a cable snaps. Trying to circle
round the long way, I stumble down
the steep hill toward the stream.
My friends have just untied their raft.
They float away and wave, "Moon River"
up and over. Where have they gone?
Kennst du das land?

I lived there for a long time.
I remember best the woods
behind the house, and what we built there,
forts, traps, rungs nailed to the side
of an enormous spruce by boys
so long ago we didn't know their names.
They'd fought in the war.

There was a boy in the class, the store,
the magazine I didn't like.
Then after awhile I liked him.
Awhile more, and I'll like him more or less
the same, or more, or less.
It's happened enough times for me to know
what's coming: not a pattern
exactly, for it's always different;
more a vehicle that you can climb
inside at any point. You can leave, too,
but it will be the hardest thing you ever did.
You've gotten used to seeing it one way,
and who's to tell you you're not right?
"A painter sees a hairbrush in the butter, and to him
it's all reflected light." Virgil said that,
Virgil Thomson. Later the same night,
he made the rounds among his guests,
a wicker basket filled with withered pears
hanging from his hands, and squeaked,
"The harder they are, the better they taste."

In which meaning is a quantity,
a participle, meaning that the range
of permutations in a band of time
is evened out and frozen, life the plinth
for ice sculptures of growing love, abiding
love, and the collapse of love through perfidy
or blind neglect   in which the moment is
the only one there is   a day at a time
is too long   have a second, then another
second   ragged men in elephant bells
in a meeting room on St. Mark's Place
holding off another bottle for another
moment   you've had a successful moment,
the only one there is, the point
at which the denouement's epitomized
in stylized gestures, when the whole ballet
depends on how it looks, which hinges
on the way it feels, its definition
like good cheekbones, their quality obvious
enough to make you first a movie star
and then a princess   you never dreamed
you'd get that far, but then you never thought
you'd have gotten this far, either

in which you share a common symbol
for each thing, and wouldn't know
the thing at all without its symbol
a city of amnesiacs who paste
the names of objects on the things themselves
to start a hundred years of solitude   anything
can happen here, and anything does
the freedom of the moment is the freedom

of the aquarium, the gay ceramic
turrets of the castle through whose windows
goldfish swim a blur
behind the glass that buttresses their world
outside the window, fish food falls,
settling on the sills like snow
if you were an Eskimo, you could call it one
of twenty names, depending on the way
it looked, a notion of abundance
determined by the names one knows
I've died a thousand deaths, a wealth of deaths,
while waiting for you here   I was afraid
that something might have happened to you, something
terrible   and that you wouldn't come

in which you find it easy, almost glib,
to marshal forces and to summon up
the feelings and the memories for the sake
of structures you would sometimes rather torch:
the mediocre bandshell, or the pavilion
with broken steps and vulgar sentiments
carved into the crossbeams by a hundred years
of self-important boys with knives
this was their place, and you'd just as soon
send the whole thing up in smoke
first the planks   then the walls that arch
around the windows   then the roof   then
the trees and the whole wood   then the lake
then the air   then the earth
but not the way you'll talk about it later

in which the blackened husk contains the seeds
of everything you burnt away, grown back
when another moment's light expels
the dark your eyelids buttressed in your eyes
not a thing has changed, only its significance
the way a drawing by a genius when erased
by another genius is another work of art,
completely new   if not a world, its map

Night goes up in . . . smoke? No, fog.
A. C sharp. C sharp. A. G.
Foghorn into symphony
needs another medium

than the words with which I make
my art. Wagner comes to mind,
the insufficiency of line . . .
leitmotivs to light the depths.

Scientific instruments,
aimed precisely at the ships,
map them out as little blips,
but could never catch the rays

jaundiced through a hangdog mist,
tumbling wisps that dramatize
thin beams that will energize
them away in minutes now.

As the planet warms, I heat
coffee the ten-thousandth time.
Words, alas, aren't music. I'm
glad to be here all the same.

Go gently into that good morning,
Go gently into that good day.
Don't leave a trace behind
of the love that you will find.
You've got more good reasons for leaving, boy,
than to stay.

Peter, Paul and Mary sang that to me in a dream
when I was sixteen. It's stayed with me.
Later on, it made me feel a kin
of Jeanne D'Arc. Somebody was calling,
somebody I couldn't see. I didn't know
the voices, but I could tell that they
were strong. I thought of stripping off
the clothes my father bought me, standing
naked in the style of Francis ("free"),
my father's patron saint and mine.
I'd wanted other-worldly intervention
for so long, the angel
who'd tell me there had been a terrible
mistake, my fortune and my father
were in another place, please follow . . .

In all the places where I've spent
the moments, I've known it was my song.
How could I be sure?
In a world that's constantly changing,
how could I be sure?

I feel it. I feel it
in my bones.

O say, can you see?
Jess, I can see very well. And the Mexican
waved from the top of the ballpark flagpole.
That's a joke, son. I turned on the cartoons
to turn him off. Has anybody here seen my old
friend Kelly with the Irish eyes?
He's as bad as old Antonio. 200 pounds
of twisted steel and sex appeal. You'd never
believe it, but your father was thin
when I married him. And light on his feet.
There's a painting of the major transportation systems
outside a Southern or a Western city
breaking down—planes crashing, station wagons
hurtling toward the ditch—and the souls
of passengers ascending light as fog
into the air. They're
wearing long white robes, like Klansmen
or the children visited by Peter Pan.
I never wanted to grow up and be
like he was, and now I haven't.

Fresh as red air of Tuscany, the dawn
of the twelfth-century Renaissance, a dry
run for the full-blown windstorm, centuries down

the rough track from Firenze, he would be
of countenance. Something Frank there, Frankish as his name,
a monicker brought back from shopping sprees

by nouveau-riches embarrassing parents,
the Bernadones, merchants to grandees,
mongers of cloth for vestments

exquisite as smoky parades of preening
clerks whose every gesture rubrics mapped,
whose purses turned to pouts when students leaning

in doorways hurled processionward their japes,
sparking absurd exchanges: "Prig!" "Young lout!"
"Old queen!" "Barbarian!" "Fatso!" "Jackanapes!"

My namesake jeered the loudest, irresponsible
and drop-dead charming as I might have seemed
in my best moments, halfway through a full

tumbler of Scotch (my second), two away
from that blissful, combustible insouciance
when anything—a gaffe, a gorgeous lay,

the loss of friends—was possible, and came
to pass more often as I passed the blacked-
out bulb that marked my limit, or in flames

passed out. Francis passed out through the city gates.
He knew of nothing worthwhile that he lacked—
top school, designer threads, a string of dates,

with sylphs—but someone older, wise and still,
a father-figure to replace the hair-
trigger-tempered draper, and to fill

the space left by his fawning. In the wood
he stumbled down a stony path to where
the tumbledown San Damiano stood,

a broken chapel. Then a sudden lurch,
as if sodden or uncertain of foot
when someone's voice said, "Build my church."

He raised it stone on stone, as troubadours
build words on music, probably employing
conventions in inverted commas, new or

clever usages for timeworn slabs
of hewn granite, repairing cracks,
painstaking as, home from his cluttered lab,

a chemist builds a fireplace brick by brick in
the cleared thicket between lawn and wood,
my father in the summer half-light, kneeling

with trowel and barrow.
He used it to burn trash
when he finished it. I don't know

how Francis used St. D's. His days were full
of roles: jongleur de Dieu, gentle seafarer
to sultanates, ambassador to wolves,

finally living like one, in a stinking
cave, the native freshness drained
out of his narrow face into the sinking

hollows of his eyes, like classic form
drained of all referents but a multitude
of fashions through the years, or men in uniform

of burnt sienna sack,
museum keepers of the holy sites
of history, builders of shrines to way-back-

when phenomena, his life's blood leaching
out of his wrists into black Umbrian soil
as if an I.V. had been yanked, and reaching

past swarms of sounds for the right words,
the ones he'd heard once only, his ears
large for them as a spindly deer's. I heard

a voice, know the words it used,
but did I get my father's meaning right?
All of it gets confused

except the question, beaten half to death,
a swarm of bees that chase a fat-legged toddler
all the way home, a temple out of breath.

To Walter Lowenfels

You had four real ones of your own, so why
did you write *To an Imaginary
Daughter*? I found it in the Books
for a Buck bin at Barnes & Noble,
your signature inside, a copy you'd inscribed
to someone whom you'd just rejected
for one of your anthologies of wooly
Movement writing, to which you gave your life
in language of your time, the Great Depression.
It's depressing how unrecognizable
your name's become; with Hemingway and
Henry Miller, one of the three
most prominent and best expatriate
writers in Paris; author of *Steel*,
the pamphlet that made bosses of the day
see Red. Your popularity
like vaunted winds of change, swept through
the corners of the world lit by Left-Lit
and out the window, like the wind today
that drove me into Barnes & Noble.
It's cold out there when no one knows
your name. Spokesman, working-class
Whitmanic bard, poet of the brave
new world, speaker of demotic
democratic truths, mover and shaker, shock-troop
of the Revolution, too-accessible
parent of forgotten books: I know your slim
affected and affecting offspring
only because some miffed, less-than-forgotten
scribbler sold it off for change.
The verdict of the History you used

as engine and excuse is not in yet,
you'd say. I'll stick around.
But I'm haunted by the lack of rhyme
and reason in how power dwindles down
from clarity and massive sweep
of language to a garrulous old man
in Peekskill serving French bread and Bordeaux
to luncheon guests. "He wore a black beret;
the old days were important to him."

Father of vanished texts, where went your truth?
The wind has cleared away your agitprop,
your art, your bromides, your imaginings
of world, or word, or children strong of grip
enough to clasp, to spare your voice.

Hercules becomes Celestial
Hercules. The son whose flesh
is eaten by the faithful once a year,
stripped from his bones, his bones
burnt, his ashes smeared across their brows,
grows slowly brighter through the centuries
and rises skyward, Sonny to sun.
Some of the farflung 'burbs confused him
with Apollo—bright chariot in the air,
flames painted on the side, chrome trim, and Steve
Reeves driving, as in "Hercules Unchained"
(the farts-and-popcorn-on-a-rainy-day
smell of the Majestic Theater, where
the picture filled the house . . . how did he make
his pecs so shiny?) Think of all that beef
whetting the most private imaginings
of throngs of kids who walked out blinking
at the strong sunlight which had changed the sky
outdoors while they were helping Joe Levine
stay rich. It's a rich life
when you stop being a host or victim
and when your mother no longer can tell you
what to do—feed the guests, son—
and your father hands you a piece of the family
business, till the day he leaves
to be much spoken of, but never seen
and there you are at the reins, waving
at the kids you shared a movie with
a long time ago, as you pass the stretch
of wood and head toward Westfield. Getting older
isn't what you thought; it's gradual
and pleasant, and has something to do
with healing, the way a cut dries up

and closes on its own, with time.
Hercules was interchangeable
with Aesculapius, once he began
his journey to the sky, taking over
where the old king left off, trajectory
predictable as missiles homing in,
a notion indicating that a home
presents itself at some point down the trail,
though present time seems not to hold it, just
the intimation of a happy splashdown
and the start of one more orbit, another day
filled to the brim with light.

Exult now, all you angels and archangels,
You citizens of heaven and of Cobble Hill,
Who touch a spark to tinder in a Webber grill
And sprinkle points of light from taper

To slender candles trembling in the knobby fists
Of old woman and callow teen
And all the ages in between
The nervous shadows on their faces veiled in mist

Of incense and the ancient import
Of texts announcing someone risen for their sake
Ejected from a tomb at daybreak
The planet his new mother, on his way to short

And mystifying conversations
With friends before departing for his Father's side
A presence in the world, as though he never died
Coloring the darkness with anticipation

Together with the smoke and tapers
It brings to mind a hillside on a summer night
When "We Shall Overcome" by torchlight
Projected from a thousand throats, across the acres

Of tombstones for the war dead, more dead
Each day across the ocean, and a man who'd tried
To stop the killing but had died
Before he had the chance, planted among them

We waited for his wife and children
The Cardinal Archbishop said a hurried Mass
And from an altar torch a fragile flame was passed
Out to the candles held by adolescent pilgrims

Whose reedy song was drowned by jet noise
Of aircraft dropping from the sky like burning gel
To land a mile away, at National
Where at the runway's end my father closed his eyes

His earphone in, relaxing in the Ford
And listening to pilot-tower
Communications by the hour
He'd sit all evening that way, never growing bored

I passed the flame to Jack O'Hara
He passed it to a monk in casual attire
In the confusion, Judy Jenkins' hair caught fire
We smothered it, and smothered laughter

Solemnity derailed by sudden fright
As some creep with a pistol had derailed our dreams
For darkness can hold anything, although it seems
To dissipate so easily for candlelight

In this dimly lit place, dim hour
We raise our voices and our song
We'd thought him dead, but were dead wrong
He's risen as he said, with endless grace and power

Where Is Art?

Georgia Brown in a dingy
period costume in a dingy
Soho room in a faded
photo of a Broadway stage,
asking in a melody
in a rhyme on a scratchy
LP, Where is what she cares
about the most, and it's the first
image that springs (spring
forward, fall back) into my mind
when I wonder, where is what
I used to care about the most,
the art of it, not artifice
like sweeteners I despise
but a thing I cared about,
care about losing touch with
enough that when the adjective
"artful" provokes an unsavory
image (Artful Dodger) I wonder
if that's the kind of art I was
making all along, clever and evasive,
like framing the question in lines
that fit too easily into what appears
to be a poem, as if to write it
that way were enough, when what
it needed was philosophy, the love
of wisdom (Where is love?) and something
behind the words when emptiness begins
to pass as profundity, to fill up
the heart when a dearth of energy
starts to pass as openness to life

and I'm running on nerves alone
and I think that's "romantic," compounding
the vulgar interest in a cheap facade

there is language behind whose clarity
stands the masterpiece that Malevich
never got around to painting   and
there is the rococo church behind
which is all the alcohol and caffeine
of the past ten years

Old man, look at my life
thirty-five and still alive   apart
from that we're more alike
every time I look   I'm
learning that the edge of night
is not the brink the starved
coyote tumbles from in his compulsive
hunt for an elusive fowl
in Saturday cartoons   nor do
I want to think the night so huge
as to resemble those sheer canyons
down which the coyote falls
to splatter with a sound
unheard by the above-it-all
observer, who notes how insignificant
such pain and disappointment seem
in this vast landscape   I want
to see the night as where the glow
thrown out by the campfire stops
and see the light as gravity
drawing the annoying creatures
of the wood as near its heart
as they can bear   where
absence is a hole chewed in a garment
by the ones we find it inconvenient
to have around   and every feeling
from exhilaration to a sense
of loss begins with intimations
that the borders which define the homely
and the unfamiliar always fray
the way that constellations draw the eye
to where the light has punched
its way into the squares of darkness
outside the windows of a lighted room

October

for Duncan Hannah

An afternoon of steady light
That clears the air, and clearly shows
Each imperfection in the skin,
Each gap within the ragged rows

Of stalks and dusty gleanings left
When crops were harvested and sent
To cities where the people shop
For seasoning, for nourishment.

As though lit from within, the strips
Of earth across the gentle hill
Glow with the fiery colors of
The dying leaves, or, fiercer still,

Are shadowed by the sleeping vines
That stiffly curl and seem to die,
And on a cart, someone to watch
The empty fields, the empty sky.

Dear heart, wish you or I were here or there . . .
No. That's not true.
I wish I knew that you
were happy now, and sure at last
of being loved. I loved
our long talks late at night
when all the others were in bed. We'd fight
about the war and Watergate, and sip
Virginia Gentleman (one was your limit).
Your image doesn't dim; it
resonates through all my life.
So many times I've wanted
to call you up or walk downstairs
to your domain, the basement
with its toolbench and pine-paneled
walls, you in a dark mood slouching
over your ham radio, to coax you
back into the light, make you laugh.
Above my desk I have the photograph
of you kneeling beside me in the garden
that the wood absorbed. I'm two and nervous
in the little plastic pool. You're
having a good time with your Number One Son,
smiling more broadly than I can recall
outside of snapshots, though I can remember all
your other faces: stolid in the pew
at church, sublime intentness of a natural
engineer at your electric saw, or soldering
a new attachment to the jerrybuilt
shortwave, red with fury
over being baited or some imaginary
provocation, but mostly
when someone didn't listen.

I see your face the times I wasn't there,
as well: weeping to me on the phone
about the total failure of your life
for a good two hours (I couldn't
decide if you were going bonkers or having
a Pascal-like moment of clear light),
or how you looked the night
of your attack, feeling it come
over you as Ted Koppel asked pithy questions
on the little screen, unable to call out
in answer or for help. I've learned
the difference between a silence
and an absence since your quick
departure. There's no "where"
there, wherever you are. When I talk
to you these days, I end up trying
to convince myself that I'm pretending,
and failing to. It makes me think of you
tapping out a signal like a blind man
on your Morse code key, to strangers
who could understand the special
language that you used, projecting it
along a wire from underground
into the air, into the world.

GERRIT, BAGEL AND

The revolution started here
the night that Judy Garland died,
and Lou Reed used to live upstairs.
Now all that's changed. I'm tired and tied

to quotes from both our histories
provoked by places that we pass
en route to movies, meals with friends
and denouement downstream. Alas,

our manuscripta gather dust
with youthful promise, youthful pouts
we used to mask the case of nerves
behind the looks that knocked them out.

But old? Nay, young, now that we've stopped
believing in our favorite lies.
Ahead, the bright uncanny blue
we saw tonight in Cadmus' eyes.

HERE COMES THE BRIDE

Ironweed, beggarweed, joe pye weed,
the Huck-Finn-threading-his-raft-among-the-stiffs-
and-driftwood feeling that a fellow gets
slapping with his paddle at the silt
and the gaseous muck he slogs through on the trek
to land. Then a cloud moves.
All those purple flowers that the streak
of purple on the endless-shades-of-green
shore signified from a midafternoon
midriver point of view become a hundred
sheaves of light. I learned their names from a book
that someone gave me in another world,
the one I came from, where adrenalin
runs like a river through the jittery day.
I've come out of the current like a girl
who thinks it's time to change
her name to something simpler, and is looking
for a way. They say folks out here work
while the light lasts, the light that outlasts them.
It's hard to tell what time it is this time
of day; these parts don't change until the sun
breaks through and bathes the river in the gentlest
glow I know. I've been there.
I'm wedded to the notion of a living
and a life awash in it, a series of tableaus
as self-contained as frames of film
where change comes imperceptibly. "That field
was carpeted in purple just a week ago;
now it's all gone to seed." When I was single,
I had the most insane adventures.
Now that I'm married, I've nothing

but the path in front of me, the wide one
to the house with the big front porch
whose light will go on in a little while.

DESTALINIZE THE SKY

Somebody up there is brooding. I think
it's Joseph Stalin, who winks

as he calls us his chickens. But
he's wrong, dead wrong. What

he thinks, he wants to be making
my urgent business. But I'm taking

the day off, starting now. Here
I'm in the shadows, see shadows as I peer

across the block of space lit
evenly, despite the beams crisscrossing it

and paved with a dark mass of metal: cars.
In Rudy's photos, short men with cigars

crisscrossed here once, bright smears
of ash across an open shutter. It's been years

since they were in the space I fill
today, although their frozen image will

persist like dead Antarctic travelers, as long
as things stay cool. Joe Stalin's strong

and monolithic visage could freeze blood,
and frosty plasma with which helicopters flood

the settings of major catastrophes—
blood in a bag, for ease

of transport, like the pond
inside my veins, directed by a fond

and strangely burly heart along the freeways,
garden paths, and St. Lawrence Seaways

whose traffic cops and traffic don't intrude
beyond the bristling borders of the rude

dictatorship enclosed within a bag of skin,
for all of its protective systems, wearing thin

and itching sometimes to admit the outer
world, unlace the sack and let the shouter

with the shopping bags, the Negro teen, the gay
clerk/typist in. But there's no way

to do it. Just keep pointing
and calling names. Joe Stalin is anointing

a successor like one chooses words,
carefully, as though it matters. Birds

skid like afterthoughts down planes
geometricians dream. The brain's

deep thoughts are worms beneath a rock.
The rock's the thing metaphysicians talk

about, the flip side of the sky's cheery
monolithic blue. Joe Stalin's weary

as he fills his coffee cup,
overturns the rock, and makes us up.

MORAL IMAGINATION

Dark puddles
turn to ice
and the insect-
shaped machines
dig out the basement
of the Loew's State Theatre
memorial construction site.
So many days the graceful
columns of its faux-
Greek-temple fourth-
through-fourteenth-floor
facade would punctuate
my work. I'd punctuate
a sentence, then gaze
beneath the perfect ovals
that the ad hoc flock
of pigeons traced
above Times Square, through air
that had replaced the ovals
cannonading from the Camel
cigarette signboard of old,
to warm brown stone. I thought
the way I made a sentence
and the way the colonnade
defined the space above marquees
and burger dives were congruent
occupations, classic forms
imposed upon the chaos
of images from dreams and traffic.
There were headlines, and then
there were the people making them.

There were bylines. One of them
was mine. There were parts
of speech as if the flow
of life churned up and acted
out within my sightlines
could be chopped up into act
and actor; as if the actors
eking out a living as the extras
in the story I perceived
as writing or as being written
in another sphere showed up
in their real lives to cash
the pittance of a check
that I allowed them as their due;
or as if life really "flowed"
at all, like lava from an old
volcano, that chugs to life
in a national park when the trails
are clogged with tourists
for whom the sudden transformation
from dream vacation to dinosaur
movie gives a new twist
to what "force of nature" means;
the words, I mean. For things
themselves possess no meaning,
needing none. By opening
the lens, one turns them
into language. There are shadows
darkening behind the buildings
whose no-nonsense facades
were blocked by other buildings
which have been torn down.
There are dark and shiny towers

in the future of this space.
A story is aching to be written
about the people who will fill
them up; what they'll wear,
and whether they will feel
the same perplexed exhilaration
looking out across the new frontiers
of space defined by acts and objects
as one does; as I do.
Their possibilities are a machine
that makes the day an ocean
not a river. Somewhere
out there is a wave
of smoke from a volcano
leveling the Douglas firs
and speeding down the valley
toward the delighted scientist.
This is a beach, the junction
of two elements. My choice
is less how to perceive it
than whether to jump in
with resolution—the kind
that makes an artist pick up
his tools, not the kind
that tells him when to stop.
It comes together
in the electric pulse
across the spaces in the brains
whose structures are enough the same
for language to embrace them
with a word. You hear it once,
and from then on you use it
as a way of seeing, and of making

others see. But there is another
way of knowing. I was walking
down a street in Paris, thinking of
the Costa Rican girl with whom
I was in love when I last walked
along that street, in '74.
Then I thought about our friend
the novelist. He had a special
fondness for the girl. When she
and I broke up later that year,
he found her an apartment
in the Village. With my head
full of memories, I turned
a corner, and there was
the novelist, who greeted me
with warmth, then asked about
the girl. I hadn't thought
of him, or of her, for a long time,
until the very moment when I met him
on the Paris street. I believe
there are no accidents. But
I believe as well intentionality
in its most drastic sense
resides outside the human heart
and that the process of adjusting
the lenses is a less important
occupation than the willingness
to live inside a work of art
as part of it, without a clue
to what it looks like, or
will look like, but for moments
like the one Paris,
when the patterns conk you

on the head. They punctuate
the flaccid hours like the formal
columns of a building
surrounded by an insane mob;
and stay to light the darkness
of the waves that stain
the beach like smoke
the way the colonnade
that lingers in the memory
imposes order even after
it's torn down, because
it once was there. I
was there, too. In a way,
I'll always be there,
and be here, too, inside
the big picture. A little man
is fuming as he tries
to make sense of his life.
Smoke puffs out of his ears
in perfect ovals. But
I'm not he. The greatest
story ever told is being
written as I write
and as you read, and you
and I are part of it.

AWASH IN ANGELS

America, I've given you All
and now I'm Ivory Snow.
Hie me down to the Marilyn Chambers:
dim rooms papered with iconic stills
from MM films. A multiple-use space:
former convent, former pied-à-terre
of famous quints, ex-crash pad. Now
a soon-to-be-accredited academy
in which new-fangled nuns instruct
their postulants in MM lore. Math:
how many Kennedys go into Marilyn?
Music: moebius tape loop of breathy
"Happy Birthday Mr. Prez" at MSG.
Szechuan food (*her* fave)
for lunch. Then on to the seminar
in MM synchronicities. Ever notice
(and here Sister Bunny smirks) how
the titles of her movies never failed
to mirror what her real-life issues
were at any point? *How to Marry
a Millionaire*: meets DiMaggio.
The Seven Year Itch: seven years
since screen debut. *Some Like It
Hot*: acme of goddess function,
the largest quantity of body heat
generated among men and boys in any
year of reign. *The Misfits*:
replay math class. Birth and death
bound a closed system, a post-conciliar
version of scholastic thought. We dig deeper
as the focus narrows, until the laser

generated by our concentration
is strong enough to slice through steel.
Remember James Bond, tied down
and spread-eagled as the white-
hot beam headed northward
from a point between his thighs?
The thongs that bound him
and the flipflop thongs
kicked under MM's bed
left the same welt, which
in another language
means "the world."

FAN MAIL FROM SOME FLOUNDER

Alberta
Hunter sings "Two cigarettes
in the dark" in the light
of midday mid-March window
on Times Square, where manifold
and ruminating centers
of semi-consciousness
wend along crisscrossing
vectors through the hubs
of transit. In this mess,
Alberta's voice is a center
of gravity, as irretrievable
in time as that furred Negress
leaving Xanadu appears in space.
Above her head, the stare
of culture hero billboards:
actor from the planet Vulcan
selling VCRs, semi-nude
ex-athlete selling BVDs.
Marketing's as seasonal
as this my planet, meaning
images, like Presidents, can serve
for just so long. So long,
old friends. You're part
of history now, the name
I give the condo complex
in my heart where you still live.
Alberta's voice sings there,
inside the Cookery. There
Duff's is packed with artists:
Kenward, Steven, John
and David, Edwin, Rudy, Joe,

Ned casting pearls, Ed
gossiping, my thirtieth birthday
party packed with former
lovers, surrounded
by those mammoth Broadway
poster frames and green
glass lampshades.
The blue glow there
is cast by much-loved
moments from TV: Bullwinkle
and Rocky in a rowboat or sailing
through the sky with Captain Peter
"Wrongway" Peachfuzz on a pile
of Upsadaisium, my element of choice.
And there, a blurred succession
of Miss Rheingolds rules—how
nerve-wracking it was to wonder
which contestant would be crowned!
Fragments of a day, blown away
like trash by updrafts.
I'm here to catch and spangle
my heart with them, like strips
of Mylar on a pantry wall.
My boundaries enclose them
as my chest encloses air
I breathe while sleeping,
while love and culture sleep
within my breast. A nest
of memories: acuity
of this face, that face
with whom I shared my space
and time, shadowed by the glow
of cigarettes to light the darkness
in all the bedrooms, billboards
or little screens of long ago.

RETROVIR

Turn
back oh man
and see how where you've come from
looks from here: the light-
filled leak of sunrise, drone
of morning's clarity and fleeting sense
of firm direction, lunch with wine,
siesta and the afternoon you're part of.
Here the sky is always blue
and white, the colors of the pills
that poison you while they extend your life,
inoculating you with time
that draws you back with fingers
curved around the bowstring.
You are not the target, you're the arrow
and the dirty wind that hits
your face on summer streets these
too-long evenings means you're moving
faster than you know, a shrill
projectile through the neutral air
above a world war, headed for the flesh
of someone's notion of croquet
at twilight on the lawn. The thickening
damp crowds out the light, as green
of grass and fountain separates
to blue and white.

NEW HAVEN AND MANHATTAN

1988-1990

THE CERTITUDE OF NIGHT

November street in a small
New England city: views
of double decker houses,
old cars, leaf-choked postage-
stamp front yards. Of all
these, which are clues?

The cold wind scatters
refuse as ebullient and foul-
mouthed children in the street
scatter as a car bears down
upon their game, which matters
not to the preoccupied and owl-

ish driver, a Puerto Rican
in a big sedan. A ball
bounces down a gutter, propelled
by a sharp gust the people
of archaic cultures might have called
the breath of gods. No way we can

buy that dream, though ours
are equally fictitious: a pot of
gold from Lotto, books that readers
will remember years from now, a love
so perfect that the thought of
it makes grown men weep. Flowers

in a window on a frozen street
make a spot of color, red ray
from a sunset past the houses
makes a spot of light. Don't say
anything that stirs the heart
resides there, anything you meet

in dreams. Mothers open doors
to step into the cold and call
their children home. The gray
and drab block darkens. Say
the certitude of night is all,
when all's arranged, that's truly yours.

COME IN FROM THE RAIN

Stick that bumbershoot
in elephant's-foot

brolly stand behind
the big door. Mind

your manners at High Tea.
Hi, you. High ve-

locity hailstones cream
passersby beyond the panes. I dream

of Jeannie, starring Bar-
bara Eden, of Eden, star-

ring Eve and Adam, of Adam
Cartwright, a.k.a. the let-'em-

have-it-with-all-candor
Trapper John. Pander

to the mass-man mass-taste,
that's my motto. Waste

the day, the life, the villain
with depression, fill-in-

the-wrong-blanks misap-
prehension, dum-dums. Nap

an hour through the Buddy
Ebsen as a perspicacious fuddy-

duddy whodunit. Then produce
the silver teapot, loose

Earl Grey and table water
slabs. Somebody's daughter

carries on the grand tradition
in the grandma manner. Wishin'

you were here don't place you
in the old wing chair. Face you

in the photos, china, art
on parlor walls. It's raining in my heart.

NO VOICE

No voice left except
a small still youthful
and persistent whisper
you wake up straining
to hear, which the street
whose shriek drowns out
the traffic of the heart
can't muffle. It hangs
like smoky songs in winter:
"I'm the Sheik of Araby."
On now-chic Avenue A,
you're on the B List:
broke. bombed. bewildered.
Boys come and go, become the men
with gray suits, farther
from your boastful arms
than the places where
they moved: Park Slope,
Upper West Side . . . "Death",
you'd sniff. But you're the one
who's dying. You made pissing away
your gifts look like an art form,
but striking a profile
with your arm akimbo
on the moving sidewalk headed
toward the precipice cheapens
every death, not just your own.
I think of J.J., with you
the only person I could be sure
of finding in the Anvil when
I made my entrance at 7 a.m.

on a Sunday in the years before
the dockstrip turned unstylish;
high on drugs as you for art-world
generations, he got sober
only to lose a lover then his own
life to AIDS. He faced
the unavoidable with grace
and brilliant humor of a sort
you once were capable of showing.
I'm grieved that he's a shade now,
but furious that you're a shadow
hurtling through your dying
at the speed of crack
while accusing everyone else
of making it tough for you to be
both happy and a baby at age 43.
There are beautiful things
you've destroyed: poems, paintings,
friendships and great loves. But
your magnum opus is the demolition
of yourself: beaten dough
of your cheeks, unwashed hair,
smelly clothes, junkie
malnutrition written into
every cell. Connoisseur, observe:
that self-absorption and gray
beard don't make you Whitman.
You're acting like a houseguest
kicked out by your life
as if your life were some rich painter
who thought you were delightful
once, but got fed up.
Any fantasy that puts you

on the streets is useful
when your veins are full of
shit. But when you lift
the lid beneath your chatter
and the stench of nothing
that your wit can comprehend
surrounds your wrist like manacles,
listen to the voice
that whispers when your own
gives out. It's telling you
that not even in death
do you have power
to make the wreckage of your life
less than your very own.
Scarecrow, genius, major
minor artist and the keenest
critic of your brief
excruciating day: it's no faux pas
to want to stay.

THE TRAPS

We covered them with boughs,
with bows and raucous
mock-respectful hooting luring boys
from other older gangs to tear
down coiling paths to tear us
limb from limb in the wood
unsuspecting of the snare until
a sneaker hit the artful disarray
of brush and disappeared
into a hole we'd dug,
leveling the lug

who chased us. And we raised
fortresses of woven boughs
(*Boys' Life* showed us how)
conducting war with sticks
as swords to music of a trap
drum, borrowed from the set
of a brother in a band. We
traipsed in bands, constricting
brows at snaps of twigs
beyond our walls—a sneak
attack by big kids? Then a squawk
and curse as some miffed birder
tripped into a trap, cried Murder,
threatened us with cops and jail.
We turned tail

and fled, half-blind from tears
of glee at his fat plight.
What right had he to flail
through brush into our wild place,
anyway? He was a larger
version of the larger boys
we teased and would become.
No fort could keep our fierce
delight from thickening
into the darkness of the men
who called us home
at dusk, who shoveled
sand into our pitfalls,
who read the paper in upholstered chairs.
Skirting our own traps, we walked
into theirs.

WEST 22ND STREET

Lapsang souchong

the favorite tea

of David Kalstone

has a *purple* taste

on a winter day

in 1976

in a parlor crammed

with books

one of which

(*Women of the Shadows*)

I'll never return

ASH WEDNESDAY

Raisin bran, not pancakes,
for Fat Tuesday breakfast.
Then wish kneejerk Alleluias
Happy Trails. It's time

for packing up the glad rags,
peeling Magic Tape off backs
of Christmas cards left dangling
on the doorframe past their prime

and burning strings from last year's
palms in the pantry
sink, the cracked spears
yielded to the sacristan for ash

to be smeared on foreheads
of a mob in cruciform, the logo
of a fierce imperial army
branded on their brows. Quick flash:

nuns with smudges in the Irish
slums, penitents in sack
at the cathedral door,
red-faced sissy in the public school

in shirt of candy-
stripes with fruit loop yanked
by hoods, embarrassed that his secret
piety and far more secret wish for cool

behavior have converged. Here's mud
in your eye and you forgot to wash
your face. Hold back: you can't
take on the world. Deep breath,

and give it up for Lent,
turn it over, like the 45s
with giant holes whose flip-sides
soothed when hit songs played to death

lost their fizz. The background
music of a life, indelible
and unremarkable as breakfast food.
There's a trip to take, whose sights

invigorate the more they drop away.
Dust accumulating on its own
is different from dust on furniture.
To see, turn off the lights.

PALMER

The words are less important than the wood
The journey less substantial than the ground
The feelings and the flights from feeling
As transitory as the snow
That keeps the ground from breathing
That saves the ground until the time
Of breath in light

The light is coming up behind the mountain
Gray and white as clouds and chimney smoke
Across the thick pond and the patchy snow
Of late March in Vermont

And grass across the graves as tangled
As the hair of a derelict and thick with frost
Flashes in the morning to the groan
Of buckling ice, sharp and impersonal
As noises of a dead man
When the useless air inside him
Leaks out to rejoin the atmosphere
That freezes on my upper lip
And makes me grateful

To gulp the only substance
Connecting me with all that lives
Brushing all flesh
And howling in my face now
From the gap between the peaks
The sine curve of the strip
Of birches on the brow
Through which a shadow passes

Like the pools of dark that
Cross my heart

I've traveled a long way
For these souvenirs of holy days
Gleaned from fields the harvesters
Have swept with fine-toothed combs
Leaving for the poor the useless
The stalk, the husk, the crumpled leaf

Changing them from mulch
Into a pilgrim's flag
In a culture where a rind
Signifies that one has eaten
Of the fruit of the tree
Of the knowledge that the knowledge
Of good and evil is someplace else
Someplace one would go if one knew how
To get beyond the mountains
That block the path as they delay
The sunrise and obscure the light
The way unpleasant facts
Prevent even a wanderer
From being king of his own life
By throwing up a story in his face
Like faces in a drive-in movie
When the Rambler's parked too close
To the enormous screen

One desires refreshment in the dizzy
Primitive perception that the only things
That matter are the ones you'll never see
So you start to walk
And end up dozens or a hundred

Units of your culture's measurement
Of space away, dozens
Or a hundred units of your planet's
Measurement of time from when
You first set out, having found
A world replete with everything
But what you sought

It would be an easy thing
To loosen the adrenalin and stride
Down city sidewalks drunken
On engaging scenes, delighting in
A world that howls into your face
As long as you keep moving

But that would be like drinking a mirage
To slake a thirst the depth
Of which has grown beyond your body
In the time it took
To get from Go to the impasse
Where the world and you stand now
Cross my palm

With silver shot with light
Intensely as the ice on knotted grass
And I will tell a fortunate a fortune
That rises in the crystal like a point
Of sun across a heaving pond

One day you'll be on the road
And suddenly the things that fill
Your field of vision will be of a piece:
A seamless whole you're part of

Like a perfect wave that breaks
All the way down the continent,
One you can ride for weeks while standing
In the same position on your surfboard
Until you'd swear that you're not moving

Nothing changes but the light
And the certainty some jetty
Down the line will spoil the fun
Which widens to a pool
Of disappointment that a thrill
Could be so simple
And might never stop

Then you blink and you're back
In the mud room in your duck shoes
And the polished wood you stood on
Has widened to a thick scuffed floor
For a moment, words
Grabbed you by the hair and dragged you
Outside of the place you breathe
But words are less important than the wood
That corrugates the mountain and the ground
Above the snow like lines that
Cross your brow

The tracks of early episodes
The way the scars across a skating pond
Are evidence of long-gone parties
Where feelings may have raged
Between a high school boy from Weston
And his steady girl, a 4H honcho
From another town

The choked ice yields
Its evidence like tablets
Thrust from a long-forgotten tomb
By a string of earthquakes
To which the international relief
Community responds with tons of wheat
And lap robes like the one beneath which
Lovers in a sleigh can bundle
A furtive episode that turns
Into a paradigm for greeting cards
So distant from the way it felt
The setting is unrecognizable
On later visits

It's not the hearts that generations
Of blades have etched upon recurring layers
Of ice that matter, it's what lies beneath
The groaning of the frozen water
Or a dead or dying man that holds them up
And paves the surface for a set
Of arabesques a pilgrim
By constitution tries to turn
Into the weight of elements
That populate the narrative
He needs to keep him moving
To keep the feelings tamped down
In an atmosphere where crystal ice
Forms sun dogs, minor lights
Refracted through a cold
So thick the air's gelatinous

To save the feelings for the time
When breath and light are synonyms
And blare of bright diversities
And yarns of high adventure on the road
Break off as palmers try
To listen for awhile
To a language that can tell them
Anything except a story
And never move a hair as it takes them
Everywhere they've walked, then sets them down
To float upon the emptiness that buoys
The wood   the ground   the air
And all the light

ORDINARY TIME

Which are the magic
moments in ordinary
time? All of them,
for those who can see.
That is what redemption
means, I decide
at the meeting. Then
walk with David wearing
his new Yale T-shirt
and new long hair to 103.
Leonard and Eileen come, too.
Leonard wears a shark's tooth
on a chain around his neck
and long blond hair.
These days he's the manager
of Boots and Saddles ("Bras
and Girdles," my beloved
Bobby used to say) and
costumer for the Gay Cable
Network's *Dating Game*.
One week the announcer is
a rhinestone cowboy, sequin
shirt and black fur chaps,
the next a leatherman, etc.
Eileen's crewcut makes
her face light up.
Underneath our hairstyles,
23 years of sobriety, all told—
the age of a girl who's "not
so young but not so very old,"
wrote Berryman, who flew
from his recovery with the force

of a poet hitting bottom.
It's not the way I choose
to go out of this restaurant
or day today, and I
have a choice. Wanda
the comedian comes over
to our table. "Call me
wicked Wanda," she smirks
when we're introduced.
Why is New York City
awash in stand-up comics
at the least funny point
in its history? Still,
some things stay the same.
People wonder what the people
in their buildings would think
if the ones who are wondering
became incredibly famous,
as famous as Madonna.
Debby Harry lived in Eileen's
building in the Village
in the early seventies, and she
was just the shy girl
in the band upstairs.
Poets read the writing
of their friends, and
are happy when they like it
thoroughly, when the work's
that good and the crippling
sense of competition stays away.
Trips get planned: David
home to California, Eileen
to New Mexico, Chris and I
to France and Spain, on vectors

which will spread out
from a single point, like ribs
of an umbrella. Then
after the comfort of a wedge
of blueberry peach pie and cup
of Decaf, sober friends
thread separate ways home
through the maze of blankets
on the sidewalk covered with
the scraps of someone else's life.
Mine consists of understanding
that the magic isn't something
that I make, but something
that shines through the things
I make and do and say
the way a brooch or scrap of fabric
shines from the detritus
to catch Leonard's eye
and be of use for costumes,
when I am fearless and thorough
enough to give it room,
all the room there is in ordinary
time, which embraces all
the people and events and hopes
that choke the street tonight
and still leaves room for everyone
and everything and every
other place, the undescribed
and indescribable, more various
and cacophonous than voice
can tell or mind conceive,
and for the sky's vast depths
from which they're all
a speck of light.

EROSION

All the things I hear
this morning I'll write down.
All the things I learned
last night I'll make a list
recounting. Counting
dark spots on the skin, dark
moods, *Dark Victory* (Miss
Davis as a proto-PWA), dark
light through the crystal
on the drawstring of the blind
that overlooks the tangled garden.
Choose to see it either way,
Louise Hay / Gabby Hayes.
Tarnation, Roy, that horse
is dead. Stop beating
(not my heart), stop waiting,
stop being so dark, think
positive! I choose
the Black Madonna, the weeping
Christ of the Petit Palais,
the unforgettable canard
at the only decent restaurant
in Arles that's open
on a Monday night. No light,
no path, no crystal
on my shade: I dreamed
them up. No day
unless I'm part of it, unless
my stories of the days
I've passed through pass
like rain down mountainsides,

appropriating all that glitters.
What I write's erosion
of a time, what I claim as mine
is gravel on the corniche road,
chips off an old block
to which I have no claim
except that I was there
the moment that they skidded
down the cliff, and lay
where the trucks pass, where
the tourists go. I saw them,
and I told you so.

ET IN ARCADIA EGO

Lo I the man, once masked in widower's weeds
with bloat, blood and adrenalin engorged
now stumble down a grassy ambleway
where ticks adhere to motions that I forged

in smithies of desire, furnace of lust,
and cool plunge of companionship to harden
and shape a goodly form, tempered and quite
as useless as a cocktail in the garden

as organizing principle for strolls
into the foliage horizontal eyes
scan for a human form behind the brush.
Within the brush, a slew of moustached guys

perspired once like a forest dripping sap
from every limb each summer, thick to burn
away like fever, boil away like rain
in sickly jungles. Flowers that I learned

the names of, nectar and deliriant,
too late to stem the growth and prune the bine,
lace memories with tendrils that have choked
vanishing nature, vanished friends of mine.

FRIENDS SERVICE

Does light
emerge or gently
blast, as in smut,
as in thrown-off
heat, to merge
with molecules,
to gently scrape
the painted surface
with pure energy
impressive for its
silence as much
as for its skid
delineated by
the dust this
side of leaded panes,
light that floats
inside a voice
like motes
across a beam
intruding from
the outer world
in an exercise
the strength of which
depends on sitting
still, on listening
for rays suffusing
deeper than the heart-
less heartbreaking
world of romance or
of nature, a spot
that throbs with

revelation independent
of what anybody thinks
or has to have to say
keeping speech at bay
like dogs until it
starts to glow, grows
irresistible? Hold
back the words
until they turn
to light.

SIGNS OF MADNESS

Recognizing strings
of coincidence as having
baleful or hermetic meaning,
e.g. the fact that each
of Ronald Wilson
Reagan's three names has
six letters, Mark of
the Apocalyptic Beast,
languorous and toothless
though it would have to be
to fit that application.
Smelling burning flesh
or sulfur, or a sweet
antibiotic sweat that
leaches into sheets
and pillows, like the smell
my mother had when she was
dying, or the one I suddenly
developed in the weeks before
I came down with AIDS.
Muttering at motorists
in other cars, hearing
one's own voice pronounce
unspoken imprecation.
Wanting to impose Islamic
law for lapses of behavior
or taste within the city limits.
Limiting one's television
fare to programs one recalls
from childhood. Wanting
to call childhood friends

and ask them how they're doing,
how their lives have changed
since junior high. Memorizing
names of senators, bishops
of the church, or nominees for
Vice President from major
parties, and reciting them
at night to get to sleep.
Listing signs that all
may be no more right
in one's mind than is right
in the world, and feeling
less anxiety from identifying
symptoms in one's thinking and
behavior than comfort
in the list's existence
and delight at having
called it forth.

ALL SOULS DAY

Faithful depart in swarms, like holiday
Or weekend mobs that throng the underground
Republic of commuters, on their way
Against the odds to someplace nicer. Round
My hospital bed, rosebuds, and beyond
Yellow hibiscus on the windowsill,
Gauze crisscrosses blue sky. Is it a fond
Evasion to imagine that we will
Relax into a gently-lit eclipse
So porous and expansive it derails
Time like a train, absorbing dark details
Life's action-painter imitation drips
Each second on each soul that aches to be
Revived, restored, on all souls? Probably.

PARABLE

(after Mark 4: 11-12)

Within the yarn, a needle
has been hidden. That's
the point, whatever message
one can find behind the words.
That dishwater contains
shards of a crystal tumbler
might be more important
than submerged utensils' function
at meals or as metaphor,
at least to the humming hausfrau,
one of the domestic types
who populate this sort of narrative.
She's wearing yellow Living Gloves
that reach up to her elbows.
Their deep cuffs are a pleasure.
It's a good clean feeling
to plunge one's hands
into those great white suds,
but what one grasps may be
no fruit plate, but the sharp
and sinking insight that within
the homeliest arrangements
lurks a secret that can change
one's life or cause
real pain. You see
the cut and hear the scream,
but don't perceive or understand
and aren't supposed to,
lest you be forgiven.

POWERLESS

I was a mess. I felt like crying
all the time. No matter what
I said, how charming I would try
to be, my friends, old friends
I thought I could depend on,
looked at me like I was crazy
or depraved. They were the ones
I'd called for years on mornings
after blackouts I perceived
as rip-roaring adventures.
"What happened? Was I too
outrageous?" These days
the answer was obviously yes, but
I was powerless to stop. I didn't know
the drinking was the cause; I thought
it was the upshot of the sad
departure of my looks and mind and hope
and friends and gifts and sense
that anything could ever feel other
than stripped of joy and dropped
into the sea in concrete overshoes again.
I was dying, lying
in a bed I couldn't even lure
a hustler into, in a rock-and-roll
motel on Santa Monica
where Madness partied all night
by the pool, and Tom Waits
used to live, a place I thought was cool
to say I stayed at, though I didn't
feel so hot when I awoke
to light that made me want
to vomit, reaching for the Bud
I'd passed out next to, thinking
that if I could choke down last night's

beer it was a form of completion
at a time when I could never finish
anything, and couldn't even
step back from the panic anymore
with a drink to make me think
my pain was my participation
in the life of poetry I'd chosen.
I wanted to be stoic at the lot
I'd drawn by being such an artist.
I wanted to be captain of my soul,
but I was out of control at the helm
of a scow I'd steered into the rocks,
horrified to watch its cargo
of self-involved self-pity
poison the environment I loved.
I couldn't stop the dark
from spreading, couldn't plug the leaks,
couldn't scrub the filth away, and
it was all my fault.
Then something odd happened.
I woke up in my motel room
in the middle of the night.
No one else was there,
but I had the strongest sense
that somebody was with me,
sitting on the bed, in fact.
It was as if my hand were being
held. I thought of that old film
The Haunting, where something
similar happens to Julie Harris.
But this wasn't scary. I lay there
and felt myself surrounded by the presence
of the gentlest, most compassionate
and loving—person? I'm not sure—
that I had ever known. There was

no hand that I could see, but
I clung to it. There was no voice
as such, and yet I clearly heard the words,
"Everything will be all right." I wondered
if this could be a visit from the Virgin Mary,
the kind I always wanted as a kid.
I was surprised how calm
and undramatic it all was.
I let the love wash over me
until I fell asleep again.
The next day was Mother's Day.
I made a call and went to my first
meeting a few blocks away. I'd been wondering
where all the healthy, handsome people
in West Hollywood had disappeared to.
I found out. An old guy
with a shaven head and twenty years
spoke first. He said, "I say
two prayers each morning. The first
is 'Thank you.' The second is
'Don't let me fuck this up.'"
I say those prayers today.
These things took place five years ago.
I didn't dream them up
or make them happen.
I was powerless to change
the horror and the shame
that had infected my whole life.
I know that they were lifted
by the power of whatever
held my hand that night.
This is not about religion,
not about belief. I know what happened.
I was there; *it* was there.
Nothing can change that.

G-9

I'm at a double wake
in Springfield, for a childhood
friend and his father
who died years ago. I join
my aunt in the queue of mourners
and walk into a brown study,
a sepia room with books
and magazines. The father's
in a coffin; he looks exhumed,
the worse for wear. But where
my friend's remains should be
there's just the empty base
of an urn. Where are his ashes?
His mother hands me
a paper cup with pills:
leucovorin, Zovirax,
and AZT. "Henry
wanted you to have these,"
she sneers. "Take all
you want, for all the good
they'll do." "Dlugos.
Meester Dlugos." A lamp
snaps on. Raquel,
not Welch, the chubby
nurse, is standing by my bed.
It's 6 a.m., time to flush
the heplock and hook up
the I.V. line. False dawn
is changing into day, infusing
the sky above the Hudson
with a flush of light.
My roommate stirs

beyond the pinstriped curtain.
My first time here on G-9,
the AIDS ward, the cheery
D & D Building intentionality
of the decor made me feel
like jumping out a window.
I'd been lying on a gurney
in an E.R. corridor
for nineteen hours, next to
a psychotic druggie
with a voice like Abbie
Hoffman's. He was tied
up, or down, with strips
of cloth (he'd tried to slug
a nurse) and sent up
a grating adenoidal whine
all night. "Nurse . . . nurse . . .
untie me, *please* . . . these
rags have strange powers."
By the time they found
a bed for me, I was in
no mood to appreciate the clever
curtains in my room,
the same fabric exactly
as the drapes and sheets
of a P-town guest house
in which I once—partied? stayed?
All I can remember is
the pattern. Nor did it
help to have the biggest queen
on the nursing staff
clap his hands delightedly
and welcome me to AIDS-land.
I wanted to drop

dead immediately. That
was the low point. Today
these people are my friends,
in the process of restoring
me to life a second time.
I can walk and talk
and breathe simultaneously
now. I draw a breath
and sing "Happy Birthday"
to my roommate Joe.
He's 51 today. I didn't think
he'd make it. Three weeks
ago they told him that he had
aplastic anemia, and nothing
could be done. Joe had been
a rotten patient, moaning
operatically, throwing chairs
at nurses. When he got
the bad news, there was
a big change. He called
the relatives with whom
he had been disaffected,
was anointed and communicated
for the first time since the age
of eight when he was raped
by a priest, and made a will.
As death drew nearer, Joe
grew nicer, almost serene.
Then the anemia
began to disappear, not
because of medicines, but
on its own. Ready to die,
it looks like Joe has more
of life to go. He'll go

home soon. "When will *you*
get out of here?" he asks me.
I don't know; when the X-ray
shows no more pneumonia.
I've been here three weeks
this time. What have I
accomplished? Read some
Balzac, spent "quality
time" with friends, come back
from death's door, and
prayed, prayed a lot.
Barry Bragg, a former
lover of a former
lover and a new
Episcopalian, has AIDS too,
and gave me a leatherbound
and gold-trimmed copy of the Office,
the one with all the antiphons.
My list of daily intercessions
is as long as a Russian
novel. I pray about AIDS
last. Last week I made a list
of all my friends who've died
or who are living and infected.
Every day since, I've remembered
someone I forgot to list.
This morning it was Chasen
Gaver, the performance poet
from DC. I don't know
if he's still around. I liked
him and could never stand
his poetry, which made it
difficult to be a friend,
although I wanted to defend

him one excruciating night
at a Folio reading, where
Chasen snapped his fingers
and danced around spouting
frothy nonsense about Andy
Warhol to the rolling eyes
of self-important "language-
centered" poets, whose dismissive
attitude and ugly manners
were worse by far than anything
that Chasen ever wrote.
Charles was his real name;
a classmate at Antioch
dubbed him "Chasen," after
the restaurant, I guess.
Once I start remembering,
so much comes back.
There are forty-nine names
on my list of the dead,
thirty-two names of the sick.
Cookie Mueller changed
lists Saturday. They all
will, I guess, the living,
I mean, unless I go
before them, in which case
I may be on somebody's
list myself. It's hard
to imagine so many people
I love dying, but no harder
than to comprehend so many
already gone. My beloved
Bobby, maniac and boyfriend.
Barry reminded me that he
had sex with Bobby

on the coat pile at this Christmas
party, two years in a row.
That's the way our life
together used to be, a lot
of great adventures. Who'll
remember Bobby's stories
about driving in his debutante
date's father's white Mercedes
from hole to hole of the golf course
at the poshest country club
in Birmingham at 3 a.m.,
or taking off his clothes
in the redneck bar on a dare,
or working on *Stay Hungry*
as the dresser of a then-
unknown named Schwarzenegger.
Who will be around to anthologize
his purple cracker similes:
"Sweatin' like a nigger
on Election Day," "Hotter
than a half-fucked fox
in a forest fire." The ones
that I remember have to do
with heat, Bobby shirtless,
sweating on the dance floor
of the tiny bar in what is now
a shelter for the indigent
with AIDS on the dockstrip,
stripping shirts off Chuck Shaw,
Barry Bragg and me, rolling
up the torn rags, using them
as pom-poms, then bolting
off down West Street, gracefully
(despite the overwhelming

weight of his inebriation)
vaulting over trash cans
as he sang, "I like to be
in America" in a Puerto Rican
accent. When I pass,
who'll remember, who will care
about these joys and wonders?
I'm haunted by that more
than by the faces
of the dead and dying.
A speaker crackles near
my bed and nurses
streak down the corridor.
The black guy on the respirator
next door bought the farm,
Maria tells me later, but
only when I ask. She has tears
in her eyes. She'd known him
since his first day on G-9
a long time ago. Will I also
become a fond, fondly regarded
regular, back for stays
the way retired retiring
widowers return to the hotel
in Nova Scotia or Provence
where they vacationed with
their wives? I expect so, although
that's down the road; today's
enough to fill my plate. A bell
rings, like the gong that marks
the start of a fight. It's 10
and Derek's here to make
the bed, Derek who at 16
saw Bob Marley's funeral

in the football stadium
in Kingston, hot tears
pouring down his face.
He sings as he folds
linens, "You can fool
some of the people some
of the time," dancing
a little softshoe as he works.
There's a reason he came in
just now; *Divorce Court*
drones on Joe's TV, and
Derek is hooked. I can't
believe the script is plausible
to him, Jamaican hipster
that he is, but he stands
transfixed by the parade
of faithless wives and screwed-up
husbands. The judge is testy;
so am I, unwilling
auditor of drivel. Phone
my friends to block it out:
David, Jane and Eileen. I missed
the bash for David's magazine
on Monday and Eileen's reading
last night. Jane says that
Marie-Christine flew off
to Marseilles where her mother
has cancer of the brain,
reminding me that AIDS
is just a tiny fragment
of life's pain. Eileen has
been thinking about Bobby, too,
the dinner that we threw
when he returned to New York

after getting sick. Pencil-thin,
disfigured by KS, he held forth
with as much kinetic charm
as ever. What we have
to cherish is not only
what we can recall of how
things were before the plague,
but how we each responded
once it started. People
have been great to me.
An avalanche of love
has come my way
since I got sick, and not
just moral support.
Jaime's on the board
of PEN's new fund
for AIDS; he's helping out.
Don Windham slipped a check
inside a note, and Brad
Gooch got me something
from the Howard Brookner Fund.
Who'd have thought when we
dressed up in ladies'
clothes for a night for a hoot
in Brad ("June Buntt") and
Howard ("Lili La Lean")'s suite
at the Chelsea that things
would have turned out this way:
Howard dead at 35, Chris Cox
("Kay Sera Sera")'s friend Bill
gone too, "Bernadette of Lourdes"
(guess who) with AIDS,
God knows how many positive.
Those 14th Street wigs and enormous

stingers and Martinis don't
provoke nostalgia for a time
when love and death were less
inextricably linked, but
for the stories we would tell
the morning after, best
when they involved our friends,
second-best, our heroes.
J.J. Mitchell was a master
of the genre. When he learned
he had AIDS, I told him
he should write them down.
His mind went first. I'll tell you
one of his best. J.J. was
Jerome Robbins' houseguest
at Bridgehampton. Every morning
they would have a contest
to see who could finish
the *Times* crossword first.
Robbins always won, until
a day when he was clearly
baffled. Grumbling, scratching
over letters, he finally
threw his pen down. "J.J.,
tell me what I'm doing wrong."
One clue was "Great 20th-c.
choreographer." The solution
was "Massine," but Robbins
had placed his own name
in the space. Every word
around it had been changed
to try to make the puzzle
work, except that answer.
At this point there'd be

a horsey laugh from J.J.
—"Isn't that *great*?"
he'd say through clenched
teeth ("Locust Valley lockjaw").
It was, and there were lots
more where that one came from,
only you can't get there anymore.
He's dropped into the maw
waiting for the G-9
denizens and for all flesh,
as silent as the hearts
that beat upon the beds
up here: the heart of the drop-
dead beautiful East Village
kid who came in yesterday,
Charles Frost's heart nine inches
from the spleen they're taking
out tomorrow, the heart of
the demented girl whose screams
roll down the hallways
late at night, hearts that long
for lovers, for reprieve,
for old lives, for another chance.
My heart, so calm most days,
sinks like a brick
to think of all that heartache.
I've been staying sane with
program tools, turning everything
over to God "as I understand
him." I don't understand him.
Thank God I read so much
Calvin last spring; the absolute
necessity of blind obedience
to a sometimes comforting,

sometimes repellent, always
incomprehensible Source
of light and life stayed
with me. God can seem
so foreign, a parent
from another country,
like my Dad and his own
father speaking Polish
in the kitchen. I wouldn't
trust a father or a God
too much like me, though.
That is why I pack up all
my cares and woes, and load them
on the conveyor belt, the speed
of which I can't control, like
Chaplin on the assembly line
in *Modern Times* or Lucy on TV.
I don't need to run
machines today. I'm standing
on a moving sidewalk
headed for the dark
or light, whatever's there.
Duncan Hannah visits, and
we talk of out-of-body
experiences. His was
amazing. Bingeing on vodka
in his dorm at Bard, he woke
to see a naked boy
in fetal posture on the floor.
Was it a corpse, a classmate,
a pickup from the blackout
of the previous night? Duncan
didn't know. He struggled
out of bed, walked over

to the youth, and touched
his shoulder. The boy turned;
it was Duncan himself.
My own experience was
milder, didn't make me flee
screaming from the room
as Duncan did. It happened
on a Tibetan meditation
weekend at the Cowley Fathers'
house in Cambridge.
Michael Koonsman led it,
healer whose enormous paws
directed energy. He touched
my spine to straighten up
my posture, and I gasped
at the rush. We were chanting
to Tara, goddess of compassion
and peace, in the basement chapel
late at night. I felt myself
drawn upward, not levitating
physically, but still somehow
above my body. A sense
of bliss surrounded me.
It lasted ten or fifteen
minutes. When I came down,
my forehead hurt. The spot
where the "third eye" appears
in Buddhist art felt
as though someone had pushed
a pencil through it.
The soreness lasted for a week.
Michael wasn't surprised.
He did a lot of work
with people with AIDS

in the epidemic's early days,
but when he started losing
weight and having trouble
with a cough, he was filled
with denial. By the time
he checked into St. Luke's,
he was in dreadful shape.
The respirator down his throat
squelched the contagious
enthusiasm of his voice,
but he could still spell out
what he wanted to say
on a plastic Ouija board
beside his bed. When
the doctor who came in
to tell him the results
of his bronchoscopy said,
"Father, I'm afraid I have
bad news," Michael grabbed
the board and spelled,
"The truth is always
Good News." After he died,
I had a dream in which
I was a student in a class
that he was posthumously
teaching. With mock annoyance
he exclaimed, "Oh, Tim!
I can't believe you really think
that AIDS is a disease!"
There's evidence in that
direction, I'll tell him
if the dream recurs: the shiny
hamburger-in-lucite look
of the big lesion on my face;

the smaller ones I daub
with makeup; the loss
of forty pounds in a year;
the fatigue that comes on
at the least convenient times.
The symptoms float like algae
on the surface of the grace
that buoys me up today.
Arthur comes in with
the Sacrament, and we have
to leave the room (Joe's
Italian family has arrived
for birthday cheer) to find
some quiet. Walk out
to the breezeway, where
it might as well be
August for the stifling
heat. On Amsterdam,
pedestrians and drivers are
oblivious to our small aerie,
as we peer through the grille
like cloistered nuns. Since
leaving G-9 the first time,
I always slow my car down
on this block, and stare up
at this window, to the unit
where my life was saved.
It's strange how quickly
hospitals feel foreign
when you leave, and how normal
their conventions seem as soon
as you check in. From below,
it's like checking out the windows
of the West Street Jail; hard

to imagine what goes on there,
even if you know firsthand.
The sun is going down as I
receive communion. I wish
the rite's familiar magic
didn't dull my gratitude
for this enormous gift.
I wish I had a closer personal
relationship with Christ,
which I know sounds corny
and alarming. Janet Campbell
gave me a remarkable ikon
the last time I was here;
Christ is in a chair, a throne,
and St. John the Divine,
an androgyne who looks a bit
like Janet, rests his head
upon the Savior's shoulder.
James Madden, priest of Cowley,
dead of cancer earlier
this year at 39, gave her
the image, telling her not to
be afraid to imitate St. John.
There may come a time when
I'm unable to respond with words,
or works, or gratitude to AIDS;
a time when my attitude
caves in, when I'm as weak
as the men who lie across
the dayroom couches hour
after hour, watching sitcoms,
drawing blanks. Maybe
my head will be shaved
and scarred from surgery;

maybe I'll be pencil-
thin and paler than
a ghost, pale as the vesper
light outside my window now.
It would be good to know
that I could close my eyes
and lean my head back
on his shoulder then,
as natural and trusting
as I'd be with a cherished
love. At this moment,
Chris walks in, Christopher
Earl Wiss of Kansas City
and New York, my lover,
my last lover, my first
healthy and enduring relationship
in sobriety, the man
with whom I choose
to share what I have
left of life and time.
This is the hardest
and happiest moment
of the day. G-9
is no place to affirm
a relationship. Two hours
in a chair beside my bed
after eight hours of work
night after night for weeks
. . . it's been a long haul,
and Chris gets tired.
Last week he exploded,
"I hate this, I hate your
being sick and having AIDS
and lying in a hospital

where I can only see you
with a visitor's pass. I hate
that this is going to
get worse." I hate it,
too. We kiss, embrace,
and Chris climbs into bed
beside me, to air-mattress
squeaks. Hold on. We hold on
to each other, to a hope
of how we'll be when I get out.
Let him hold on, please
don't let him lose his
willingness to stick with me,
to make love and to make
love work, to extend
the happiness we've shared.
Please don't let AIDS
make me a monster
or a burden is my prayer.
Too soon, Chris has to leave.
I walk him to the elevator
bank, then totter back
so Raquel can open my I.V.
again. It's not even
mid-evening, but I'm nodding
off. My life's so full, even
(especially?) when I'm here
on G-9. When it's time
to move on to the next step,
that will be a great adventure,
too. Helena Hughes, Tibetan
Buddhist, tells me that
there are three stages in death.
The first is white, like passing

through a thick but porous wall.
The second stage is red;
the third is black, and then
you're finished, ready
for the next event. I'm glad
she has a road map, but I don't
feel the need for one myself.
I've trust enough in all
that's happened in my life,
the unexpected love
and gentleness that rushes in
to fill the arid spaces
in my heart, the way the city
glow fills up the sky
above the river, making it
seem less than night. When
Joe O'Hare flew in last week,
he asked what were the best
times of my New York years;
I said "Today," and meant it.
I hope that death will lift me
by the hair like an angel
in a Hebrew myth, snatch me with
the strength of sleep's embrace,
and gently set me down
where I'm supposed to be,
in just the right place.

HARMONY IN RED

The woman with the bun
and Roman face
arranges red and yellow
fruit upon a bed
of dark green leaves,
for a centerpiece the colors
of a traffic light, which
hadn't been invented yet
in ought-eight, when all this
popped up in the mind
of an artist—popped
out, rather, in his work.
Arabesques as thick and bluntly
pronged as antlers snake
up the tablecloth and up
the wall behind it, framing
clunky flower baskets
painted in the style of wacky
backgrounds from the *Jiggs
and Maggie* comic strip, though
with a broader brush. Luscious
lemons on the table, purple
sky outside above the lawn
and weird pink barn.
There's a season out there,
spring from the look of it,
and a time of day, less
conclusive. But indoors
the red of walls and tablecloth
and whatever concoction
the decanter holds would
stop time, even if this weren't

an image on a poster
for a show of Impressionist
and Early Modern Paintings
from the U.S.S.R., on the wall
above the table where I drink
my bright red breakfast juice.
Today will be as packed for me
as Matisse's dining room,
with its tasks and patterns.
May I be the woman
with the bun, intent
on lovingly composing
the abundance of the grove
outside or a fruitery
down the street from the studio
in the heart of a city
where the art of the centerpiece
can make a difference still,
as quiet as a nun, serene
as a successful nun
as I pursue my work.

ETIQUETTE IN 1969

It was an unfriendly act
to "Bogart," i.e. to
draw deeply on a bomber
as it reached the stage
of roachdom, instead
of passing it along.
A song had been written
about this; Peter Fonda
put it on the soundtrack
of *Easy Rider*. "Nigger-
lipping" was a no-no,
too; it meant to leave
the reefer soggy
with saliva. "Jesus,
Dlugos, you nigger-lipped
the joint!" A hoarse
aggrieved "J'accuse"
behind a barricaded
door in St. Cassian's dorm,
two years before I softly
kissed a black man's lips,
a black dancer's gentle lips,
for the first time.

YOUR NEW HOUSE

for Eileen Myles

Forty, sign of plentitude
or fullness in Semitic myths:
forty thieves, a surfeit
of desperation and bravado,
galloping on steeds through rooms
of someone else's house, a big
one with a fence and a name;
forty days in the wilderness
eating roaches, wearing leathern
straps, a downtown lifestyle
touch in the Synoptic
Gospels; forty nights of rain,
the pitching deck resounding
with the screeching animals
(make this madness stop!);
forty years until I lead you
by the hand to the place
I have prepared for you especially.
All that went before is
so much furniture. Welcome
to your new house, full
of everything you need in a land
of light. It belongs to you now.
Its name is Today.

TURNING

Michael McClure is turning into Gary Snyder.
Gary Snyder is turning into Pete Seeger.
Pete Seeger is turning into the Rev. Al Sharpton,
who's turning into a made-for-TV movie, *The Revenge of Fat Albert*.
Albert Innaurato is turning into a successful playwright
with his new play. With his new book,
Kenward Elmslie is turning into Basho, a surprise
to the latter, who's been waiting for Gary Snyder
to turn into him for some time now.
Joe Brainard's turning into Jean Cocteau
but better (those expressive lines).
Jean Cocteau could never get turned on
in his last years, though early in his life
he was notorious for his ability to come
to orgasm by merely thinking of sex.
He turned into an opium addict
and fell in love with Jean Marais.
Jean Marais turned into a forgotten actor.
America is turning into a culture
with reruns instead of a memory.
Andy Warhol turned into a culture hero.
I remember nothing of the one conversation
I had with him, not even where it happened;
some opening, I suppose. A blond
with acne in green pants was with him,
and I kept turning my head to cruise the boy,
a rerun of my bad behavior drinking in New York.
New York is turning into an unlivable city,
and all of us are slowly turning into the dead.
But the sky is turning that deep backlit blue,
as dark as purple though more delicate,
that Joseph Cornell noticed when he turned
his field of vision skyward, and saved for us
inside a wooden box.

I used to love an architect,
which is why I cannot pass
a building without weeping.
But now I am within
your walls, O Jerusalem:
Jerusalem, built as an artichoke
in which the sweetest regions
are the dark, the undersides
of leaves that turn like hands
to cup the rain. We overturned
the clots the frost had changed
clay into, and found
pieces of a Huckleberry Hound
glass tumbler. These bones
are dry, son of man; it's time
they had a drink. It rained
and rained and washed away
the prints of hands and feet
from the garden. I played
there long ago, surrounded
by a wall of smiles: Ike's,
Mom's, the perspiring grin
of the full Kool-Aid pitcher.
The moving finger writes,
as carefree and uncaring
as the day, a flirt
whose smile seems full
of intimations as it tries
to catch your eye, then bolts
into the shadow of the tree
on your neighbor's property
that fills a corner of your lawn

with apples from the boughs
that overhang. It's a source
of nourishment and consternation
as well as homes for countless
worms. Parallel worlds
of animals that don't resemble
each other or you until you
learn their elemental gestures,
how cells move and motions
the appetites provoke. It's dance
and festival time, the party
to which the people go down
on roads from everywhere
to this vast enclosure. Once
you could have changed things,
built another city; but now
you're stuck with it the way
it is, the elevations
and the master plan, drawn out
like a howl from yonder dungeon
by a man with calipers
and a sharpened sense
of how to organize and fill
the space, a place to grow
the memories you treat
as artifacts, and mulch
the older memories to enrich
the dry but shady corner
of time where you can gorge
on windfall. Let go
and the elements break up
the clots into their elements,
the dark remains. Overturn,
overturn, overturn them.

I'm as sick as my secrets.
They're ice-blue.

SONNET

I didn't want to tell you that I kept
What I collected when the typhoon swept
Through Pakistan in 1969.
I emptied the donation box to dine
In style with friends. The millions that I raised
For UNICEF years later never blazed
To burn away a theft I chose to hide.
For want of what I stole, how many died?

Nor did I want to share the afternoons
In grungy storefronts stalking horny goons.
Sex of a sort—dispirited, forlorn.
Damp walls, waist-level holes, and grainy porn.

Bravado masked my faithlessness and shame.
One secret left: my life's one love's real name.

IT USED TO BE MORE FUN

It used to be more fun to be a poet
start the day with coffee and a sense
of bowling over people in a public space
with words that tell how I'm bowled over
this minute by the light
that pours across the city and its various shoes
and uniforms of occupation
troops whose ways of life I'd never share
but for the spaces
we separately passed through
I thought that I was different as I filled
those yellow pads with words
written in the styles of heroes
I wanted to be famous as, but younger,
the New York Ingenue School
of poetry and life   but now I know
that saying that I'm different
from the rest because I make a poem
instead of shoes and uniforms
is how I drove my car toward death
too long—it wasn't sloth
or lust or self-absorption
that put me where I ended up,
I was a poet, the same excuse
and boast my heroes used—the one
who was too drunk to see
the headlights coming, the one
who never left his bed, the connoisseur
of cure and re-addiction, the messed-up
child   it used to be more fun before I knew
that what I thought I was and wanted

was death and my embroidery a shroud.
Say it loud, I'm not proud
of handiwork like that. I used to think
that poetry could serve the revolution
and that the revolution would transform
the world because the only way
that I could see things ever
changing was from outside
so I hitched my fortune to a threadbare star.
It was more fun to write against the war
when we thought the gifts our heroes
the downtrodden of the world
bore were truth and justice
instead of one more scam   in Vietnam
my poems and self-righteous voice
helped give birth to boat people   in Cambodia
to unspeakable crimes   and now
my "US Out of Nicaragua" rap gives succor
to another ominous bunch of agrarian
reformers, this one with a top cop
whose first name is "Lenin," a touch
straight out of a darkly funny novel
by Naipaul or Evelyn Waugh
It used to be more fun when other places
seemed better and more noble than America
even the obsessive money-grubbing swamp
of sanctimony that's America these days
it used to be more fun when poetry
didn't cost so much   and when I didn't need
the government to give me money to write poems
I liked what poetry could do
to street life, even and especially
when it came from the streets   I liked

the poise and energy and grace
of black poets and gay poets and Dadaists
and unschooled natural artists
who fell into the workshops through the open doors
it was more fun before the mass
of canny grant recipients of many hues
took over   it was more fun in my director's chair
writing poems in an attic
than as a director, hurting friends
regretfully in the service of collective goals
it was more fun before I knew
my poetry could never be a spaceship
to speed me far away, or that I'd always be
outside it, like a parent,
seeing its resemblance to
my old intentions but unable
to make it work
and trusting it less
for the truths it told
than for the lies it didn't

THE FAR WEST

The city and the continent
trail off into cold black
water the same way: at
the western edge, a flat
stretch with precipitous
planes set perpendicular
and back from the beach
or beach-equivalent, a blacktop
margin where the drugged
and dying trudge, queue up
for Hades. Bolinas
had its junkie lady with gray
skin, gray sweater, stumbling
through the sand with the short-
burst intensity and long-run aimlessness
of crackhead hustlers on the West Street piers.
Dreams of Bolinas haunted me for years
before I saw it. I'd huddle
at the foot of the cliff in a cold
wind late at night, wrapped
in Indian blankets, waiting
with strangers as the tidal wave
or temblor hit. Tonight I walk
with old friends in a new dream
past a vest-pocket park of great
formality and charm in the far
West Village. My disaffected
former confidant has grown
a pony tail and cruises up
the street on a "hog," a "chopper,"
which seems a perfect locomotive choice.

I walk out to the quay where gondola
after enormous gondola departs
for "the other side," not New Jersey
anymore, anymore than something
prosaic as another mass of land
past the bright horizon
could function as a mirror
of the chopped-away Bolinas hill.
O western edge, where points
of interest on maps of individual
hearts and bodies disappear
in waters of a depth unfathomable
even in a dream, I had thought
that sleep was meant to blunt
your sharpness, not to hone
and polish with the lapping
of the hungry waves of Lethe.

STATION

When I'm this blue
about my total lack
of organizing skills to solve
the problem with my taxes,
assignments due,

paper bags stuffed full
of papers in what Chris
refers to as the world's
largest In box, my
spacious home, my dull

mind for the task
at hand, glazed eyes, a second cup
of coffee makes me wired then
tired not sharp, on top
of crisis of the day—don't ask—

and trussed to fears of mine:
will I die like Frank
O'Hara, wander through
mad life with bad teeth
a la the divine

John Wieners, live in shame
as a dependent baby like Rene
or Jimmy in his crazy years?
Be where you are, heart, mind:
all roads end at the same

place, the destination
and the embarkation point
this chair, desk, view
of shadows, wind
of feelings, station.

PRAYERS, WORKS, JOYS, AND SUFFERINGS

Centering Prayer by Basil
Pennington's the Lenten reading
of Thomas Carey, postulant
at Little Portion. *Burpee's
Catalog* is mine. I'm centering
myself inside my life, that wheeze
and brightness, in my office
"high above" or "in the throbbing
heart of" Fire Prevention Square,
the name the Mayor
posted on the sulfur streetlight
that perches on the spit
of yonder traffic isle. He stepped
into a cherry-picker's basket
and ascended skyward, waving a fire-
fighter's hat. Cameras clicked
although the contrived cognomen
never has: always was and always will
be Times Square, inspiring
the same sense of changelessness
and hopelessness at the inability
to change that an avalanche
freeze-framed in mid-course
from mountain peak to nestled
village can provoke. Underneath
the *Heidi*-sequel eaves
of one of those chateaux,
I'm having dinner with my friends:
Duncan! Karen! Michael! Ann!
Basil! Chicken! Candlelight

laps at the alpenhorn above
the mantle. Far away, New York
is mantled in new snow. At dawn,
the Time-Life Building's alpenglow
indicates a night of intimacies
deeper than one knows outside of sleep.
Then work, followed by a visit to
the drunken artist in his rubber gloves.
He works in shining poison.
I make my art of thinner substance
though I like to think
the finished pieces shed a kind
of light, a view you'd share if you
were looking out the same train window
as me, as little gardens whiz past
with their compact charms,
charms to which I'm not ashamed
to say I'm no longer immune.
In each garden, there's a summer house
for tools, and tea, and *Burpee's Catalog*.
Let's sit there for awhile, and enjoy
the light that fills this part of Belgium.
I'll only pass this way one time;
therefore whatever I can possibly
remember, let me use it in a poem.
Dearest, I offer you my prayers, works,
joys and sufferings of this day,
for all the intentions of your sacred
heart, in reparation for all my sins,
for the good of all my friends, especially
for those most in need of mercy.

SAYING IT SIMPLY

Tuna, celery, mayonnaise
and good brown bread
center me in kitchen sun.
Living with the hunger
drives me crazy.
I'm drawn to one today
and called to the other,
to emptiness that makes me
sing. What are the words?
Maniac with pangs or sweet
believer with a Buddha smile,
keep them simple either way.

VIRGINS AND MARTYRS

As cause of sainthood,
"virgin" sounds like a reversal
of a Thomist's definition
of evil, virtue by virtue
of an absence. But
there is a gung-ho aspect
to the type, especially
the virgin martyrs. Agatha
and Agnes wouldn't marry
pagan boys, and paid
with their breasts, their
heads, their lives. Maria
Goretti, age 15, died screaming
"No, Francesco" to the rapist
who today is an ex-con
penitente somewhere in Calabria.
Their cults seem plausible
as monuments to every woman
victim of male violence, but
that's not why they made
the kalendar. These deaths
are venerated by the church
as a form of fidelity
to a Lover who demands
a heart's devotion totally.
Rather than resisting domination,
the virgin martyrs spurn
the louts that kill them
in the interest of staying
tight with the most demanding
male of all, if one can call

the après-Resurrection Jesus
"male" with any meaning. Can
one call him anything with any
meaning? Other kinds of martyrdom
evince the same ambiguity.
Janani Luwum, the archbishop
murdered by Amin: was he ready
to die for Christ, or did he
think that not even a maniac
would kill his country's primate?
The "Martyrs of Memphis," nuns
who died while nursing typhoid
patients: did they throw their
lives into the swamp with joy,
or were they simply victims
like everybody else that summer?
Gonzaga nursed the dying
in Rome until he caught
the plague himself and died,
but he's no martyr. Martyrdom
requires an act of violence
to make it work. But is
that all it takes? Martin
Luther King's on the kalendar
for the first time this year:
martyr, maybe; saint, no way.
A guy who screwed two women
and slapped around a third
the last night of his life ought
not to be classed with Goretti.
Saddest of all are
the "confessors," also-rans
of martyrdom, those condemned

to die by imperial decree, who
through imperial caprice
were freed before their executions:
old men showing scars
of jailhouse tortures on a PBS
special about years of oppression
years after oppression ceased;
widely, mildly admired, but never
the real thing, part of the pantheon,
muttering until some humdrum form
of dying carried them away,
"I could have been a contender."

RADIANT CHILD

for Keith Haring

A baby in a desert
boom town wears a T-shirt
on which is an image
of the Radiant Child.
The infant is no larger
than a young man's hand,
the generous hand of the artist
who died this afternoon.
By the time she's old enough
to crawl like the child
in the drawing, his hand
will wear a coat of dust,
or long ago have been
reduced to ash. Ashley
Noel Snow, my lover's niece,
a brand-new life in a T-shirt
from the Pop Shop, in a snapshot
he would have loved to see.

February 16, 1990

THE TRUTH

Every time I use
my language, I tell
the truth. A cat
in a white collar,
like a priest with calico
fur, walks across the dead
grass of the yard, and out
through the white fence. The sun's
strong, but the colors of the lawn
were washed out by the winter, not the light.
February. Stained glass window of the house
next door takes the sun's full brunt.
It must look spectacular
to the neighbor in my head,
a white-haired woman with an air
of dignity and grace, who
through pools of the intensest
colors climbs the flight of stairs.
I've never seen it,
but I know it's there.

FOOLS FOR CHRIST

for Brother Thomas Carey

"All it takes
to start a religious
community in the Episcopal Church
is two queens and a sewing machine,"
a nun once told me. Your droll tales
of how your own foundation came to be
reminded me of that. Lunatic, perfervid,
Catholic by self-definition,
their heads full of Franciscan habits
learnt from plate impressions
in novels of Sir Walter Scott . . .
could Christ's own Fool himself
ever have been so impossible?
The obstacles to fleshing out
his fantasies were similar
to theirs, of course. This is
a respectable community
and family and I won't have my son
bolting out the door of the showroom
to the wood, where he'll be singing
idiotic songs and hugging lepers.
No good will come of a sissy
like you running off to India to found
a Kipling nightmare of a Hindu-
Anglican devotional menage; saffron
robes and floral pattern tea set.
Stay away from tramps and shiftless
boys; they'll beat you up
and give you lice. And what a girl

of your background ever could see
in spending hours on her calloused knees
before the communion breadbox,
I'll never understand. It's tempting
to romanticize "the little way"
when burgherly objections are so
easily lampooned. But most or all
of these characters in sack
were what we might call maniacs
without a lapse of charity.
Called to community, yet loathing
life in common; drawn to fidelity,
yet scrambling down the track
to Rome and back as if it were
the IRT; living out their dreams
against the hopes of family
without a twinge of guilt or sense
of irony, as if to want to wear
medieval clothes while herding goats
across the lawn of a Long Island
mansion were the least exceptional
ambition in the world. The social
disconnections that dangle
from their model like a fringe
of unplugged cords from countertop
appliances can seem as monumental
in their rejection of the ethic
of convenience as Francis
in the history of the church.
It may not be about perception
of divine will, finally;
it may be a gathering of egos
drunken on their vision of a life

they can control and have fun living,
which poses enough of a problem to others
to make the ones who choose it
feel special or important.
But through the open seam where basting
of the givens of a normal life
to motions of the heart has pulled away,
the hanging threads denote the emptiness
which waited to be there from the beginning,
and contains the mystery they seek.
Through the torn fabric, light
pours in, illuminates the dance.
Christ works through, not despite, extravagance.

HEARTLESS WORDS

> *Words cannot be wholly transparent.*
> *And that is the "heartlessness" of words.*
> —George Oppen

Black of pavement and snow-covered cars
like the black of brooks
that run between snow-covered rocks

Cheshire, Woodbridge, Bethany
can the names of towns
or names of colors

sum up how it "is" or "feels"
to raise a shade and let
all of that great gray light

reflecting from the snow
into a living room
a living man inhabits

as if the match of architecture
space and memorabilia
formed another body

loose and disconnected
itself enclosed by language
like a wall of bricks

the snowy light bombards
and permeates the way the cold
inexorably soaks through winter clothing

layer by layer
a February morning
lit by an enormous atmosphere

that wraps the day's experience
like foil and flies
like arrows through the language

to the room and through it to the skin
toward a heart that is itself a word—
a heart of what? Where

does morning's core
locate itself, if not
within the snow outside,

the breathless cold
that keeps a man from speaking
the heartless words that make his day

THE SIXTIES

When boys of 25 explain
the Sixties to me
I want to rip their tongues out

"a period when every structure
was besieged but cooler
heads prevailed

and now we're on the high road
back to basics"—hell,
I lived through it

the impulse wasn't wrong
and didn't fail, the people did
Kent State was the watershed

when it became crystal clear
we'd have to shoot the SOBs
to change things, and we slunk away

the lice-infested longhaired
derelicts in Santa Cruz and Key West
signify no greater failure

of nerve than all the former
McGovern volunteers on Wall Street
psychedelics are a helpful lens

for understanding too
acid let the TV babies know
that fitness of a human action

depends on how it feels inside
the heads and chests of individuals
not on how it looks on network news

satanic factories of false desire
still belching noxious bromides
acid was not the first breath

of Aquarian dawn, it was the final gasp
of a perspective in which to inhabit
the moment was an impulse

worthy of respect and trust
acid took the chains off
and magnified the heart

visions on the trip itself were less
impressive than the knowledge that the warp
and woof of the quotidian

like every fabric was composed
of threads, and a human possibility
existed to see through them to the light

behind, beyond, within
unmediated by the senses
or what "the senses" usually denotes

that was the excruciating part
of trips gone sour, the contemplative
inexorable aspect, and was why

you couldn't find a single tab
that wasn't cut with speed
after 1969—keep moving,

don't look, don't slow down,
disco acid of the Seventies
bearing no resemblance to its parent

but today after so many years
in which more chains and blindfolds
have fettered deadened hearts each day

the 25-year-olds without a clue
are right in one respect: the tools
for freedom that we used back then

aren't powerful enough to cut
the mustard, loose the shackles
of the Age of Cable

we need something stronger than acid
stronger than a common fight
against an insane war

strong as the willingness
to pay attention to the feeling
that the light is near

and that its simple presence has
the power to destroy
the prisons we mistake for lives

MEHR LICHT

were the last words
of Goethe on his
deathbed as the darkness
closed around him.
But Mayor Licht
was also the chief
executive of Providence,
Rhode Island in the early
Eighties. I'm dreaming
of the best political
commercial of all time—
Weimar in the 1830s,
Goethe gasping "Mehr licht,
mehr licht"—and suddenly
Mayor Harry Licht of Providence
appears to pump the paw
of the poet, and save the day.

GOOD MORNING

I've got nothing to say
but it's O.K.
it's Special K
I'm loading up with fruit
and downing
to stoke my fires
as I steam toward the chapel

Good Morning,
it's wonderful that I can inhabit
your element, this typical
New Haven fog,
my normal cloud-nine
maunderings through which
the rote of liturgy
will cut like toddlers with their
blunt-edged scissors, defining
forms du jour with dogged
imprecision and alarming grunts

the way I drank
the way I drove
my car and drove myself,
the way I fell apart,
you'd think that I'd be dead
by now, but I'm
delighted to report that
that is not the case

if all life is a journey
it's brought me to this single point,
here and now, the setting
for the secret message
that inheres in cereal
and misty dawn, like the voice
on the tape player hidden
in the breadbox
on *Mission Impossible*

"Good Morning, Mr. Phelps,"
it says, and the secret
agent replies, "Good?
It's perfect!"

SWEDE

Michael Friedman's humorous pet name
for his penis is "The Swede"

I think of this because I'm reading
Michael's new collection of poetry portraits

lots of which are about girls he's known
and loved, especially blondes

and because I have to make
a reservation at the Hotel Suede

in Paris in the next few days
for my boyfriend Chris, a big

Midwestern Swede, and me
Chris would be annoyed I told you that

"I'm an American!" I can hear him say
"Why do people who grow up

in the East identify each other
by their forebears' place of origin?"

so let me correct myself: "a big
Midwestern Swedish-American"

whose forebears came from Norkoping, which sounds
like something people do in Sweden

something useful
and vaguely mysterious

the only real Swede I have ever
known was a girl who smoked cigars

and had a black producer boyfriend
her name was Jonna Bjorkefall

we worked together for a little while
in Washington a long time ago

Jonna's introductions to the mysteries
of America were the stuff of office legend

when she caught the flu and had to see
a doctor, she was asked how she would pay

"I'll stop at the post office on the way
and get a voucher," Jonna declared

another time, she misplaced a huge stack
of checks that public-minded citizens

had sent to help Ralph Nader's work
"Where are those checks?" screeched the boss

and Jonna replied, "Oh, I put them
somewhere," which I and my boyfriend

at the time, an English-American
named Randy Russell, thought was hilarious

though it strikes me just this minute
that both the stories are a lot

more humorous when you throw in
the Swedish accent

my favorite Jonna anecdote
is not a story, but a picture

Jonna and her boyfriend took the Wilson Line
down the Potomac one romantic night

I imagine them, she so blonde,
he so black, watching by the rail

as the city slips away and the darkening
woods of Maryland touch the shore

then Jonna walks alone to the prow,
lights a thin cigar, and contemplates her future

in silhouette against a backlit sky
like the greatest Swede of all,

Greta Garbo, going into exile
at the end of *Queen Christina*

PARACHUTE

The Bergman image of a game
of chess with Death,
though not in a dreamscape
black-and-white as melancholy
films clanking with symbols,
but in a garden in Provence
with goldfish in the fountain
and enormous palms whose topmost
fronds cut into the eternal
blue of sky above the Roman
ruins and the dusty streets
where any door may lead to life's
most perfect meal: that is what
I think of when I remember
I have AIDS. But when
I think of how AIDS kills
my friends, especially
the ones whose paths
through life have least
prepared them to resist
the monster, I think of
an insatiable and prowling beast
with razor teeth and a persistent
stink that sticks to every
living branch or flower
its rank fur brushes
as it stalks its prey.
I think of that disgusting
animal eating my beautiful friends,
innocent as baby deer. Dwight:
so delicate and vain, his spindly

arms and legs pinned down with needles,
pain of tubes and needles, his narrow
chest inflated by machine, his mind
lost in the seven-minute gap
between the respirator's failure
and the time the nurses noticed
something wrong. I wrapped
my limbs around that fragile body
for the first time seven years
ago, in a cheap hotel by the piers,
where every bit of his extravagant
wardrobe—snakeskin boots, skin-tight
pedal pushers in a leopard print,
aviator's scarves, and an electric-
green capacious leather jacket—
lay wrapped in a corner of
his room in a yellow parachute.
It's hard enough to find a parachute
in New York City, I remember thinking,
but finding one the right shade
of canary is the accomplishment
of the sort of citizen with whom
I wish to populate my life.
Dwight the dancer, Dwight the fashion
illustrator and the fashion plate,
Dwight the child, the borderline
transvestite, Dwight the frightened,
infuriating me because an anti-AZT
diatribe by some eccentric
in a rag convinced him not to take
the pills with which he might
still be alive, Dwight
on the runway, Dwight on the phone

suggesting we could still have sex
if we wore "raincoats," Dwight
screwing a girl from Massapequa
in the ladies' room at Danceteria
(he wore more makeup and had better
jewelry than she did), Dwight planning
the trip to London or Berlin where he
would be discovered and his life
transformed. Dwight erased,
evicted from his own young body.
Dwight dead. At Bellevue, I wrapped
my arms around his second skin
of gauze and scars and tubing,
brushed my hand against
his plats, and said goodbye.
I hope I'm not the one
who loosed the devouring animal
that massacred you, gentle boy.
You didn't have a clue
to how you might stave off
the beast. I feel so confident
most days that I can stay
alive, survive and thrive
with AIDS. But when I see
Dwight smile and hear his fey
delighted voice inside my head,
I know AIDS is no chess game
but a hunt, and there is no
way of escaping the bloody
horror of the kill, no way
to bail out, no bright
parachute beside my bed.

BREATHING IN CONNECTICUT

slow the noose
fast the holy day
dark the rasp
light the cigarette

and dare to see our father
wheezing through this state
dare to say our father
with the lighted match

we smoke his brand
and flaunt the same bravado
at the same bad news
in femoral pulse or flash

borne to us on waves
as goddesses are borne upon the sea
the spume of clubs
where Jane Morgan is trapped

in proto-paparazzi flash
and a taste for narrative
that grows on one
like the taste of Pall Mall straights

the tract-house satisfaction
of blue smoke-shot light
that streams through kitchen windows
like spotlights on Jane Morgan

before the war
before the warning signs
before a man gets old enough
to make it stay alive with words

HOOSIER RHAPSODY

I'm in seed corn
and into the horizon.
Writing that may be a form
of advertisement for myself,
the silo that crops up
like a refrain throughout
my work. It's filled
with an abundant mass
of color, like the sky
the weight of which is balanced
on the corn's enormous ears,
never mussing their fine
tassels, as silky as the hair
of a girl in a portrait
in an ad for Breck Shampoo.
Who painted all those Breck
Girls, anyway? Ralph
William Williams, that's who.
He had a summer house
near where we used to stay,
a lake with fifteen syllables
in its name. Living
in America's a fulltime job,
so much to remember and to learn.
I'll bet you'd rather be
in Paris, knocking back a tall
Ricard or three at the cafe
beloved of you and Picasso.
It's the hour, not the company
that counts when it gets late;
I don't mean *too* late, merely

later than you think. I never
think at all after eleven.
"Wonny" Firbank dying in a room
with wretched wallpaper—that's
the image that cropped up
inside my head just now.
It's after eleven, and I monitor
the images the way a TV addict
switches channels. I learned
something new this evening
through the fog of your thick
voice: your father, whom I'd
always dreamed the epitome
of country doctor horse-
and-buggy horse sense, thinks
of himself as coming from
Detroit, where he went to
med school. The image
of his class reunion sticks
with me: a busload of distinguished
doctors carted in from Dearborn
to sample the charms of the East-
Berlin-in-1960 lookalike
where they once were boys. When you
revisit your life as an artist,
is the rubble piled as high
as the blasted buildings
of Detroit? Sufficient unto
the day is its detritus.
Sheaves of paper blow away
like pages torn from a calendar,
their versos filled with verses
scrawled in the enormous hand

of "Wonny" Firbank. I'm thinking
of him downing bottles of champagne
and gorging on peaches;
filling up those big blue
postcards with about ten words
apiece, then throwing down
his pen in exhaustion, which is
how his books were written;
unable to bear the company
of other writers; and locked in
the obliterating whimsy out of which
he drank himself to death. Death
back home is more dramatic than that.
Farm machinery that turns
on one without so much
as a warning snarl; seizures
in the middle of a sermon or lugubrious
example of Herr Luther's hymnody;
or the thin scream of desperation
from the girl with the perfect
hairdo who teeters on the edge
of the bridge across the Wabash.
Its current and the sky
absorb the sound. The vaunted
emptiness of cornfield
after cornfield's an illusion;
the air and the unfolded
topsoil is a silo for the produce
of the human heart, grotesquely
crabbed or giant as if some Hoosier
Chernobyl sprayed its steam
across the fields that feed us.
I'm still hungry, aren't you?

There's a bistro where we'll get
a bite, the one we liked
in the Seventh. I can go there
with you in my head, but
that doesn't put me back in Paris
or you anywhere else but bombed
in your apartment, a hundred miles
away. Nor does it put us
back in Indiana, turbulent
and seething hotbed of a million
personal tragedies. Somewhere
Tippecanoe rages, Dreiser writes
his advertising songs, James Whitcomb
Riley modestly accepts the plaudits
of a gaggle of admiring boobs.
You can't get there from here.
Our one and only option is the next
step, the next minute, the next course
on our plate, a prospect as capacious
as a big midwestern sky, to be filled
with our choices.

GOODBYE TO CHRYSIS

The surest way to
oblivion for an underground
star is to accept a role
in a major Hollywood film:
Charles Ludlam dead of AIDS
soon after filming *The Big
Easy*, Divine collapsing
into death the week that *Hairspray*
opened, and now International
Chrysis, model of sobriety
and transsexual charms, dead
of cancer on the eve
of her big break in *Q & A*
the same cancer that killed off
Candy Darling, occupational
hazard of those who would change
the chemistry of body to become
what they behold in their imaginations
Chrysis was a bombshell with
extraordinary assets: thirty-eight,
twenty-six, thirty-six, nine
but there was no measuring the love
behind the gentle way in which
she welcomed newcomers
at the Red Door Thursday nights
when she chaired the meeting
or the honesty with which she shared
the story of her work to turn
a madcap party of a life into a day-
at-a-time practicum of principles
for quiet joy, though "quiet"'s

not an adjective that springs
to mind when Chrysis is singing
and swinging on the imagination's stage
I missed her service at the UN
Chapel, of all places
Why there? asked my sponsee
of a downtown colleague of the artist
who replied, After all, my dear,
she *was International* Chrysis

AS ALIVE

as the old man risen
early to ascend the stoop
of the Puerto Rican tailor,
turn and flick his cigarette
to the street

the wren that hops away,
dodging the fire

and I, febrile,
cooled by morning air,
lungs misted with the clouds
of pneumocystis, this first day
of the month when I was born

SLEEP LIKE SPOONS

There is a bed on 83rd
which like a Gileadic balm
can soothe the soul. I lay me down
to sleep there, and to find the calm

that lives within your shoulder blade,
beneath the cool and freckled skin
that makes my midnights white as those
in settings Scandinavian

where cry of loon and forest sighs
not car alarms and salsa beat
drift upward through the window cracks
and mitigate the summer heat.

No way to mute the blaring horns,
nor open hearts that don't discern
the trove of tenderness within
the tangled postures lovers learn

in sex and rest, limbs juxtaposed,
exhaustion mingled with delight.
We close our eyes and sleep like spoons
inside the silverchest of night.

ANNE FRANK HOUSE

There's no way to prop up the bright bouquets
next to the statue of the little girl
and so they strew the pavement, roll away
in stiff spring breezes. Amsterdam unfurls

like banners advertising the immense
and undigestible bite of "van Gauche"
the tourists try to swallow, or the dense
sweet cannabis smoke trailing from the roach

of an attractive boy who, leaning out
his Westerkerk-view window, simply stares
at coltish German teenagers who shout
and tussle till they climb the secret stairs

to where she waited, where she tried to sleep.
Beside the Prinsengracht, I start to weep.

LAGOON CAPRICCIO

The land and water are what will remain
long after taste or nature strips the shore
of pyramid and folly. But it's more
complex than that. For one thing, the terrain

looks like a treacherous flat of shifting mud
even a gondolier would need a chart
to cross. Its edges, frozen in the art
of Canaletto, shift with every flood

and ebb tide in the world of weather. Haste
or painterly ebullience packed the banks
with architectural wonders, little thanks
to any monument that ever graced

Venice or any other town. Check out
the crouched nude on the pedestal, a wacky
if pulchritudinous Stylites. Tacky
Franciscan-looking saints wave from the stout

tempietto's roof, their blessings to impart.
Then shift back to the skyline, thick, unkempt
with towers like a ragged frieze. Attempt
to represent? No way. So where to start

the search for what is real and what will last?
Not in the land nor in the history
of architecture, nor the mystery
of why an image from a dream, recast

and fleshed out, suddenly appears within
the memory of a place one used to live
the laws of which allow the walls to give
way and the inner world to cascade in

as water flushes the canals each night,
but in the simple fact that someone made
the image as he made it, and it stayed
to challenge and to tease notions of "right"

representation. The mistaken view,
the misremembered vision is no lie
but cornerstone, reordering the sky.
Landscapes spring leaks, interiors poke through,

the way a half-remembered masterwork
two centuries old, on a museum wall
is changed forever by a poem scrawled
inside a dark apartment in New York.

TURANDOT

When I try to imagine
what heaven will be like,
I think of Puccini's Pekinese
court, ruled by a big Joan Sutherland
type wearing an enormous headdress,
where riddling has metastasized
from a show of wit into a burning
passion, consuming all the time
that passes in the progress
toward an end that never comes,
and everyone, not only the sympathetic
slightly ridiculous Ping, Pang and Pong,
has long since been sated by the marvels
of the capital, and just wants to go home.

D.O.A.

"You knew who I was
when I walked in the door.
You thought that I was dead.
Well, I am dead. A man
can walk and talk and even
breathe and still be dead."
Edmond O'Brien is perspiring
and chewing up the scenery
in my favorite film noir,
D.O.A. I can't stop watching,
can't stop relating. When I walked down
Columbus to Endicott last night
to pick up Tor's new novel,
I felt the eyes of every
Puerto Rican teen, crackhead,
yuppie couple focus on my cane
and makeup. "You're dead,"
they seemed to say in chorus.
Somewhere in a dark bar
years ago, I picked up "luminous
poisoning." My eyes glowed
as I sipped my drink. After that,
there was no cure, no turning back.
I had to find out what was gnawing
at my gut. The hardest part's
not even the physical effects:
stumbling like a drunk (Edmond
O'Brien was one of Hollywood's
most active lushes) through
Forties sets, alternating sweats
and fevers, reptilian spots

on face and scalp. It's having
to say goodbye like the scene
where soundtrack violins go crazy
as O'Brien gives his last embrace
to his girlfriend-*cum*-Girl
Friday, Paula, played by Pamela
Britton. They're filmdom's least
likely lovers—the squat and jowly
alkie and the homely fundamentally
talentless actress who would hit
the height of her fame as the pillhead-
acting landlady on *My Favorite Martian*
fifteen years in the future. I don't have
fifteen years, and neither does Edmond
O'Brien. He has just enough time to tell
Paula how much he loves her, then
to drive off in a convertible
for the showdown with his killer.
I'd like to have a showdown too, if I
could figure out which pistol-packing
brilliantined and ruthless villain
in a hound's-tooth overcoat took
my life. Lust, addiction, being
in the wrong place at the wrong
time? That's not the whole
story. Absolute fidelity
to the truth of what I felt, open
to the moment, and in every case
a kind of love: all of the above
brought me to this tottering
self-conscious state—pneumonia,
emaciation, grisly cancer,
no future, heart of gold,

passionate engagement with a great
B film, a glorious summer
afternoon in which to pick up
the ripest plum tomatoes of the year
and prosciutto for the feast I'll cook
tonight for the man I love,
phone calls from my friends
and a walk to the park, ignoring
stares, to clear my head. A day
like any, like no other. Not so bad
for the dead.

NOTES

Abbreviations:

Cooper   Dennis Cooper: *Coming Attractions: An Anthology of American Poets in Their Twenties.* Los Angeles: Little Caesar Press, 1980.

CPR   "Tim Dlugos: Twenty Early Poems." Edited by David Trinidad. *Columbia Poetry Review* (No. 21, 2008).

EN   *Entre Nous.* Los Angeles: Little Caesar Press, 1982.

HT   *High There.* Washington, D.C.: Some of Us Press, 1973.

JSEA   *Je Suis Ein Americano.* Los Angeles: Little Caesar Press, 1979.

Liu   Timothy Liu: *Word of Mouth: An Anthology of Gay American Poetry.* Jersey City, New Jersey: Talisman House, 2000.

Merla   "Lost Voices: A Tribute to Tim Dlugos." Edited by Patrick Merla. *The James White Review* (Vol. 17, No. 2; spring 2000).

Powerless   *Powerless: Selected Poems 1973-1990.* Edited by David Trinidad. New York and London: High Risk Books/Serpent's Tail, 1996.

SP   *Strong Place.* New York: Amethyst Press, 1992.

PHILADELPHIA: 1970-1973

COSMOGONY
Circa 1970. On typescript, TD wrote: "(one of my first poems)." The film *Easy Rider* had been released the previous year.

"SIT ON THE MOUNTAIN, YOUNG GENTLEMEN."
Circa 1970.

BEYOND THE LIGHT AND THE ROCKS
Written in either 1970 or 1971.

GUILLAUME DE LORRIS
Dated "9-30-70." First published in *Janaad* (No. 2, fall 1970), under

the name Timothy Dlugos. On typescript of this poem, TD wrote: "dedicated to John A. Dlugos [TD's brother], on whose birthday this was written." Inspired by Guillaume de Lorris's 13th-century allegory of courtly love, *The Romance of the Rose*, in which a twenty-year-old lover, during the month of May, enters a garden, comes upon the Fountain of Narcissus, and falls in love. TD had turned twenty the month before writing this poem.

SURF MUSIC, TEA WITH HONEY
Dated "1-23-71." First published in *Grimoire* (Vol. 2, 1971), under the name Timothy Dlugos. *Grimoire*, the undergraduate literary magazine at La Salle College, was faculty advised by Richard Lautz, to whom TD would later dedicate *Entre Nous*. TD worked on the staff of the magazine.

NIGHT KITCHEN
Dated "1-26-71." First published in *Grimoire* (Vol. 2, 1971); reprinted in *CPR*. TD acknowledged borrowing the title from children's book author Maurice Sendak, whose *In the Night Kitchen* was published in 1970.

LINDFORS AS MOTHER COURAGE
Probably written in March 1971. TD saw actress Viveca Lindfors (1920-1995) perform the title role of *Mother Courage* (George Tabori's American version of Bertolt Brecht's *Mother Courage and Her Children*) in the 1970/1971 season at the Arena Stage in Washington, D.C. Also mentioned in "For Years."

LOON DANCE
Dated "3-25-71."

LAST POEM, FIRST MORNING
Circa April 1971. After completing this poem, TD put together a sheaf of six poems and titled it "Dreamburg," using Timothy Dlugos as his author name. This was apparently his first attempt at compiling a selection of his work. "Dreamburg" consists of "Guillaume de Lorris," "Surf Music, Tea with Honey," "Night Kitchen," "Lindfors as Mother Courage," "Loon Dance," and "Last Poem, First Morning." TD gave stapled copies of "Dreamburg" to his family and friends.

"I REALLY LIKE YOUR POEMS,"
Handwritten manuscript dated "11-14-71." First published in *Salt Hill*

(No. 26, 2011). Dick Gallup and Ron Padgett are poets associated with the New York School. According to Padgett, he and Gallup read at the Y in Philadelphia around the time TD wrote this poem. TD also describes this meeting in the ninth stanza of "A Fast Life."

"WHO WILL HAVE WHOM IN THE NEXT LIFE?"
Dated "2-22-72." First published in *CPR*.

"I COULD NOT FIND A PEN"
On handwritten manuscript (dated "2-26-72"), TD wrote: "(drunk-poem)." First draft written on the back of a flyer for a dance held at the Gay Activists Alliance in Washington, D.C., on March 18, 1972.

MICHAEL
Dated "4-20-72."

"NICOTIANA-SENSATION"
Dated "5-12-72." First published in *CPR*.

DAVID CASSIDY
Dated "5-27-72." First published in *CPR*. Teen idol David Cassidy appeared in the television sitcom *The Partridge Family* from 1970-1974.

LAST LETTER
Dated "4 Sept 72." First published in *Grimoire* (1973); reprinted in *HT*. This poem was originally titled "Last Letter to Michael."

"ALL THE POEMS I EVER WRITE WON'T TELL ME"
Dated "4 Sept 72." First published in *CPR*.

POEM FOR PASCAL, I'M GOING AWAY
Dated "9 Sept 72." First published in *CPR*.

AFTER PARTING
Circa 1972. First published in *CPR*.

"HERE IS THE BLOND WORLD OF SUNDAY MORNING:"
Dated "17 Sept 72." First published in *CPR*.

AN UNDELIVERED CLASS PRESENTATION ON
THE SUBJECT OF GAY CONSCIOUSNESS
Handwritten manuscript dated "19 Sept 72." First published in *CPR*.

"DAVID CASSIDY, I WANT TO FUCK YOU!"
Circa 1972. First published in *CPR*.

A NOTE
Circa 1972. First published in *CPR*.

HEADING INTO THE CITY
Circa November 1972.

NIAGARA
Dated "15 Nov 72." First published in *Grimoire* (1973); reprinted in *HT*.

WATCHING *PSYCHO* FOR THE FIRST TIME
Dated "15 Nov 72." First published in *CPR*. Anthony Perkins also
stars in Frank Perry's film version of Joan Didion's novel *Play It As It
Lays*, released the year TD wrote this poem.

FOR MICHAEL LALLY
Dated "29 Nov 72." In August of 1972, TD heard poets Ed Cox (1946-
1992) and Michael Lally give a reading at Catholic University of
America in Washington, D.C. Inspired by their openly gay poetry
(Lally was a professed bisexual at that time), TD went up to them and
proclaimed, "You guys are my heroes!" He soon became friends with
both of them.

FOR MY COUSIN, CHRISTINE SPRING (1948-1971)
Dated "6 Dec 72." Published in *HT*. TD describes the death of his
cousin in the third section of "Death Series."

WERE WOLF
Dated "13 Dec 72."

SMALL POEM
Dated "13 Dec 72." First published in *CPR*.

"HOW LONG CAN ONE BE BLACKLY HUMOROUS?"
Dated "13 Dec 72." First published in *CPR*.

MORNING OFFERING
Circa 1972. First published in *CPR*.

JOHN TONGUE
Dated "6 Feb 73." Published in *HT*.

AFTER SEPARATION
Dated "12 Feb 73." First published in *Mass Transit* (No. 1, summer 1973); reprinted in *HT*.

SHELLEY WINTERS
Dated "13 Feb 73." First published in *CPR*.

LETTER POEM
Dated "19 Feb 73." Published in *HT*; reprinted in *Court Green* (No. 6, 2009).

ALLENTOWN
Dated "11 Mar 73." Published in *HT*.

ON TV
Dated "18 Mar 73." Published in *HT*.

"FELL ASLEEP STONED SECOND"
Dated "22 Mar 73." Published in *HT*.

DAN PROPPER
Dated "26 Mar 73." Published in *HT*.

POEM AFTER DINNER
Dated "26 Mar 73." First published in *Hanging Loose* (No. 23, summer 1974); reprinted in *HT*, *EN*, and *Powerless*. Also included in *Persistent Voices: Poetry by Writers Lost to AIDS*, edited by Philip Clark and David Groff (Alyson Books, 2010).

NOTE TO BOB CHAMBERLAIN
Dated "28 Mar 73." First published in *CPR*.

ASH WEDNESDAY – 5 POEMS
Circa 1973. Published in *HT*.

CHRIS STREET
Dated "30 Mar 73." Published in *HT*. This poem was originally titled "Above the Street."

CHRIS STREET II
Dated "11 Mar 73."

FRIDAY NIGHT
Dated "early April 1973." First published in *CPR*.

JOE
Dated "5 Apr 73." Published in *HT*. An early boyfriend, Joe was an important figure for TD. In other poems, he appears as Joey and by his nickname, Spinner. His last name is unknown.

CRABS? NO CRABS
Dated "15 Apr 73." First published in *CPR*.

SECOND ANNIVERSARY
Dated "16 Apr 73." First published in *CPR*.

WASHINGTON, D.C.: 1973-1976

CRAZY
Circa 1973. Published in *HT*.

DEATH BY DROWNING
Dated "5-24-73; rev. 6-4-73." Published in *HT*.

NINETY-ONE DEGREES
Dated "4 June 73." First published in *Mass Transit* (No. 1, summer 1973); reprinted in *HT*.

THINGS I MIGHT DO
Dated "6 Jun 73." First published, with an introduction by David Trinidad, in *The Poetry Project Newsletter* (No. 216, October/November 2008). Saint Geraud was the pseudonym of poet Bill Knott. Poet Terence Winch was at that time the poetry book buyer for Discount Books just off Dupont Circle.

ON SEEING GARY COOPER WAKE UP IN BED WITH
WALTER BRENNAN IN *THE WESTERNER*
Dated "14 June 73." Published in *HT*.

COMPENSATION
Dated "21 June 73."

HIGH THERE
Dated "30 June 73." Published in *HT*. Originally titled "Herschel."

NEXT CHAPTER
Dated "6 July 73." Published as "Chapter Two" in *Mass Transit* (No.
5, fall 1974).

THE WAY WE ARE NOW
Dated "11 July [1973]." Published in *HT*. TD met and became friends
with Mary Ellen O'Donnell in 1970, when they were both students at
La Salle University in Philadelphia.

TWO THINGS A STAR WOULDN'T DO
Dated "10 Aug 73." First published in *Salt Hill* (No. 26, 2011).

HAIKU
Dated "10 Aug 73."

MESCALINE
Dated "21 Aug 73." Published in *HT*. Original dedication read "for
Blaine Fairchild."

FAMOUS WRITERS
Dated "11 Sept 73." First published in *Mass Transit* (No. 3, January
1974); reprinted in *Angels of the Lyre: A Gay Poetry Anthology*, edited by
Winston Leyland (Panjandrum Press / Gay Sunshine Press, 1975).

SEPTEMBER 12
Dated "12 Sept 73." Published in *EN*.

TEN MOVIES
Dated "24 Sept 73. found poem." First published in *The Thursday Book*
(June 1975).

FLAMING ANGEL
Dated "15 Oct 73." First published in *Hanging Loose* (No. 23, summer 1974); reprinted in *JSEA* and *EN*.

OUT OF LOVE
Dated "27 Oct 73."

NIGHT LIFE
Dated "31 Oct 73." First published in *Painted Bride Quarterly* (Vol. 1, No. 3; summer 1974); reprinted in *Angels of the Lyre*.

INCREDIBLE RISKS
Dated "9 Nov 73." Published in Cooper. Also published as a postcard by Hard Press in 1981.

THE HIGH AIR
Dated "1 Dec 73."

AFTER ANNE HERSHON'S PARTY
Dated "8 Dec 73."

POEM FOR JEANNE
Dated "21 Dec 73." Published in *Mass Transit* (No. 3, January 1974) and *Four Quarters* (Vol. XXV, No. 1; fall 1975); reprinted in *JSEA* and *EN*.

THE THIRD SEX
Dated "21 Dec 73." First published in *Court Green* (No. 5, 2008).

AFTER A LINE BY TED BERRIGAN
Dated "22 Dec 73." First published in *The American Poetry Review* (Vol. 39, No. 4; July/August 2010).

NYC DIARY
Dated "4 Jan 74." First published in *Electronic Poetry Review* (No. 8, 2008). Record of trip TD made from Washington, D.C., to Manhattan, January 1-3, 1974. His traveling (and sleeping) companions were poets Michael Lally and Terence Winch, and Ramon Osuna, owner of the Pyramid Gallery in Washington, D.C., where Lally curated a poetry reading series. TD mistakenly says that he wakes up late on Saturday; it was actually a Wednesday. "SOUP" stands for Some of Us Press, who had recently published TD's chapbook *High There*.

NOTE AND SONNET
Dated "5 Jan 74." First published in *Electronic Poetry Review* (No. 8, 2008).

SO FAR
Dated "12 Jan 74." First published in *Phoebe* (Vol. 3, No. 2; 1974); reprinted in *JSEA*, *EN*, and *Powerless*.

GANGSTER OF LOVE
Dated "6 Feb 74. found poem." Introducing this poem at a reading in 1974, TD stated text was taken from *The Christian Science Monitor*.

DAY LIGHT
Dated "10 Feb 74." First published in *Gay Sunshine* (No. 23, 1974); reprinted in *Angels of the Lyre* and *The Son of the Male Muse: New Gay Poetry*, edited by Ian Young (The Crossing Press, 1983).

MALLARMÉ
Dated "13 Feb 74." Published in *Phoebe* (Vol. 3, No. 2; 1974) and ZZZ (1974); reprinted in *None of the Above: New Poets of the USA*, edited by Michael Lally (The Crossing Press, 1976).

DREAM SERIES
Dated "26 Feb 74."

DEATH SERIES
Dated "27 Feb 74." First published in *Salt Hill* (No. 26, 2011).

HOMAGE TO P. INMAN
Dated "27 Feb 74." TD refers to this poem in the first stanza of "The Death of a President." Helen Hayes appeared in the 1970 movie *Airport*.

TOO FAR
Dated "5 Mar 74." Published in *Mass Transit* (No. 4, spring/summer 1974) and ZZZ (1974); reprinted in *EN*.

AMERICAN BASEBALL
Dated "19 Mar 74." First published in ZZZ (1974); reprinted in *None of the Above* and *Powerless*.

GILLIGAN'S ISLAND
Dated "30 mar 74." First published in ZZZ (1974); reprinted in *None of*

the Above, EN, and *Powerless.* Selected by David Trinidad for inclusion in *Dark Horses: Poets on Overlooked Poems,* edited by Joy Katz and Kevin Prufer (University of Illinois Press, 2007).

THE BLACK FOREST
Dated "1 Apr 74." First published in *The Thursday Book* (June 1975); reprinted in *JSEA.*

UNDER THE SKY
Dated "6 may 74." First published in *Salt Hill* (No. 26, 2011).

PRESIDENT TRUMAN
Dated "8 May 74." First published in *ZZZ* (1974); reprinted in *None of the Above* and *EN.*

LET'S GO / FROM JOURNAL
Dated "19 May 74." First published in *The American Poetry Review* (Vol. 39, No. 4; July/August 2010).

AS IT IS
Dated "10 July 74." First published in *Bird: A Fly-by-Night Journal of D.C. Poets* (1974); reprinted in *EN.*

WHERE I STAND
Dated "15 July 1974." First published in *Clementine* (No. 4, 2010).

NOTE TO J.A.
Dated "13 Aug 74." First published in *ZZZ* (1974); reprinted in *EN.*

GREAT ART
Dated "19 Aug 74." Published in *JSEA,* Cooper, *EN,* and *Powerless.*

THE PRESIDENT'S SON
Dated "21 Aug 74."

JE SUIS EIN AMERICANO
Dated "6 Oct 74." First published in *Hot Water Review* (1976), with the following author's statement: "I sleep with other human beings, live in the capitol of one of the major powers, and have a hard time believing I will ever die." Reprinted in *JSEA* and *EN.*

TAROT FOR MY HISTORY
Dated "29 Oct 1974." Published in *Little Caesar* (No. 6, 1978). Ron Schreiber (1934-2004) was a poet, English professor, gay activist, and co-founder and co-editor of Hanging Loose Press.

GREAT BOOKS OF THE 1950s
Dated "27 Dec '74." First published in *Hot Water Review* (1976); reprinted in *JSEA*, *EN*, and *Powerless*.

SOME
Circa 1974. Published in *JSEA* and *EN*. In drafts, this poem was dedicated to Anne Waldman.

STANZAS FOR MARTINA
Circa 1974; only section 7 is dated ("July 12"). Sections 2, 5, and 7 were published in *Mass Transit* (No. 5, fall 1974). Poem appeared in *JSEA*, *EN*, and *Powerless*. Martina is the poet Tina Darragh.

CLUBS I'VE JOINED
Circa 1974. First published in Merla.

"LIGHT SHINES THROUGH THE LEAVES"
Circa 1974.

A FAST LIFE
Dated "Washington, D.C. 1974-1975." Published as chapbook (in an edition of 350) by David Trinidad's Sherwood Press (Los Angeles, February 1982). Reprinted in Merla.

PRISONERS OF THE HEART
Dated "14 May 75." First published in *Little Caesar* (No. 4, 1977); reprinted in *EN*.

AT THE POINT
Dated "16 May 75." First published in ZZZZZ (1977); reprinted in *JSEA*, Cooper, *EN*, and *Powerless*.

POPPERS
Dated "4 July '75." First published in *Personal Injury* (No. 2, January 1976); reprinted in *JSEA*. David E. Thompson (1939-1996), whose pen

name was Davi Det Hompson, was a multimedia artist active in the Richmond, Virginia, arts community.

POWDER PUFF
Dated "5 July 75." Washington, D.C., poet Ann Darr (1920-2007) was one of the first women military pilots to serve in WWII as a Women's Air Service Pilot (WASP).

STRONG FEELINGS
Dated "1 sept '75." First published in *Little Caesar* (No. 4, 1977); reprinted in *EN*. In drafts, this poem was dedicated to Vernon Ishikazi.

POLES APART
Dated "4 sept 75." First published in ZZZZZ (1977); reprinted in *EN*.

FOR YEARS
Dated "13-14 Oct 1975. Washington." Published as chapbook (in an edition of 200, of which 26 copies were signed and numbered by TD) by Doug Lang's Jawbone Press (Washington, D.C., 1977).

SLEEP WITH PAUL
Dated "10-16-75."

LUNCH WITH PAUL
Dated "21 Oct 75." First published in Andrew Lundwall's webzine *Seconds* (2009).

SONNET ("MY NIXON IMITATIONS CUT ACROSS")
Dated "10-28-75."

SONNET ("A FAST LIFE   ROSCOE'S, 4 P.M.")
Dated "11-75."

DAY FOR PAUL
Circa 1975. First published in ZZZZZ (1977); reprinted in Cooper, *EN*, and *Powerless*.

YOU ARE THERE
Circa 1975. First published in ZZZZZ (1977); reprinted in Cooper, *EN*, and *Powerless*.

KNOWING IT
Circa 1975. Published in *JSEA*.

SONG FROM DREAMS
Circa 1975.

THE DEATH OF A PRESIDENT
Dated "9 Mar 76." Published in *JSEA* and *EN*.

SONNET ("THE RIVER FILLS WITH SHINING RAIN, THE WAY")
Dated "April 76. DC." Published in the "Rimbaud issue" of *Little Caesar* (No. 5, 1978).

WHITE PETALS
Dated "4-1-76. DC." First published in *Four Quarters* (Vol. XXVII, No. 4; summer 1978); reprinted in *JSEA* and *EN*.

2 FRAGMENTS FOR STEVE HAMILTON
Dated "April 11, 1976. DC."

JET
Dated "21 Apr 76. DC."

MANHATTAN AND BROOKLYN: 1976-1988

THOMAS MERTON LIVED ON PERRY STREET
Dated "6 July 76. NYC."

NOTE TO MICHAEL
Dated "26 sept 76. nyc." Published in *EN* and *Powerless*.

TERMINAL DAYS
Circa 1976. First published in *Mag City* (No. 6, 1979); reprinted in *JSEA*.

"COOL AIR IN MY CHEST   IT'S"
Circa 1976.

I REMEMBER SPINNER
Circa 1976. Poem retrieved from handwritten drafts.

NEW HOPE
Dated "12 jan 77. nyc." Published in *JSEA*, *EN*, and *The Son of the Male Muse*.

SONNET ("THE NIGHT HE LEAVES, YOU FIND A SHINY DIME")
Dated "NYC. 28 July 77." Published in *JSEA* and *EN*.

KEY STROKES
Circa January/February 1978. Published in *JSEA* and *EN*.

SONNET ("FRONDS PLUMMET FROM THE TREEBELT TO THE STREET")
Circa January/February 1978. First published in *Bingo Chow* (No. 3, fall 1978); reprinted in *JSEA* and *EN*. The dedication is an acrostic.

TO JB FROM KW
Dated "Key West. 23 Feb 1978." First published in *Bingo Chow* (No. 3, fall 1978); reprinted in *JSEA* and *EN*.

CROSS DRESS
Circa 1978. First published in *The World* (No. 31, 1978); reprinted in *Out of This World: An Anthology of the St. Mark's Poetry Project, 1966-1991*, edited by Anne Waldman (Crown, 1991). Cut-up from author Jan Morris's *The World of Venice* (1974). Morris is a well-known transsexual. TD recycles the last line of the third stanza in section 4 of "The Lions of St. Mark's."

IN LONDON
Circa 1978. Published in Cooper. Cut-up from actor Michael Chaplin's autobiography *I Couldn't Smoke the Grass on My Father's Lawn* (1966). Chaplin is the son of Charlie Chaplin.

BINDO ALTOVITI
Circa 1979. First published in *Adix* (Vol. 1, No. 3; August 1979); reprinted in Cooper, *EN*, and *Powerless*. Raphael's painting *Portrait of Bindo Altoviti* is housed at the National Gallery of Art in Washington, D.C., where TD undoubtedly saw it.

TETRACYCLINE DAYS
Dated "Mamaroneck, NY. 17 July '79."

THE BEST OF GAUCHO

Dated "30 Nov 79, NYC." Published in *EN*. "The Legend of Gaucho" was published in *The Faber Book of Movie Verse*, edited by Philip French and Ken Wlaschin (Faber and Faber, London/Boston, 1993).

THE YOUNG POET

Dated "1-1-80." First published in *Knock Knock: A Funny Anthology by Serious Writers*, edited by Vicki Hudspith and Madeleine Keller (Bench Press, 1981); reprinted in *EN* and *Powerless*. Poem triggered by Dennis Cooper's description of Amy Gerstler's poetry as "sharp, stylish, and oddly moving" in calendar of readings at Beyond Baroque Literary/Arts Center in Venice, California.

THE STEVEN HAMILTON SESTINA

Dated "1-8-80. Mamaroneck." First published in *B City* (No. 8, 1993); reprinted in Merla. Patrick Merla: "This poem was written nearly a decade before use of the word 'queer' instead of 'gay' became commonplace. Randy Agnew was the (reputedly gay) son of Spiro Agnew, Richard Nixon's Vice President, who (like Nixon after him) resigned in disgrace, to be replaced by Gerald Ford, father of Jack Ford, who posed pinup-style for the cover of *Interview Magazine* and partied with Andy Warhol's Factory crowd while his father was still in office."

QUM

Dated "7-9 Jan 1980." First published in *Little Caesar* (No. 11, 1980); reprinted in *EN* and *Powerless*. Included in *A Year in Poetry: A Treasury of Classic and Modern Verses for Every Date on the Calendar*, edited by Thomas E. Foster and Elizabeth C. Guthrie (Crown, 1995). Poet Donald Britton was in his early forties when he died of AIDS on July 22, 1994.

"ONCE I LET A MAN BLOW ME"

Dated "9 Jan 80." First published in *Seconds* (2009). The title is a variation on the first line of John Ashbery's "Poem in Three Parts," which reads, "'Once I let a guy blow me.'"

FLIPPER

Circa April 1980. Published in *EN*. Flipper was the nickname of artist Philip Monaghan, a boyfriend of TD's in the early eighties. Monaghan was in Italy at the time this poem was written; he and TD were in correspondence. Monaghan is also the subject of "Philip's Razor."

GONE WITH THE WIND
Dated "11-16-80. Bklyn Hts." Published in *EN.*

PASTORALE
Dated "11-18-80. Bklyn Hts." Published in *EN* and *Powerless.* TD's college friend Virgil Moore died at age twenty-four in 1975.

HOW I GOT MY BOOKS
Dated "12-17-80. Brooklyn Heights."

THE RUBBER LADY
Dated "1-2-81. Bklyn Hts." Published in *EN.*

"AS IF NANTUCKET WERE ARCHANGEL, ICEBREAKERS"
Dated "1-18-81. Bklyn Hts." Published in *EN.*

NERVES
Dated "1-19-81. Bklyn Hts." First published in *The Poetry Project Newsletter* (No. 86, December 1981); reprinted in *EN.*

"HELLO, I'M JOHNNY CASH,"
Dated "1-22-81. Bklyn Hts." First published in *Barney* (No. 1, 1981); reprinted in *EN* and *Powerless.*

AMSTERDAM
Dated "16 Feb 1981. Bklyn Hts." Published in *EN.*

THE ABSENCE OF LIGHT AND A DRAWING BY EDWARD
Dated "6 Mar 1981. Brooklyn Hts." Published in *EN.*

THE COST OF LIVING
Dated "3-19-81. Brooklyn Hts." Published in *EN.*

SONG OF BERNADETTE
Circa 1981. First published in *Snap* (No. 1, winter 1982); reprinted in *EN.*

ENTRE NOUS
Dated "March 28, 1981. Brooklyn Hts." Published in *Barney* (No. 1, 1981) and *Christopher Street* (Issue 60, 1982); reprinted in *EN* and *Powerless.*

THANKSGIVING SONNET
Dated "11-29-78, rev. 4-17-81." The mass poisonings at Jonestown occurred on November 18, 1978.

NEW YORK'S NUMBERS
Dated "Crossworld S.C. 23 April 1981."

NEGATIVE CREDIT
Dated "Bklyn Hts. May 6, 1981." Published in *EN*.

CHEZ JANE
Circa 1981. Published in *EN* and *Powerless*.

SUNDAY, BROOKLYN HEIGHTS
Dated "June 7, 1981. Brooklyn Hts." Musician John Lennon had been murdered the previous December, at the age of forty.

THE CONFESSIONS OF ZENO
Circa 1981.

GRIST
Dated "June 23-24 1981. Brooklyn Heights." Published in *EN*.

FROM JOURNAL ("PICKING UP BACKGROUND MATERIAL FOR A COPY ASSIGNMENT . . .")
Dated "24 June 81. Bklyn Hts." First published in *Mag City* (No. 13, 1982); reprinted in *SP*.

HARBOR LIGHTS
Dated "Jun 26 81. Bklyn Hts." First published in *Hanging Loose* (No. 96, 2010).

COLUMBIA LIVIA
Dated "9 July 1981. South Harwich." Published in *EN*.

FOO DOG BLUES
Dated "23 July 81. Bklyn Hts." Published in *EN*. Included in *Queer Dog: Homo/Pup/Poetry*, edited by Gerry Gomez Pearlberg (Cleis Press, 1997).

EAST LONGMEADOW
Circa August 1981. Published in *EN* and *Powerless*.

REGO PARK
Dated "3 Aug 81." Published in *EN*.

THERE'S SOMETHING ABOUT THE DYING
Dated "4 Aug 81. NYC." Published in *EN*.

PHILIP'S RAZOR
Dated "6 Aug 81. Bklyn Hts."

IF I WERE BERTOLT BRECHT
Dated "Aug 7 1981. Bklyn Hts." Published in *EN* and *Powerless*. Also included in *Persistent Voices*.

JANET'S REPENTANCE
Dated "11 Aug 81. S. Harwich." First published in *Snap* (No. 1, winter 1982); reprinted in *EN*.

TIM DLUGOS, YOUNG REPUBLICAN
Dated "14 August 81. NYC."

OBSCURE DESTINATIONS
Dated "Aug 18, 1981. Bklyn Hts." Published in *EN*.

THE GLORIOUS MYSTERIES
Dated "18 Aug 81. Bklyn Hts." Art critic and poet Gerrit Henry died in 2003, at the age of fifty-two.

TO BE YOUNG, GIFTED AND BLACK
Dated "20 Aug 81. NYC." Published in *EN*.

DESIRE UNDER THE PINES
Dated "Fire Island Pines. Aug. 22, 1981." First published in *Mag City* (No. 13, 1982); reprinted in *The Son of the Male Muse*, *SP*, *Powerless*, and Liu.

BRIAN AND TIM
Circa 1981. Published in *EN* and *Powerless*.

THE LIONS OF ST. MARK'S
Dated "August 28-31, 1981. Brooklyn Hts–Rehoboth Beach." Published in *EN* and *Powerless*.

A WAY OF LIFE
Dated "Sept 5-6 81. Dewey Beach." Published in *EN*.

THREE WISHES FOR THE MURDERED SISTERS
Dated "16 Sept 81. Bklyn." First published in *The Poetry Project Newsletter* (No. 86, December 1981); reprinted in *EN*. On December 2, 1980, three Catholic nuns and a lay missionary were beaten, raped, and murdered by a military death squad in El Salvador while volunteering to do charity work during the civil war there.

A BIRTHDAY NOTE TO KAREN
Dated "3 Oct 81." Addressed to actress Karen Allen, whose birthday is October 5, 1951; the dedication is an acrostic. TD knew Allen from the Mass Transit poetry scene in Washington, D.C., in the mid-seventies. Allen is one of the stars of *Indiana Jones and the Raiders of the Lost Ark*, which was released in June 1981.

SODOM
Dated "4 Nov 81. NYC."

WHORES DE COMMERCE
Dated "10 Dec 81. Cobble Hill, Brooklyn."

SOLIDARITY
Dated "Cobble Hill, Brooklyn. 13 January 1982." First published in *Mag City* (No. 13, 1982); reprinted in *SP*.

TWENTY-FOUR HOUR MASSAGE
Dated "4 Feb 82. Cobble Hill."

FOR DENNIS FROM DELIRIUM
Dated "Cobble Hill. 12 Feb 82." As editor of Little Caesar Press, Dennis Cooper published TD's book *Entre Nous*, hence the pun in the last line.

EPITHALAMIUM
Circa February 1982.

SOMETIMES I THINK
Dated "NYC. 30 Mar 82–5 Apr 82." First published in *The American Poetry Review* (Vol. 39, No. 4; July / August 2010).

FILM
Dated "April 6 82. Cobble Hill." First published in *Shiny International* (No. 2, 1987); reprinted in *SP*.

FROM JOURNAL ("THE APPARITION AT LA SALETTE TO THE CHILDREN . . .")
Circa 1982.

STEVE REICH AND MUSICIANS
Dated "28 April 82. Cobble Hill." First published in *Shiny International* (No. 2, 1987).

NOT STRAVINSKY
Dated "28 April 82. Cobble Hill." Published in *SP* and *Powerless*.

MAY RAIN
Dated "28 April 82. Cobble Hill." First published in *Hanging Loose* (No. 96, 2010).

THE BAR
Dated "28 April 82. The Bar, NYC." Steven A. is Steven Abbott, a young architecture student who dated TD during this period. He is the subject of "Another You"; both he and the song "Another You" are again mentioned in the final line of "Music That Makes Me Cry."

PSALM
Dated "28-29 April 82. Cobble Hill." First published in *Brooklyn Review* (No. 9, 1992); reprinted in *SP* and *Powerless*.

FROM JOURNAL ("ON MOST PERFECT SUNNY MORNING OF THE YEAR . . .")
Dated "30 April 82. NYC." Published in *SP*.

CLOSE
Dated "3 May 82. (Venus-Day)." First published in *The Son of the Male Muse*; reprinted in *SP*. Beginning in the early eighties, TD saw author Brad Gooch's therapist, Sister Mary Michael Simpson, whose office was located at the Cathedral Church of St. John the Divine in Manhattan. TD wrote the poem in the park next to the Cathedral. Per Gooch, he and TD shared a "religion fixation: partly kitsch, partly something else."

WALL STREET SAUNA
Circa 1982.

SONG
Dated "15-17 May 82. Cobble Hill-NYC." Published in *SP*.

ON THIS TRAIN ARE PEOPLE WHO RESEMBLE
Dated "17 May 82. on the subway." Published in *SP* and *Powerless*.

JUNE 25TH
Circa 1982.

"DON'T KNOW WHY"
Circa 1982.

FAILED PILOT
Circa 1982. Kip Noll and Jeremy Scott were gay porn stars in the early eighties. They appeared together in William Higgins's *Pacific Coast Highway* and *The Class of '84 Part 2*, both released in 1981.

SUMMER, SOUTH BROOKLYN
Dated "28 june 82. cobble hill." First published in *Hanging Loose* (No. 60, 1992); reprinted in *SP*, *Powerless*, and Liu.

MY DEATH
Dated "15 july 82 rev. 21 july. cobble hill."

HARDING'S BEACH
Dated "8-2-82. S. Harwich." First published in *American Letters & Commentary* (No. 2, fall 1989); reprinted in *SP*.

IF WE'RE SO FUCKING SMART WHY AREN'T WE RICH
Dated "5 Aug 82. Cobble Hill."

NEW MUSIC
Circa 1982. First published in *Gandhabba* (Vol. 1, No. 1; January 1984); reprinted in *SP* and *Powerless*.

MYRON AND MILTON'S CAPRICE
Circa 1982.

TO CLEAR THINGS UP, SCOTT
Dated "18 August 1982." First published in *Clementine* (No. 4, 2010).
Actor and writer Scott McKinley dated TD in the early eighties. He
writes: "I had a mad crush on him. I remember first meeting him
through a mutual friend at Julius's on 10th Street . . . I thought he was
gorgeous and upon being introduced to him, I instantly recognized
his name and I (somehow) conjured up the first lines of his poem
'Hello, I'm Johnny Cash.' Tim was flabbergasted and said that no one
had ever quoted one of his poems to him before. I guess it was better
than a pick-up line because we hooked up that night . . . He was older
than me and I was certainly intimidated by his talent and intellect, but
he was always so lovely and kind."

COLUMBUS DAY
Collaboration with David Trinidad dated "Columbus Day [October
11] 82. Cobble Hill, Bklyn, NYC." Written to be read that evening at
Trinidad's poetry reading at St. Mark's Church.

NO SYMPATHY
Circa November 1982. On a typescript of this poem that he sent to
Dennis Cooper in late December, TD wrote, "found this in a notebook
(I wrote it on the subway a month or so ago) & am sending it along
under the heading 'Fulmination du Jour.' Needless to say, this one is
strictly entre nous!!"

SONNET ("JOE JACKSON WALKS INTO THE NINTH
CIRCLE")
Dated "11 Nov 82. Cobble Hill."

SONNET ("STEVIE NICKS WALKS INTO THE
PARISIAN WEATHER")
Dated "3 Dec 82. Cobble Hill." Published in *SP*.

SPY OF LOVE
Dated "6 dec 82. Cobble Hill." First published in Merla.

THE NINETEENTH CENTURY IS 183 YEARS OLD
Dated "Aug–8 Dec 82. Cobble Hill." First published in *Hanging Loose*
(No. 60, 1992); reprinted in *SP*. Introducing this poem at a reading in
1984, TD said it came out of a dinner argument over a piece of music
with British artist Keith Milow.

GREEN ACRES
Dated "Cobble Hill, Brooklyn. 28 Dec 82." First published in *Barney* (No. 4, 1984).

A SENSE
Dated "8 Feb 83. Cobble Hill." First published in *The World* (No. 42, January 1992); reprinted in *SP*.

FOOT GEAR
Circa 1983. First published in *Tammy* (No. 2, 2010).

THE INFLUENCE OF ALCOHOL UPON HISTORY
Dated "21 march 83. cobble hill." First published in *Tammy* (No. 2, 2010).

THE MORNING
Dated "April 4, 1983. Cobble Hill." First published in *Santa Monica Review* (Vol. 4, No.2; spring 1992); reprinted in *SP* and *Powerless*.

PRETTY CONVINCING
Dated "7 April 83. Cobble Hill." First published in *BOMB* (No. 11, 1985); reprinted in *SP*, *Powerless*, Liu, and *Persistent Voices*.

MUSIC THAT MAKES ME CRY
Early draft dated "Cobble Hill. March 29, '83"; revised on May 5, 1983. First published in *Clementine* (No. 4, 2010).

ANOTHER YOU
Circa 1983. First published in *Tammy* (No. 2, 2010).

TONIGHT
Dated "Cobble Hill. finished 12 May 83." First published in *Clementine* (No. 4, 2010).

WEEK
Dated "May 16 83. Cobble Hill." First published in *Clementine* (No. 4, 2010).

THIS MUCH FUN
Dated "19-20 May 83. Cobble Hill." First published in *TV Generations*, catalogue for exhibition at LACE (Los Angeles Contemporary Exhibitions), February 21–April 12, 1986; literary editor, Tim Martin. Reprinted in *SP*.

LIT
Dated "New York. 7 July 1983." First published in *Hanging Loose* (No. 60, 1992); reprinted in *SP*. Dedicated to Mark Butler in draft.

SPINNER
Dated "13 July 83. Cobble Hill." First published in *Brooklyn Review* (No. 9, 1992); reprinted in *SP* and *Powerless*. From a proposed series of poems entitled "Letters to the Dead."

OCTAVIAN
Dated "Aug. 16-17, 1983." First published in *Talisman Magazine* (Hunter College; winter 1986). Also published in *The World* (No. 42, January 1992) and reprinted in *SP*. Introducing this poem at a reading in 1984, TD pointed out that it contains several Octavian references: the youthful lover of the Marschallin in Richard Strauss's comic opera *Der Rosenkavalier* and Roman emperor Augustus Caesar, who was an eighteen-year-old student when he became heir to his great-uncle Julius Caesar. TD said he "wanted to write in a semi-Marschallin voice" and that, as in *Der Rosenkavalier*, there's a monologue in the middle of the poem.

ARMAGNAC
Dated "10 Dec 83. Cobble Hill."

CAPE AND ISLANDS
Dated "Aug 1983–24 Feb 84. South Harwich–Brooklyn." Published in *SP*. In a letter to Michael Friedman dated September 21, 1983, TD wrote that he was "working on a long poem called 'Cape and Islands,' which keeps shifting its focus, which either means it will be a failure or I'll have to slug in some fairly original transitions."

"FAME THE INSATIABLE COUSIN"
Dated "Feb 29, '84."

THE FRUIT STREETS
Dated "Mar 5 1984. Cobble Hill." First published in *BOMB* (No. 11, 1985); reprinted in *SP* and *Powerless*. Dedicated to Jeffrey Simpson in draft.

FOUR ORGANS
Dated "6 march 84. cobble hill." First published in *BOMB* (No. 11, 1985); reprinted in *SP*.

WORDS FOR SIMONE WEIL
Dated "21 March 84. Cobble Hill." First published in *BOMB* (No. 11, 1985); reprinted in *SP*.

TRINIDAD
Dated "13 May 84. L.A." First published in Merla. Patrick Merla: "This is a charming example of the fluidity of Dlugos's composition and of his natural generosity. Dlugos dashed off this poem in minutes as an impromptu house gift to David Trinidad, with whom he was staying while visiting Los Angeles."

CHRISTOPHER ISHERWOOD
Dated "July 10 '84."

HEALING THE WORLD FROM BATTERY PARK
Dated "July 14-16, 1984. Cambridge–New York." First published in *Hanging Loose* (No. 60, 1992); reprinted in *SP* and *Powerless*. Also included in *The Best American Poetry 1993*, edited by Louise Glück (Scribner, 1993).

JULY
Dated "July 27-28, 1984. Sag Harbor." First published in *The Paris Review* (No. 102, spring 1987). Also included in *Earthly Delights: Garden Imagery in Contemporary Art*, catalogue for exhibition at Fort Wayne Museum of Art, Fort Wayne, Indiana (September 10–November 6, 1988); curated by Anna C. Noll. Reprinted in *SP* and *Powerless*. TD wrote this poem in the voice of painter Darragh Park (1939-2009), after visiting Park's home in Bridgehampton, New York.

KING OF THE WOOD
Sequence probably written between 1982 and 1985. "Where Is Art?" dated "9-3-82. Cobble Hill"; all other sections undated. "Dear heart, wish you or I were here or there . . ." was first published in *The Paris Review* (No. 102, spring 1987). "To Walter Lowenfels" was first published in *Washington Review* (Vol. XIV, No. 2; August/September 1988). Entire sequence published in *SP*; "To Walter Lowenfels" and "Dear heart, wish you or I were here or there . . ." reprinted in *Powerless*. "October" is based on a painting by Duncan Hannah of the same title.

GERRIT, BAGEL AND
Dated "23 Jan 86."

HERE COMES THE BRIDE
Circa spring 1986. Published in *The Poetry Project Newsletter* (No. 141, April/May 1991); issue featured memorial tribute to TD that contained three poems by TD and reminiscences and poems by Ray DiPalma, James Krusoe, Michael Lally, Eileen Myles, David Trinidad, and Terence Winch. Reprinted in *Powerless* and Liu. Poem written for collaborative lithograph (edition of 40) with painter Duncan Hannah. Entrepreneur Dean Rolston, who commissioned the lithograph, brought TD and Hannah to Athens, New York, where TD was inspired by a bridle path leading from their cabin to the Hudson River. "I think this is it!" exclaimed TD, who then sat on the cabin porch and wrote the poem.

DESTALINIZE THE SKY
Dated "2-26-87. NYC."

MORAL IMAGINATION
Dated "Jan 2, 1988. New York City." Per TD's notes: "The Paris anecdote . . . happened to and originated with Michael Lally."

AWASH IN ANGELS
Dated "NYC. Jan 26-27, 1988." First published in *The World* (No. 51, 1995).

FAN MAIL FROM SOME FLOUNDER
Dated "March 23, 1988. Times Square, NYC." First published in *Shiny International* (No. 4, 1989).

RETROVIR
Circa summer 1988. First published in *Poets for Life: Seventy-Six Poets Respond to AIDS*, edited by Michael Klein (Crown, 1989); reprinted in *Powerless*. Also included in *Jugular Defences: An AIDS Anthology*, edited by Steve Anthony and Peter Daniels (London: The Oscars Press, 1994). AZT (azidothymidine), the first drug approved for the treatment of HIV infection, was sold under the name Retrovir.

NEW HAVEN AND MANHATTAN: 1988-1990

THE CERTITUDE OF NIGHT
Circa November 1988. First published in *American Letters & Commentary* (No. 2, fall 1989).

COME IN FROM THE RAIN
Dated "New Haven. Nov 3, 1988." First published in *Poetry* (Vol. CXCIV, No. 4; July/August 2009). Also included in *The Best American Poetry 2010*, edited by Amy Gerstler (Scribner, 2010).

NO VOICE
Circa 1988. First published in Merla.

THE TRAPS
Circa 1988. First published in *Hanging Loose* (No. 96, 2010).

WEST 22ND STREET
Dated "New Haven. Nov 27, 1988." First published in *Brooklyn Review* (No. 6, 1989). David Kalstone, literary critic and professor of English at Rutgers University, died of AIDS in 1986 at the age of 53.

ASH WEDNESDAY
Circa 1989. First published in *The American Poetry Review* (Vol. 39, No. 4; July/August 2010).

PALMER
Circa March 1989.

ORDINARY TIME
Dated "NYC, 21 May 1989." First published in *BOMB* (No. 35, spring 1991); reprinted in *Powerless* and Liu. Per TD's notes: "The line from John Berryman . . . comes from 'A Stimulant for an Old Beast' in *The Dream Songs*."

EROSION
Dated "June 7, 1989. New Haven." First published in *Art & Understanding: The Journal of Literature and Art About AIDS* (Vol. 1, No. 3; spring 1992). An early draft of this poem had the following epigraph by Bo Huston: "There's no such thing as 'early death.' There's only death."

ET IN ARCADIA EGO

Dated "New Haven. Aug. 31, 1989." On a copy of the poem he sent to David Trinidad, TD wrote, "here's the poem I read to you over the phone—'The Faerie Queene Meets Sexual Compulsives Anonymous.'"

FRIENDS SERVICE

Dated "New Haven. Aug 31, 1989." Published in *Shiny* (No. 6, 1991; issue dedicated to the memory of TD) and *The Poetry Project Newsletter* (No. 141, April/May 1991).

SIGNS OF MADNESS

Dated "New Haven. Sept 3, 1989." Published in *Art & Understanding: The Journal of Literature and Art About AIDS* (No. 1, fall 1991) and *Chemical Imbalance* (Vol. 2, No. 3; n.d.); reprinted in *Powerless*. Also included in *Jugular Defences*.

ALL SOULS DAY

Dated "Roosevelt Hospital, NYC. 2 Nov 1989." Published in *Art & Understanding: The Journal of Literature and Art About AIDS* (No. 1, fall 1991) and *Santa Monica Review* (Vol. 4, No.2; spring 1992); reprinted in *Powerless*. The dedication is an acrostic. Amy Gerstler, the dedicatee, has said that TD gave her a copy of the poem when she visited him at Roosevelt Hospital, and that TD was reading Charles Dickens's *Our Mutual Friend*, a novel he had been reading, off and on, since at least 1981.

PARABLE

Dated "Roosevelt Hospital, NYC. 4 November 1989." Published in *Powerless*.

POWERLESS

Dated "Roosevelt Hospital, NYC. 9 Nov. 1989." First published in *Brooklyn Review* (No. 7, 1990); reprinted in *Powerless*. The "rock-and-roll / motel on Santa Monica" was the Tropicana Motor Hotel in West Hollywood, where TD regularly stayed, in the early eighties, on visits to Los Angeles. In 1982, he wrote that the place was "delightfully seedy as ever, with the beautiful boys and stoned members of obscure rock bands trooping through the lobby." The hotel was torn down in 1987.

G-9

Dated "Roosevelt Hospital, NYC. 15-16 November 1989." First published in *The Paris Review* (No. 115, summer 1990). In her final issue as poetry editor of *The Paris Review* (No. 124, fall 1992), Patricia Storace noted that "Tim Dlugos's extraordinary AIDS poem" was among the poems she was "particularly proud of publishing." Reprinted in *Powerless*. Subsequently published in *Things Shaped in Passing: More "Poets for Life" Writing from the AIDS Pandemic*, edited by Michael Klein and Richard J. McCann (Persea Books, 1997); *Up Is Up, But So Is Down: New York's Downtown Literary Scene, 1974-1992*, edited by Brandon Stosuy (New York University Press, 2006); and in the "Queering Language" issue of *EOAGH: A Journal of the Arts* (No. 3, 2007), edited by CAConrad, kari edwards, Paul Foster Johnson, Erica Kaufman, Jack Kimball, Tim Peterson, and Stacy Szymaszek. In 1992, a wooden lectern with brass plate commemoration to TD was installed in the patient lounge on the G-9 (AIDS) ward at Roosevelt Hospital, and copies of TD's "G-9" were made available to patients and visitors.

HARMONY IN RED
Dated "New York City. 21 November 1989." First published in *BOMB* (No. 35, spring 1991); reprinted in *Powerless*.

ETIQUETTE IN 1969
Dated "NYC. 22 Nov 89." First published in *Shiny* (No. 6, 1991); reprinted in *Powerless*.

YOUR NEW HOUSE
Dated "NYC. 10 Dec 89." Written for Eileen Myles's fortieth birthday party, at which TD recited the poem. Published in *The Poetry Project Newsletter* (No. 141, April/May 1991).

TURNING
Circa 1989. First published in Merla. Patrick Merla: "The references in this 'list' poem are typically wide-ranging: from the disparate poets Michael McClure, Gary Snyder, Kenward Elmslie, and Basho; to the activist folksinger Pete Singer (persecuted by the federal government's House Un-American Activities Committee in the 1960s), the controversial activist/agitator Al Sharpton, and TV actor/educator/comedian Bill Cosby's popular character Fat Albert; to playwright Albert Innaurato, author of *Gemini*, a 1977 Broadway hit about a sexually confused young man, later made into a film starring David Marshall Grant (whose beauty Dlugos remarked on to friends after seeing him in 1979 in *Bent*, Martin Sherman's play about gay victims of the Nazis, and who went on to star, after Dlugos's death, in *Angels in America*), and writer/filmmaker Jean Cocteau and his

lover and frequent star, Jean Marais; to the artists Joe Brainard, Andy Warhol, and Joseph Cornell."

"I USED TO LOVE AN ARCHITECT,"
Circa 1989.

"I'M AS SICK AS MY SECRETS."
Circa 1989.

SONNET ("I DIDN'T WANT TO TELL YOU THAT I KEPT")
Circa 1989. First published in Merla.

IT USED TO BE MORE FUN
Circa 1989. First published in *The American Poetry Review* (Vol. 39, No. 4; July/August 2010).

THE FAR WEST
Circa 1989.

STATION
Circa 1990. First published in *Santa Monica Review* (Vol. 4, No.2; spring 1992).

PRAYERS, WORKS, JOYS, AND SUFFERINGS
Circa 1990.

SAYING IT SIMPLY
Circa 1990. First published in Merla.

VIRGINS AND MARTYRS
Circa February 1990.

RADIANT CHILD
Dated "Feb 16 1990." First published in *BOMB* (No. 35, spring 1991); reprinted in *Powerless*. Written on the day artist Keith Haring died of AIDS, at age 31.

THE TRUTH
Dated "Feb 19 1990. New Haven." First published in *Poetry* (Vol. CXCIV, No. 4; July/August 2009).

FOOLS FOR CHRIST
Dated "Feb 23 1990. New Haven." Published in *Anglican Theological Review* (Vol. 73, No. 3; summer 1991). Written after TD attended a workshop given by poet and Franciscan friar Tom Carey at Berkeley Divinity School at Yale University. Carey spoke about the Franciscan movement in the Anglican Church.

HEARTLESS WORDS
Dated "New Haven, 24 Feb 90." First published in *Hanging Loose* (No. 96, 2010).

THE SIXTIES
Dated "February 25, 1990. New Haven."

MEHR LICHT
Circa 1990. First published in *Poetry* (Vol. CXCIV, No. 4; July/August 2009).

GOOD MORNING
Circa 1990. First published in *Brooklyn Review* (No. 8, 1991); issue dedicated to the memory of TD.

SWEDE
Dated "April 26, 1990. New Haven." First published in *Washington Review* (Vol. 16, No. 6; April/May 1991); memorial issue, "Remembering Tim," contained reminiscences and poems by Ed Cox, Tina Darragh, Cheri Fein, Michael Friedman, Beth Joselow, Michael Lally, Bernard Welt, Terence Winch, and others. Reprinted in *Powerless*. Also included in *Full Moon on K Street: Poems about Washington DC*, edited by Kim Roberts (Plan B Press, 2010).

PARACHUTE
Dated "May 7, 1990. New Haven." First published in *Long Shot*'s "AIDS in America" issue (No. 10, circa 1991); reprinted in *Powerless*. Also included in *Things Shaped in Passing*.

BREATHING IN CONNECTICUT
Circa 1990. First published in *Salt Hill* (No. 26, 2011).

HOOSIER RHAPSODY
Dated "May 14-15, 1990. New Haven."

GOODBYE TO CHRYSIS
Dated "May 16, 1990. New Haven." First published in *The World* (No. 51, 1995). In Alcoholics Anonymous, a sponsee is someone who is guided through the Twelve Steps by a more experienced member, who is called a sponsor.

AS ALIVE
Written on August 1, 1990. Published in *Art & Understanding: The Journal of Literature and Art About AIDS* (No. 1, fall 1991); reprinted in Merla.

SLEEP LIKE SPOONS
Written in August 1990. First published in Merla. Also included in *Persistent Voices*. TD's lover Christopher Wiss lived on West 83rd Street in Manhattan.

ANNE FRANK HOUSE
Dated "8-8-90, NYC." First published in Merla. In a July 9, 1990 letter to Joe Brainard, TD wrote, "the big event in Holland was a visit to the Anne Frank House. After all the images & words abt. the Holocaust to which we've all been exposed over the years it is amazing to me that the most overwhelming expression of the horror is a little girl's bedroom with magazine clippings, puppets, kittens and movie stars pasted at little girl eye level on the wall. To know that this room was a hiding place because the most powerful people in Europe hated and wanted to kill that little girl, and succeeded, overwhelms me more than all the death camp photos I've ever seen. A busload of German teenagers were visiting at the same time we were; they entered noisy and cheery like typical teenagers, and were clearly shaken when they left. Which is worse, I wonder: To be a German adult who remembers the madness, or to be a German kid who realizes for the first time that his parents or grandparents may have had complicity in the horrors?"

LAGOON CAPRICCIO
Dated "8-11-90, NYC." First published in *Washington Review* (Vol. 16, No. 6; April/May 1991).

TURANDOT
Dated "Aug 18, 1990. NYC." Published in *Outweek* (No. 79/80; January 9, 1991) and *Shiny* (No. 6, 1991); reprinted in *Powerless*.

D . O . A .

Dated "Aug. 29, 1990. NYC." First published in *Outweek* (No. 66; October 3, 1990); reprinted in *Powerless* and Liu. Also included in *Editor's Choice III: Fiction, Poetry & Art from the U.S. Small Press (1984- 1990)*, edited by Morty Sklar (The Spirit That Moves Us Press, 1991); *Jugular Defences*; *Things Shaped in Passing*; and *Persistent Voices*.

PRIVATE "STRONG PLACE" MANUSCRIPT

In late 1982, TD prepared a manuscript entitled "Strong Place." Sixty copies were Xeroxed and, in January 1983, privately distributed to friends as a New Year's present. The contents were as follows:

Close; Sonnet ("Joe Jackson walks into the Ninth Circle"); Whores de Commerce; Sometimes I Think; Philip's Razor; Tim Dlugos, Young Republican; Twenty-Four Hour Massage; Steve Reich and Musicians; The Glorious Mysteries; Film; From Journal ("The Apparition at La Salette to the children . . ."); The Confessions of Zeno; Epithalamium; Solidarity; On This Train Are People Who Resemble; Desire Under the Pines; Wall Street Sauna; Song ("Early summer sunlight and the wise guys whistle"); Not Stravinsky; Summer, South Brooklyn; From Journal ("Picking up background material for a copy assignment . . ."); My Death; Harding's Beach; New Music; Myron and Milton's Caprice; From Journal ("On most perfect sunny morning of the year . . ."); Psalm

This compilation can be seen as a working draft of the book manuscript of *Strong Place* that TD finalized later in the decade.

"POWERLESS" MANUSCRIPT

Before his death, TD prepared his final manuscript, "Powerless," and dedicated it to Christopher Wiss. The manuscript, never published, was ordered as follows:

Part 1: Here Comes the Bride; Harmony in Red; Moral Imagination; Destalinize the Sky; No Voice; The Traps; Fan Mail from Some Flounder; Etiquette in 1969; West 22nd Street; Come in from the Rain; Swede; Lagoon Capriccio; Fools for Christ; Ash Wednesday; Friends

Service; Palmer; Part 2: Powerless; The Truth; Heartless Words; Parable; Saying It Simply; Retrovir; The Certitude of Night; Signs of Madness; Erosion; Radiant Child; All Souls Day; Parachute; Sleep Like Spoons; Turandot; D.O.A.; Ordinary Time; Part 3: G-9

Powerless was used as the title of TD's selected poems in 1996. TD's dedication to Christopher Wiss was also used for that collection.

INDEX OF TITLES

Brackets indicate untitled poems

INDEX OF FIRST LINES

Nightboat Books

Nightboat Books, a nonprofit organization, seeks to develop audiences for writers whose work resists convention and transcends boundaries. We publish books rich with poignancy, intelligence, and risk. Please visit our website, nightboat.org, to learn about our titles and how you can support our future publications.

The following individuals have supported the publication of this book. We thank them for their generosity and commitment to the mission of Nightboat Books:

Kazim Ali

Anonymous (2)

In memory of Boo

Rebecca Burrier

Jennifer Chapis

Jim Cory

Cheri Fein

Raymond Foye

Sarah Heller

Nathan Kernan

Gillian McCain

Patrick Merla

Elizabeth Motika

Maryellen O'Donnell

The Estate of James Schuyler

Kenneth A. Schwartz

Benjamin Taylor

Peter Waldor

Edgar Wells

Christopher Wiss

This book has been made possible, in part, by a grant from the New York State Council on the Arts Literature Program.

State of the Arts

NYSCA